Child Pornography

The availability of child pornography on the Internet has become a cause of huge social concern in recent years. This book considers the reality behind the often-hysterical media coverage of the topic. Drawing on extensive new research findings, it:

- Examines how child pornography is used on the Internet;
- Identifies the social context in which such use occurs;
- Develops a model of offending behaviour to help better understand and deal with the processes of offending.

Detailed interviews and offenders' own accounts are used to illustrate the processes involved in offending and treatment.

The authors argue that we need to redefine our ideas of offending, and that while severe deterrents need to be associated with possession of child pornography, a better comprehension is needed of the links between possession and committing a contact offence. Only by improving our understanding of this complex and very controversial topic can we hope to deal effectively with offenders and their child victims.

This book is an essential read for anyone involved with offenders or victims, from a psychological, judicial or social background.

Professor Max Taylor is Professor of Applied Psychology at University College Cork, and director of the COPINE Project. He is a Chartered Forensic Psychologist, with extensive experience of research in areas related to the criminal justice system.

Dr Ethel Quayle is a College Lecturer in the Department of Applied Psychology at University College Cork, and a researcher with the COPINE Project. She is a clinical psychologist with extensive experience of work with offenders.

Child Pornography

An Internet Crime

Max Taylor
and Ethel Quayle

Brunner-Routledge
Taylor & Francis Group
HOVE AND NEW YORK

First published 2003
by Brunner-Routledge
27 Church Road, Hove, East Sussex, BN3 2FA

Simultaneously published in the USA and Canada
by Brunner-Routledge
29 West 35th Street, New York, NY 10001

Brunner-Routledge is an imprint of the Taylor & Francis Group

Typeset in Times New Roman by
Keystroke, Jacaranda Lodge, Wolverhampton
Printed and bound in Great Britain by
MPG Books Ltd, Bodmin

British Library Cataloguing in Publication Data
A catalogue record for this book is available from the British Library

Library of Congress Cataloging in Publication Data
Taylor, Maxwell, 1945–
Child pornography : an internet crime / Max. Taylor and Ethel Quayle.
p. ; cm.
Includes bibliographical references.
ISBN 1-58391-243-6 (hardback : alk. paper) – ISBN 1-58391-244-4 (pbk. : alk. paper)
1. Children in pornography. 2. Internet pornography. 3. Internet and children. 4. Child sexual abuse–United States–Prevention. 5. Pedophilia. I. Quayle, Ethel, 1953– II. Title.

HQ471 .T39 2003
363.4′7–dc21

2002015046

ISBN 1–58391–243–6 hbk
ISBN 1–58391–244–4 pbk

Contents

Illustrations

Table

Figures

Foreword

Child pornography is an emotive topic, and discussions tend to touch raw and sensitive issues, where opinion and moral position become more important than rational debate. Perhaps this is how it should be when facing disturbing deviant behaviour. Bruno Bettelheim wrote that he 'shied away from trying to understand the psychology of the SS because of the ever-present danger that understanding fully might come close to forgiving'. The paedophile, and the public visible product of paedophilia in the form of child pornography, seems in many ways to give rise to public emotions that are like those associated with the SS. Collectively paedophiles are vilified, demonised and subject to enormous moral approbation. And in trying to develop a psychological understanding, we do run the risk of excusing, of offering a logic that seems to side-step issues of responsibility, or issues of consequences for victims, and in so doing appearing to condone if not forgive.

In embarking on this book, we were aware of these problems. But the paradox is that without understanding, the harsh world of the SS becomes that much closer as prejudice substitutes for reason, as self-righteous assertion distorts debate, and hinders the search for solutions. This book does try to increase our understanding of the processes that lead to the production and distribution of child pornography. In doing so, however, it neither offers apologies, nor does it diminish the significance of the consequences for the child victims, or for society in general. In its conclusions it places the debate firmly within a victim-centred perspective, with the ultimate aim of using psychological insights to develop better and more effective child protection strategies.

One victim in particular stands out. Thea Pumbroek died in Amsterdam on the 27 August 1984. She was 6 years old. She had already appeared in a number of child pornographic videos, and died of an overdose of cocaine whilst being filmed. As we have found in trying to reconstruct the events around her death, nobody remembers her. We know of no commemorative foundation in her name to focus attention on helping victims of child pornography, and even the records of her death seem to have disappeared or been mislaid. She seems to have been treated in death as little more than the object she had been in life. Children do not normally die as a result of involvement with child pornography, and Thea's tragic death finds few parallels in the contemporary world. But our lack of knowledge of her does mirror our lack of knowledge of the victims of child pornography, and emphasises a concern at the distortion in resources being directed towards offenders rather than victims.

In this book we are aware that we have also potentially contributed to this distortion in that we have taken an offender focus. Offenders collect and trade child pornography, have created the Internet networks that facilitate the exchange of photographs, and some of them produce child pornography. Our understanding of the processes involved must necessarily therefore begin with the offender, and clearly efforts to control child pornography must focus on the offender. But we must not lose sight of the child in the photograph, of their short- and long-term needs and situations, and of the need to ensure that the victim remains empowered throughout the process of dealing with offenders.

The research on which this book is based was undertaken as part of the COPINE Project. The history of the COPINE Project lies in a research programme concerned with disadvantaged children, especially street children, that began in 1990 with the founding of the Child Studies Unit. COPINE stands for *Co*mbating *P*aedophile *I*nformation *N*etworks in *E*urope, the name given to the EU-funded project that initiated the research programme. Over time, the Project has developed into a unique research initiative, drawing on clinical and forensic psychology to explore and understand in a rounded way the world of child pornography, and those involved in it. The success of the Project lies in its ability to cross professional and national boundaries – Project members are academics, but research has developed in collaboration with other professions and disciplines that are also concerned with the management of child pornography, especially the law enforcement world. The Project activities could not have been undertaken without strong support from the European Commission through its STOP and Daphne programmes.

The subject matter of this book, child pornography, is illegal in most Western countries. Its production, distribution and possession is a serious offence. The research reported in this book has drawn upon an extensive knowledge of child pornography, but it is important to stress that this has been acquired within a closely controlled professional and legal framework, and at all times, appropriate professional and moral controls have been adhered to. We have taken considerable efforts to not identify individuals or processes in our discussions. We are very aware of the dilemma any author faces in this area of providing sufficient information to enable appropriate professional discussion and debate without fuelling prurient interest or fantasy. We are also very aware that a book of this kind can be read with intentions very different from those of the authors, and indeed can be misused. We hope that we have guarded against this.

Many organisations have contributed to this book, in one way or another. We owe debts of gratitude to: the Governors and staff of HM Prisons Wakefield, Strangeways, Channingswood, Winchester and Wandsworth, and to Cork and Limerick Prisons; to the staff of Salford and Eccles Probation Service and the NSPCC Dove Project; to Greater Manchester Police, the London Metropolitan Police, the National Crime Squad, Hampshire Police, An Garda Siochána and

Interpol; to the Wolvercote Clinic. Amongst many individuals, we particularly wish to thank: the staff of the COPINE Project, especially Graine Murphy, Emma O'Dwyer, Mary Vaughan and Gemma Holland, and our colleague Noreen Moynihan for her secretarial help and support; Bob McClachlan, Hamish McCullough and Terry Jones and their respective staff; George Bullock and Paul Wright and their colleagues; Sarah Ward; Angela Cope and Louise Wright; Donal Findlater and Joe Sullivan. We wish also to thank the many offenders who gave permission to engage in the research that underpins this book; we hope that in telling their stories they help to redress some of the damage done. The views expressed in this work are solely those of the authors, and we take full responsibility for them.

This book was written whilst both of us were on leave of absence from University College Cork, and we wish to thank the President of the University, Professor G. Wrixon, for facilitating our leave. The table used in Chapter 2 to illustrate a typology of paedophile picture collections was previously published in *The Police Journal*, 74 (2000), 97–107 and reproduced with the kind permission of Vathek Publishing Ltd. Some of the material presented in Chapter 5 was previously published in *CyberPsychology and Behaviour*, 4(5) (2001), 597–608 and is reproduced with the kind permission of Anne Liebert Publishing Co. The authors gratefully acknowledge assistance received from the University College of Cork Faculty of Arts Research Publication Fund.

Whilst not always helped by their presence, we are nevertheless grateful for the contribution of Alice, Cathy and Josh. Tuff was a benign influence, but generally speaking Francis got in the way.

EQ and MT
Restábal and Cork

Chapter 1

Introduction

Awareness and recognition of the problems of the sexual abuse of children has grown enormously over the past two decades amongst both professional and lay communities. From being a largely unnoticed and hidden problem, it now commands government and media attention as a major social problem. However, not all aspects of the sexual abuse of children, either in the past or currently, command equal attention. Until recently, child pornography was not seen as a particularly significant element in the array of activities related to sexual abuse. If it was recognised, it was seen as a rather small and essentially specialist correlate of a much broader and more significant problem. Although we have little knowledge of the role that child pornography might play in the sexual abuse of children, this was probably an appropriate perception at least until the 1990s. However, since the mid-1990s, we have seen a change in the nature of child pornography. This is primarily but not exclusively in terms of access to it, and its distribution. Associated with this, there has been growing media attention given to child pornography, both in itself, and with respect to child pornography on the Internet. Indeed, it might be argued that the problem of child pornography has leapt from a situation of general ignorance and inattention to one of massive media and political attention. There are almost daily news reports of arrests of individuals either in possession of, distributing, or creating child pornography. The issue of child pornography has, for the moment, become a major area of law enforcement activity, and parallel social concern.

Yet, paradoxically, we know relatively little about child pornography, and it is not an area that has attracted much systematic research effort. If we move from the media dramatisation to ask questions about its nature, its relationship with sexual abuse of children, and its broader relationship with the Internet (either as a medium of distribution, or as a factor in itself) we have remarkably little knowledge. Throwing some light on to what child pornography is, how it is produced, and how and why it is distributed and collected are the central aims of this book.

At first sight, asking questions about child pornography may seem largely irrelevant. After all, it may seem obvious that the explanation lies in simply deviant sexual interests, which find expression in photographs of children. That the subjects of the photographs are children rather than adults would seem to simplify or negate any potential debate about human rights issues and freedom of access, which has dominated questions over the right to produce and access adult pornography. In the case of child pornography, as with child sexual abuse, we tend to conclude that there is an imbalance of power between the child in the picture and the adult who produced it, such that the child cannot in any meaningful sense 'choose' whether or not to be in the photograph. This might help us to place into perspective issues related to the production of child pornography; but does this imbalance equally apply to the viewer of child pornography? In what sense is the viewer engaging in the process of abuse? And given that sexual arousal related to photographs necessarily also relates to fantasy, are we in an oblique way attempting to control fantasy, rather than behaviour, when we move away from seeking to control production to controlling the viewing of child pornography? These are difficult questions to answer.

An equally difficult issue lies in deciding what actually constitutes child pornography. Examining photographs from the seized collections of offenders demonstrates that a wide variety of images are collected and in some sense used by adults sexually interested in children to fuel their fantasies. This raises complex issues about the nature of pornography when we attempt to define it by objective measures as opposed to looking at the function it has for the individual and the use to which it is put. In doing this it raises equally complex and fundamental issues about sexual interest in children, and why and how that interest finds expression in child pornography.

This book also addresses a wider context, however, in that the primary contemporary sources of child pornography relate to the Internet. We can regard the Internet as simply a medium of distribution, but, at least in the context we are concerned with, the Internet itself also has an important psychological role to play in the development and propagation of child pornography. Child pornography and the Internet represent an almost paradigmatic example of contemporary crime – the bringing together of sexual exploitation of children and the new technologies. This challenges and extends our understanding of the relationship between man and computers, and the role that the computer might play in the sexual exploitation of children. As well as exploring the role of the Internet, the analysis presented in this book also draws on work from three substantive areas – adult sexual interest in children, notions of community and virtual community, and the psychology of collecting. Pulling together the threads from these diverse areas will help to place the role of child pornography and the Internet within a broader context, with implications for law enforcement, social welfare intervention and public policy.

CHILD PORNOGRAPHY

As soon as we examine what we mean by child pornography, we begin to encounter uncertainties and confusions. The terms 'child' and 'pornography' on their own are themselves contentious, with complex and sometimes contradictory meanings.

The ways that we define what it is to be a child are socially and temporally situated, as are views about the appropriateness of adult sexual interest in children and what constitutes pornography. Given this, definitions of child pornography can therefore be quite complex.

A necessary central quality of child pornography is, of course, that a child is in a photograph. What national laws define as a child quite reasonably relates to chronological age. However, an immediate and obvious problem is that different jurisdictions set different ages for what constitutes a child. Consistent with the UN Convention on the Rights of the Child, in the West we tend towards an all-embracing view that childhood ends at 18, and seek to extend legal protection from sexual and labour exploitation to all below that age. The age of consent for sexual activity (which may or may not be related to what we mean by a child), however, is more likely to be 16 (and even 14 in some jurisdictions). In contrast, social and psychological insights into what constitutes 'a child' emphasise that it is not simply a chronological judgement, but it is also a social and cultural statement. Western concepts of childhood, with assumed relationships with parents, and the notion of dependency, are not necessarily shared in all societies, and views about the appropriateness of child labour (and child sexuality) vary between cultures.

Even in a narrow technical sense related to photographs of children, we can encounter difficulties. When viewing a picture in the absence of information about the individual photographed, attempting to determine an age may become a matter of complex judgement. Whilst decisions about whether a person photographed is a child are not problematic when the individual is very young; when we move into adolescent years such decisions, when based on visual evidence, are much more difficult to make. There are enormous individual variations in the normal development of secondary sexual characteristics, making visually based judgements about age very difficult.

However, assuming a child is involved, what then constitutes pornography? In some jurisdictions, pornography is linked to notions of obscenity; in others it is linked to sexuality and sexualised behaviour. As we will see in Chapter 2, this can make a critical difference as to how any given putative example of child pornography is regarded.

These differing criteria mean that it is quite possible for a picture to be regarded under laws that emphasise sexual qualities as child pornography but to fail in jurisdictions where obscenity or public morality definitions prevail. Photographic work that might be defended against accusations of obscenity and indecency on artistic grounds, such as the photographs of her own nude children taken by the well-known photographer Sally Mann, might well also be regarded as sexual depictions in jurisdictions where potential sexuality is emphasised. Although Mann herself rejects any accusation of sexuality in her photographs, Kincaid (1998: 320 fn 98) cites an art critic who praised her photographs 'because they beautifully demonstrate that being pure and innocent has nothing to do with being sexless', which, to say the least, demonstrates the tensions involved in making judgements about this kind of photograph. Naturist material may similarly be difficult to categorise. Naturism is a legitimate activity, and presumably photographs of naked children and adults involved in naturist activities are, in their context, appropriate.

A major difficulty relates to what, in the context of adult images, might be regarded as erotica. Pictures of this kind would generally be regarded as child pornography where reference is made to sexual qualities, but might not if obscenity or indecency criteria are used. For example, erotica can be described as sexually explicit material that depicts adult men and women consensually involved in pleasurable, non-violent, non-degrading, sexual interactions (Marshall and Barrett 1990), whereas pornography might be thought to depict activity that is non-consensual and where one of the participants is portrayed as powerless or non-consenting. In later discussions, we will explore further the issue of power as an element in the production of child pornography. If we take the view that a child cannot give informed consent, whatever the visual representation suggests, quite clearly in erotica of this kind questions related to consent could not be at issue.

At its worst, child pornography is a picture of a child being in some sense sexually abused. That is to say, at its worst, it is the portrayal of a sexual assault and as such it is therefore the picture of a serious crime in progress. In most Western countries not only the production but also the possession of that photograph (or video or cine film) is itself an offence. Generally, but not exclusively, an adult (often a man) commits the assault portrayed against a younger girl or boy. The person holding the camera is also generally an adult, who in some way directs the abusive content of the photograph. But a picture might as readily involve two or more children of either the same or different sexes. However we construe this, of course what follows is that such a picture is also the picture of a crime scene.

The media accounts of child pornography quite properly emphasise this extreme sexual quality of the pictures, and draw the inference that all child pornography is necessarily related to ongoing sexual assaults on children. When we see prosecutions associated with child pornography in the courts, however, the offences may indeed relate to the *production* of such material, but may also relate to its *possession* and also its *distribution*. The distribution and collecting of child pornography may well separate the viewer from the source, and thus, not all offenders involved with child pornography are necessarily involved in direct sexual assaults on children, but may view or collect pictures of sexual assaults. In a sense, this constitutes a form of secondary assault, as distinct from the original primary assault. But this raises the issue of the relationship between sexual assaults on children, taking such pictures, and the viewing and collecting of child pornography. Some authors have asserted that child pornography is a 'sideline' in which 'all else is subordinated to the act of molestation'. This may be the case with respect to the production of child pornography, but the active engagement of many people in its collection and distribution suggests that the situation is more complex than that. Child pornography raises issues about the nature of adult sexual interest in children, sexual assaults on children, and sexual fantasy about children. It seems to identify within the category of individuals with a sexual interest in children a range of behavioural and psychological qualities that extend our current understanding of sexual abuse of children beyond actual physical assault.

Indeed, the range of people involved in child pornography offences seems to cross boundaries of class, income and profession. Doctors, technicians, businessmen, teachers, media personalities, policemen: these are just a few of the kinds of people who have been found guilty in recent criminal proceedings of possession of child pornography. Offenders are not always adult males; women are also involved. Nor is age particularly relevant; children as young as 13 have been involved in the distribution of child pornography, and men as old as 75 have been convicted for the production of child pornography. We have no idea how many people collect or possess child pornography. Nor do we have any idea of the extent of the broader issue of adult sexual interest in children. But all our knowledge of offending suggests that the number of people involved is considerable. However, occasionally, there are glimpses we can make into this world. On 14 November 2001, abc News.com reported the results of an FBI investigation into a child pornography web site operated by Landslide Productions. This company's web site sold subscriptions to web sites offering child pornography. Landslide Productions grossed $1.4 million dollars in one month, and on investigation revealed 35,000 individual subscribers within the USA. This is the largest such site to be detected to date, but indicates the scale of both the interest, and the potential profit.

Why does this occur? What is it that sustains the behaviour of collecting child pornography that exposes those involved to what in the current climate is a very real risk of a long prison sentence if caught? What role does child pornography play that it should seemingly draw in people who otherwise might lead lives with no contact with the law enforcement authorities? These are important issues about which we are only now beginning to gain some understanding: later chapters will explore these issues in much greater depth.

The phrase 'at its worst' was deliberately used earlier in the discussion when referring to what we might call child pornography. That is because not all pictures are pictures of a sexual assault in progress. Some pictures that we might regard as child pornography are of naked children posed in sexually provocative ways; others are of clothed or partially clothed children posed, or with some degree of underwear showing. As noted above, sometimes pictures of this kind when involving adults are termed 'erotica'. The link between them all is that they in some way serve a sexual purpose, not necessarily (or even at all) for the child concerned, but for the producer and viewer. Some legal definitions of child pornography (as discussed above) recognise this, but the presence of such photographs also draws our attention to personal and essentially psychological qualities of child pornography for the viewer. The photographer creates a photograph, either deliberately or adventitiously, and the viewer constructs from that photograph some sexual meaning. It is that cycle of production and viewing that characterises the process of child pornography. Central to our understanding of this are notions of sexual fantasy, sexual arousal and sexual behaviour.

In addition, we know that those who collect child pornography do not restrict their collections to small numbers of photographs. Such people may collect thousands of images. Given this number, it is unlikely that the collector can know the detail of what he has, and most certainly an individual cannot engage sexually (through masturbation, for example) with so many pictures. Why then are collections often so large? What psychological functions might these collections play? We also know that adults sexually interested in children can be highly specific in targeting preferred pornography, which may relate to particular physical characteristics of a child or children, or may relate to activities portrayed in the images. Indeed, this may be the principle around which their collection is organised.

Clearly, child pornography has, as its primary function, some element of sexual arousal or fantasy. A central question that follows from this is what role does such material play in sexual *behaviour*, as opposed to fantasy. To answer this, we need to explore the relationship between sexual arousal and fantasy, collecting behaviour and the likelihood of actual sexual assault against a child. Certainly, in the context of adult pornography, there is some evidence to suggest that sexually aggressive behaviour may increase after exposure to photographs containing violent or coercive images. Is that the case with respect to child pornography? Or does engagement with child pornography serve to displace potential assaultive behaviour with other more acceptable forms of sexual activity (such as masturbation), thereby protecting against sexual assaults?

To continue our brief discussion of the nature of child pornography pictures, not every picture that is attractive to an individual with a sexual interest in children is necessarily pornographic or even highly sexualised in its content. Non-sexual pictures of children are, for many individuals, attractive objects to collect and presumably fantasise over. Following through on this point emphasises a fundamental difference of view between legal definitions of child pornography, and psychological accounts of what constitutes pictures attractive to adults with a sexual interest in children. Pictures are both taken and collected for a variety of reasons; the uses to which the viewer might put pictures are complex, and producers of child pornography recognise this. Legal definitions of child pornography generally fail to deal with this issue.

To add to the complexity in terms of the practical management of child pornography, quite commonly children involved in more extreme examples of its production may also have non-pornographic pictures taken of them. For example, in 2000, a 14-year-old US child who had been involved in the production of large amounts of child pornography, including a Russian pornographic video, was also extensively photographed in non-pornographic settings on numerous occasions. These pictures, entirely legal and widely available on the Internet, in many respects complement and extend the illegal pornographic material of the same child. They may provide contextual material about the child, making them more 'real' to the offender and fuelling sexual fantasies.

There is also a sense in which the legal specification of child pornography in a jurisdiction shapes what material is produced. During the year 2000 there emerged a number of commercial sites on the World Wide Web offering erotic pictures of children for payment. The pictures were erotic in the sense that the children were posed in states of partial or full undress, but the pictures had no explicit sexual content. Adults were never present in the pictures, and the poses adopted were in the main not necessarily sexually provocative (although often genitalia were focused on). The pictures appear to have been very carefully produced to fall just within the limits of what constitutes legal pictures in the country that hosted the web site. To summarise, it seems clear that, whilst we might start with a relatively simple framework from which to understand child pornography, closer inspection reveals complex themes and issues.

Throughout this book we have used the term 'child pornography' to describe its subject matter. This is, as we will see, in some cases a legal term, and in any event it is a term with wide currency. However, its continuing use does present some problems, notably in terms of the comparisons it invites with 'adult pornography'. The issue here is our often-ambivalent view of the nature of adult pornography, and the sense in which that ambivalence might leak into the way we think about child pornography. Adult pornography can be bought in respectable bookshops, it is available from newsagents (even if on the top shelf); we see frankly pornographic advertisements for new cars, we may be sent mildly pornographic calendars. There is often a sense of titillation, of adolescent manly mild rudeness, associated with adult pornography that inappropriately diminishes its abusive content.

A better term than child pornography would be 'images of sexual abuse', or more simply 'abuse images'. This unambiguously expresses the nature of child pornography, and places it firmly outside of the range of acceptable innuendo and smutty jokes – perhaps this should apply to adult pornography as well. However, notwithstanding this, we have chosen to use the term 'child pornography', primarily because it has wide currency and in the current climate at least is the conventionally acceptable term; we use it, however, in the knowledge of its inappropriateness to describe the reality of the images we are concerned with.

Concerns over child pornography

Many things drive concern over child pornography, but the principal factor for most people concerned about this area relates to child protection. With the advent of new technologies, demonstrating an interest in child pornography has moved from furtive and often expensive purchasing of magazines and videos to being able now to download vast numbers of photographs without payment, in large quantities and in the privacy of one's own home. This seems to represent a reduced risk to the individual to acquire material, allows for the size of collections to grow and creates a constant demand for new and novel material. Meeting the demand for new material inevitably means that more and more children are involved in the production of child pornography. Also, for those with a sexual interest in children, new technologies such as digital cameras mean that those interested in viewing can also very easily become producers. Both still and moving photographs can now be produced with no third-party involvement, and with apparent total security. Such technology can even allow the online abuse of children, directed by others from any distance.

But, whilst it is important to create an environment in which children are not abused, it is also necessary to recognise the limits that protection can take. In particular, recognising that individuals with a sexual interest in children might sexualise what may, in other contexts, be appropriate photographs points to the need for a discriminating approach. It is the link between child pornography and sexual abuse that makes child pornography inappropriate and illegal; it is not the fact that people might generate obscene, deviant or inappropriate fantasies around some photographs. Creating a pragmatic balance between freedom of thought and expression (and recognising that these cannot be controlled), and child protection is the challenge we face in this area.

However cautious we must be in making inferences about civil libertarian and other issues related to non-pornographic material, we also need to be aware of the context in which much of this material is produced. The case referred to above of a boy subjected to both pornographic and non-pornographic photography also serves to highlight a further, even more disturbing, factor in the production and distribution cycle of child pornography – the involvement of organised crime. The photographer of this child was allegedly paid $75,000 to produce a video by Russian organised criminal sources involved in the commercial distribution of child pornography. This is by no means a typical situation, and, for the moment, we can say that child pornography distribution, and in most cases production, remains a complex international conspiracy not primarily driven by money; but alarmingly it is one in which money seems increasingly to be a factor. But regardless of issues of payment, this emphasises the fact that the child involved in this transaction was essentially a commodity, to be used primarily in this case for the generation of profit, but in other cases for sexual fantasy. As far as the distributors are concerned the pornographic material produced is simply a product, although clearly that product gained its value from its sexual content.

What commercial involvement emphasises more clearly than domestic production is the sense in which the pictures that constitute child pornography are disembodied and disconnected; they are unreal representations, a symbol of something rather than a reality. That they are of real children is, of course, significant and crucial, but photographic representations (and video representations) are creations rather than reality. It is not the particular child that is important, but an image of a child that meets certain visual requirements (in terms primarily of looks and actions performed). But the cycle of child pornography does involve real children, and we know that the content implicit in sexual photographs of children also finds expression in reality. The smiling face of the child in a photograph is also the face of a child subject to a serious crime. Once captured on a photograph, the image remains. The child is forever frozen at its age at that time, and is available to anyone who has the means to acquire it. Child pornography therefore represents and preserves that abuse or sexualised image for as long as that photograph (or video) remains. The relatively innocent other photographs that were taken of the child referred to above (and regrettably of many others) need to be seen in this broader context.

In the past, obtaining child pornography was difficult. It required a measure of physical exposure of the person involved to being identified, in that a visit to a specialised sex shop was required, or a name and address had to be given to a mail order organisation. The private exchange of pictures between individuals also took place, but again the danger of identification remained. Pictures (in the form of single images, magazines, cine films and latterly videos) may have been costly to obtain from commercial sources, because even if they were not illegal, open acknowledgement of a sexual interest in children is not something that has ever been tolerated in contemporary Western societies. Recognising this, the retailers of child pornography could charge large amounts of money for their material. But now circumstances have changed. Whilst the open commercial sale of child pornography is now no longer tolerated in any Western country, paradoxically the availability of child pornography is easier and in more plentiful supply than ever before. This is because of the Internet. The Internet enables the speedy, efficient and above all anonymous distribution of child pornography on a global scale. Anyone with a modicum of technical expertise can access child pornography through either the World Wide Web or newsgroups. Furthermore, much of the Internet-related pornography is free. Child pornography is one of the few *commodities* that can be transferred over the Internet, in the sense that the information required to construct a picture can be rapidly and easily distributed over an existing widely available network. Thus, the Internet enables in this case not just the passage of information, but also the delivery of a product – a picture or video sequence – provided the recipient has the software to decode and construct a picture.

The information passed over the Internet that constitutes a picture is a perfect copy of an original, which can be reproduced endlessly without loss of definition or any other qualities. Once a picture has been copied and distributed over the Internet, its further distribution is wholly out of control. If a picture has been transmitted to an Internet source, removal of the original source, therefore, has no effect on the subsequent distribution. What this means is that once a picture has been copied and distributed on the Internet, it is essentially always available. It can always be further copied, it can always be distributed, and it always remains. The only certain way of eliminating a picture is to trace and eliminate every copy, an impossible task given the global scale of distribution of these images.

Such distribution of images is not random, nor do those with a commercial interest in its production solely drive it. People coming together on the Internet, to a large extent, form a community. Communities may constitute a few people or thousands. Membership of communities formed on the Internet is constantly changing and evolving as people respond to this medium. For those who have a sexual interest in children, such communities are used to normalise those interests but are also used to share and trade information, and particularly photographs of children. Individuals approached through such communities help to provide 'missing' pictures from series, help solve technical problems in the trading of material, give advice about security issues to prevent detection by the law and offer fantasy stories to complement the images of children. The communities themselves, if children are also involved, may also be used as a means of contacting children or trading information about children. Child pornography is not exclusively a cybercrime, for not all collectors of child pornography necessarily use the Internet to acquire child pornography. But the Internet is the most visible and significant contemporary medium for the distribution of child pornography. And because the commodity of visual images is uniquely a product that can be distributed over the Internet, the bringing of child pornography into cyberspace has resulted in exaggerating and adding a significant new dimension to the contemporary social problem of child sexual abuse.

CHILD SEXUAL ABUSE

The past twenty years have seen an enormous growth in concern about adult sexual abuse of children. It has become a major area of both research and practical social welfare intervention. The periodic scandals related to inadequate childcare and especially sexual abuse in residential settings have raised legitimate questions about how we treat vulnerable children. But research has also emphasised the familial base of most child sexual abuse.

There are a number of psychological and criminological theories of child sexual abuse, which stem from a variety of disciplinary foundations. These include psychodynamic, behavioural, biological, socio-cultural and global theories. Until fairly recently, the most prominent theoretical stance was psychodynamic. Essentially, the offenders' underlying motivation was constructed as being not sexual in nature, but involving the expression of non-sexual needs and unresolved life issues. Assault was then viewed as a 'pseudo-sexual act' or sexual behaviour that was used to meet non-sexual needs. This model went on to categorise child molesters into two basic types, according to the nature of their motivation. The *regressed offender* was seen as someone who had developed age-appropriate sexual orientation, but who, under particular circumstances, regresses to sexual involvement with children. The *fixated offender* was someone whose primary sexual interest was in children.

Within the last fifteen years there has been increased interest in examining the empirical relationship between child molestation and a wide variety of psychological variables. Such variables include social and interpersonal factors, cognitive states, childhood, family and attitudinal factors. Within this framework, Finkelhor's (1984) Precondition Model is perhaps one of the most widely known models of child sexual abuse. According to this model four preconditions need to be met before sexual abuse can occur:

(a) motivation to sexually abuse;
(b) overcoming internal inhibitors;

(c) overcoming external inhibitors; and
(d) overcoming the resistance of the child.

Finkelhor (1984) intended the Precondition Model to be a general blueprint for all kinds of sexual abuse, but he did, however, highlight the importance of two dimensions to classify child sexual abusers: (a) strength of motivation; and (b) exclusivity of sexual preference. According to the Precondition Model, the dimension of Motivation has three components:

1 emotional congruence – the offender has an emotional need to relate to children;
2 sexual arousal – children are a potential source of sexual gratification; and
3 blockage – adult sexual and emotional gratification are unavailable to the offender for a number of reasons, e.g. low social competence and sexual anxiety.

Although Finkelhor (1984) argued that most sexual behaviour involves some non-sexual motivation, the Precondition Model places great emphasis on sexual arousal, with respect to motivation, and sexual preference as an important dimension of child sexual abuse.

The role of fantasy in the broad issue of adult sexual interest in children is little understood but it is clearly a significant variable in child pornography. In a general sense, the relationship between fantasy and action remains obscure. Authors such as Margison (1997) asserted that in paedophilia the move from fantasy to action is critical, while Howitt (1995) noted an imperfect match between fantasy and action. He suggested that the idea of fantasy could be seen in one of two ways – in a psychoanalytic sense where the fantasy acts as wish-fulfilment and is therefore separate from everyday life (much like a safety-valve), or it could be viewed as fantasy being a precursor to action. It may be, as suggested by Seto *et al.* (2001) that those who are predisposed to sexually offend are the most likely to show an effect from pornography exposure and are also the most likely to show the strongest effects. Predisposition to offend is likely to mean the seeking out of pornographic and fantasy material, which is less likely in those without a sexual interest in children.

An important conceptual consideration highlighted in recent years in the academic literature is the role played by cognition or thought processes in adult sexual interest in children. Such cognitions include the decisions made by the person with a sexual interest in children that place him at risk for offending, the high-risk situations that threaten his control, and the thoughts and feelings that can lead to offending behaviour. Nelson *et al.* (1988) stated that a number of common risk factors can precipitate offending behaviour. These include the presence of a potential victim, the use of disinhibitors such as alcohol or drugs, interpersonal conflict, rationalisations for engaging in the behaviour (such as those obtained from support networks on the Internet) and negative affect or mood. Cognitive distortions are regarded by many as the 'sine qua non of the paedophile' (Howitt 1995: 92). Although there is no one conceptual model which addresses cognitive distortions alone, there are many theories and models of child sexual abuse which refer to cognitive distortions as an important facet of such offending behaviour. Cognitive Distortions, according to Howitt (1995) 'provide offenders with an interpretative framework that permits them to construe the victims and motives of others as sexual and allows them to justify and excuse themselves (and others) their offending behaviour' (93). As with the majority of cognitive explanations, it is unclear whether the faulty cognitions, such as 'Having sex with a child is a good way for an adult to teach a child about sex' are post-offence rationalisations, or are in existence prior to offending. This whole area is one of great significance in understanding child pornography, and is discussed later in much greater depth.

THE PAEDOPHILE

The person who is sexually interested in children is often termed a paedophile. The Paedophile Liberation Front, a mutual support group for those with a sexual interest in children, define a paedophile as 'an adult that is sexually attracted to children. "Sexually" means that this person may like to touch you, rub your body against his, be very affectionate and cuddly. He (or sometimes she) may also wish to touch your private parts, or have you touch his. In short, a paedophile likes to do with children what everybody else likes to do with adults.'

As portrayed in accounts like this, paedophilia is not only a sexual orientation but also a way of life and has a whole subculture to support it. Within this subculture, discriminations are made between paedophiles and child molesters (sometimes called predators). From this perspective, child molester is a negative term, and is generally used to refer to people who sexually abuse children, whereas paedophilia indicates a sexual interest in and love of children, which may never be acted upon. Indeed, within the context of the Internet, many paedophiles would argue that looking at photographs provides a safe outlet for feelings that might otherwise lead to a contact offence.

Using the term paedophile in some measure draws on positive connotations. The term paedophile in origin means 'lover of children', a socially positive and on the whole desirable state. However, the context most commonly used, and of concern to us, makes reference to sexual love or desire. Within Western society, such sexual love is a source of concern when the object of that emotion is a child. A better term may be to refer to adults with a sexual interest in children, but this is both unwieldy and lacks common acceptance. In this book, paedophile is sometimes used for the sake of brevity of expression. It should be noted, however, that use of the term does not imply a blurring of the distinctions between affection and sexual desire, nor does it imply an acceptance of the appropriateness of sexual interest in children.

Lanning (1992) developed the first typology of paedophilic computer offenders, which proposes two broad categories. The *Situational Offender* (dabbler) is described as being either a teenager who searches online for pornography and sex or an impulsive/curious adult who has discovered an unlimited access to pornography and sexual opportunities. He describes the behaviour of such 'dabblers' as being less persistent and predictable than that of preferential offenders. The *Preferential Offender*, in contrast, is either sexually indiscriminate with a broad interest in sexually deviant activities or a 'paedophile' who has a definite preference for children. He distinguishes these two subtypes by assserting that the paedophile will collect mainly child-focused material whereas the indiscriminate preferential offender will have a wide-ranging collection, which will include pictures of children.

According to Lanning the sexually indiscriminate offender will be less likely to commit a hands-on sexual offence with a child (especially a prepubescent child) than a paedophile. Also included are other 'miscellaneous' computer offenders such as journalists who trade child pornography as part of a news story, pranksters who are playing dirty tricks, older boyfriends who are attempting to entice adolescent girls or boys and concerned citizens attempting to combat the problem (Lanning 1995: 13). Central to this classification is an assumption that those who are active on the Internet begin with the intent of actively seeking paedophilic material, and/or to join a paedophilic community. This implicitly suggests that the preferential paedophile poses a significantly greater risk of committing a hands-on offence.

An area of obvious great concern is the relationship between paedophile interests, child pornography and sexual offences against children. It must be noted that we have very little systematic evidence on the relationship between involvement with child pornography and sexual assaults on children. We do know, however, that not all who are convicted of sexual assaults on children express an interest in, or knowledge of, child pornography. What systematic evidence there is that addresses these issues primarily relates to adult situations, and effects on child-related offending can really only be suggested by inference. The most intensively examined area relates to the effects of pornography on indicators of rape. In a paper reviewing the effects of pornography in the aetiology of sexual aggression primarily directed at adults, Seto *et al.* (2001) concluded that 'overall, there is little support for a direct causal link between pornography use and sexual aggression', although it should be noted that the evidence can be contradictory. They also noted that the role of pornography in other areas such as child molestation is much less well researched.

Durkin (1997) outlined paedophilic misuses of the Internet emphasising that it acts as 'an outlet for sexual gratification and as a social consolidation mechanism'. He also raised the issue that the supportive environment available on the Internet to paedophiles may be influential in encouraging some of them to commit sexual abuse of children. The Internet has made a huge impact on paedophile networking allowing communication and access to unlimited numbers of likeminded people (Durkin and Bryant 1995). The supportive environment offered by the Net involves both social consolidation and validation, and, because of that, Durkin and Bryant suggested that there is a distinct possibility that some paedophiles may refine or act upon their deviant proclivities because of their exposure to the Internet. This, they note, is an unprecedented development in the area of paedophilic behaviour.

THE INTERNET

The relationship between the individual and the Internet is a fascinating one. In one sense, the Internet is merely a means of communication, facilitating the exchange of information in unique, rapid, convenient forms. There is increasing evidence, however, of the Internet itself, and the social and psychological processes that are involved in accessing it, being both a process and factor in its own right that is both cumulative and additional to other means of communication. In the context of concern to this book, there is growing evidence of the Internet playing a part in the facilitation of adult sexual interest in children, not merely through the transfer of child pornography, but by providing a supportive context and by changing opportunities individuals might have for contact with children through chat rooms, web sites and e-mail.

The existing models of offending behaviour tend to examine the attributes of the offender without reference to the process of offending. Many of the offender models tend to be static rather than dynamic, the problem lying within the individual rather than in the socially changing and constructed interaction between the individual and his world. However, Granic and Lamey (2000) have suggested that through Internet experiences people have come to reinterpret society, relationships and even the self. The possibility that people are changed by and subsequently contribute to change through the Internet is highly relevant to the area of sexual offending. Through the Internet we see a potential change in the offender's beliefs, values and cognitive styles. The fact that through the Internet users can in the main go anywhere and say anything without any official governing body restricting those actions means that for some people this will be their first experience of acting outside the confines of a conventional hierarchy. Granic and Lamey made the important observation that 'conventional hierarchies are disrupted by a distributed, decentralised network in which power is spread among various people and groups and one voice does not dominate or pre-empt others' (*ibid.*: 104). Such experiences may empower some people such as sex offenders who have otherwise been marginalised in conventional society. Those who have never been able to function at an optimal level in the real world may feel that they have the chance to do so now that conventional structures are broken down. Holmes *et al.* (1998) have even suggested that the computer might act as a catalytic or facilitating mechanism for new forms of deviant behaviour and that the computer can be a mechanism of metamorphosis.

Not only is it apparent that for some individuals the Internet presents an opportunity to access material that may be problematic from a judicial perspective, but also there is emerging a literature that suggests that the nature of the Internet itself may be problematic for the user. A study by Morahan-Martin and Schumacher (2000) suggested that in their sample men were four times more likely to have a problem controlling their use of the Internet than women. They asserted that this was possibly because males were more likely to use applications, such as Internet games, Netsex and Internet gambling, that these authors associated with more compulsive use. They also gave some understanding about the experience of being 'online', which has relevance for those sexually interested in children. 'On the Internet, one can self-present from the relative safety of a computer screen. Social contact over the Internet does not involve face-to-face communication and can even be anonymous, which can lessen social risk and lower inhibitions' (Morahan-Martin and Schumacher 2000: 25).

This is similar to the findings of Turkle (1995) who suggested that the Internet allows users to try out new ways of relating, new roles and identity and even to switch genders. It has even been suggested that the Internet can produce altered states of consciousness, which are the result of intense and immediate interactive feedback (online) that responds to other users' individual commands and which differentiates it from other, more passive, entertainment and communication technologies (Bromberg 1996).

The effects of the Internet *per se* may be evident in other ways. The media frequently contain comments related to the amount of pornography on the Internet. This comment is usually made with reference to adult pornography, although it could as readily be made with respect to child pornography. The nature of the Internet, however, makes quantification of comments of this kind very difficult, but there is some evidence that the use of the Internet as a medium for the distribution of pornography has changed the type of at least adult pornography available. Barron and Kimmel (2000), in a comparative study referring to adult pornography available from magazines to video to the Internet, suggested there has been an increase in 'both the violence and the amount of misogyny – women as victims – contained in the images'. In many ways, child pornography is necessarily non-consensual, and although sadistic child pornography or the portrayal of violent scenes involving children is relatively rare, the processes described above may well be reflected in the increased availability and qualities of child pornography. Certainly, there is at the moment some evidence that the age of children in new child pornography is getting younger.

In terms of the management of child pornography, and its control by law enforcement agencies, the Internet presents special difficulties. One essential quality of the Internet is that it knows no national borders, and presents equally to all who can access it an enormously valuable resource. A user can as readily access a site in his or her own country as in any other, and information can be almost instantaneously passed around the world at virtually no cost to the user. In terms of the concerns of this book, however, this presents quite special problems. For example, what is legally appropriate in one location may not be elsewhere, but access to it through the Internet cannot in the main be controlled by any national jurisdiction. Given that a picture is uniquely in Internet terms a commodity, that commodity can be moved between people with ease. And given the nature of the Internet, and the way information is organised, unless special procedures are put in place it is essentially untraceable if the sender wishes it to be. Both formal and informal means of contact between people is possible using the Internet, adding further to the complexity of its management and control.

Control of the Internet

Attempts to control child pornography on the Internet have brought into focus critical issues related to the nature of the Internet as a medium of information transmission, and the social context in which that information is transmitted. A central issue for policy makers is the problem of reconciling freedom of speech and limitations on censorship of the Internet with the very evident child-protection problems presented by the production, distribution and viewing of child pornography. International co-operation in terms of legislative harmonisation has tended to separate the regulation of child pornography from broader censorship issues of the Internet. In part, this has been done as a means of avoiding controversial problems related to differing national perspectives on censorship, and also as a way of encouraging the development of e-commerce by minimising the regulatory framework applied to the Internet. A particular problem in regulating the Internet is the sense in which no single national framework can apply to it.

Focusing attention on the management of child pornography has undoubtedly helped in the development of a common international agenda in the emergence of protective legislative frameworks. However, this development has also tended to divert legislative and policy attention from the broader problem of the regulation of adult pornography, and explorations of features in common with child pornography. At least for some individuals, an interest in child pornography is a step along a path of access to pornographies in general; this emphasises the more general issue of the need to encourage the development of a broader regulatory environment (see Edwards 2000 for a discussion with respect to British obscenity laws). The increasing evidence of organised criminal involvement in the trade in child pornography and its links to the sex industry adds further emphasis to this point. The recent Cybercrime Convention, if ratified by individual states, will make some significant changes in international police practice and legal harmonisation. But despite the fact that the Convention contains specific reference to child pornography, it largely has an anti-terrorism focus, rather than a child-protection one, and its practical significance remains to be demonstrated.

The distributed and essentially uncontrollable qualities of the Internet present enormous challenges for law enforcement agencies tasked with the management of child pornography on the Internet. A central area of difficulty relates to who will actually take ownership of investigations into, for example, cases of production of new child pornography, when all that is known is that a new picture or series of pictures has emerged? If a picture contains no clues as to location, then what police force will take the responsibility for investigation? Given the geographical basis on which police forces operate, this is a very real problem. International agencies such as Interpol obviously have a role to play in terms of co-ordination, etc. But Interpol does not have the authority or capacity to mount national investigations.

It can be argued that the Internet industry occupies a critical role in any discussion about regulation of the Internet. Initiatives to encourage self-regulation amongst Internet Service Providers (ISPs) offers an alternative to legislative intervention, with the added bonus of a significant international dimension, at least amongst the larger ISPs. Recent US legislation will facilitate this development, as will the emergence of national structures, such as the Irish Government's Internet Advisory Board. A critical issue relevant to this is a recognition of the link between child pornography picture collection, and engagement with chat and other forms of communication with likeminded individuals. Much of this communication relates to exchange of fantasy (but presumably, at times, real) accounts, although there is clear evidence of individuals learning security procedures, and gaining information generally about the location of supportive material. In practical terms, meaningful legislative attempts to control fantasy and personal communication are difficult in the extreme to develop, and impossible to apply, as well as presenting major human rights issues. A more effective way of addressing this problem is through individual ISPs, through their terms of service, which will effectively allow control over chat rooms and other communication protocols where obviously illegal material, such as pictures, is not involved. The challenge here, of course, is the development of effective international self-regulatory frameworks for ISPs.

LOOKING AHEAD

In the following chapters, we will attempt to explore what child pornography is, how it relates to the Internet, and crucially, how the Internet uniquely creates and develops processes that facilitate the collection and distribution of child pornography. Child pornography is an emotional issue, and quite naturally the debate around it has largely been characterised by strong moral and political imperatives, rather than reasoned debate and understanding. One of the main objectives of this book is to try to develop a systematic and reasoned understanding of child pornography. It does not seek to diminish its seriousness nor to condone or excuse its production, distribution or collection. But this work is produced in the belief that understanding and knowledge will help better control and limit its availability.

Throughout the book the significance of three broad themes are stressed as being central elements that help our understanding of child pornography and the Internet. The first theme obviously relates to *sexual behaviour* and *sexuality*. Child pornography is sexual both in intent, and in reality. However, it is important to recognise that associated with sexuality are notions related to power and control. The second theme relates to the significance of a sense of *community*, which finds virtual expression in the context of the Internet. In the sense used here, community embraces an array of facilitative and supportive elements, as well as serving a normalising role. The third theme relates to *processes*, which in Internet terms find expression in collecting; it may also embrace notions of risk taking and the significance of anonymity.

The book is structured in terms of chapters addressing individual issues. Chapter 2, 'The nature of child pornography', explores the factors involved in the production of child pornography, and considers its nature and content. It places child pornography within a historical context, particularly relating it to social and political changes in the 1970s and explores what constitutes contemporary child pornography as reflected in the material collected. Based on empirical analysis it develops a classification taxonomy, illustrating the above through empirical and case study examples. Chapter 3 explores the area of 'Adult sexual interest in children' reviewing our understanding of adult sexual interest in children, with a particular emphasis on psychological approaches. This includes offender typologies, cognitive accounts, empathy, theory of mind and insider accounts.

Chapter 4 brings together the major themes of 'The Internet, Child pornography and Adult sexual interest in children'. This chapter introduces those aspects of the Internet that relate to and facilitate adult sexual interest in children. This includes the computer as a catalyst, the process of normalisation, access to and manipulation of images, and accessing both adults and children. In Chapter 5 we introduce 'Metamorphosis'. This chapter explores contemporary knowledge about how people engage with the Internet and how, through that engagement, they may be changed. Particular points of reference include self-representation, new roles and identities, changing socialisation and new ways of relating, and reinterpretation of society, relationships and the self.

Developing further the theme of the role of the Internet, Chapter 6 introduces the notion of 'A virtual community'. In this chapter we examine the importance of community in relation to offending behaviour. In particular, we explore how offending behaviour is facilitated and developed by virtual structures on the Internet. It uses examples from Internet Relay Chat involving paedophile communication to demonstrate two aspects of community: a hierarchy of membership and developing ways of protecting 'the group'.

Chapter 7 moves the discussion on towards more psychological issues, in a discussion of 'The process of collecting'. This chapter explores the psychology of collecting behaviour, with particular reference to the effects of the Internet. It focuses on collections of pornography to illustrate the processes involved, comparing and contrasting Internet-mediated collecting with other forms of collecting. It also examines how aspects of both collecting and organising behaviour may function socially, and the role this may have as forensic evidence. Extending the psychological discussion, Chapter 8 addresses 'A model of problematic Internet use'. This chapter presents a process model of problematic Internet use, emphasising the various factors influencing both the development of the offending process, and offending behaviour. The final chapter, Chapter 9, 'Issues for concern and conclusions', draws together issues arising in earlier chapters, with a particular emphasis on the role of changing technologies, the role of the ISP industry and societal ambiguity towards child sexuality.

CONCLUDING COMMENTS

This book does not contain any pictures, or indeed any descriptions that reveal the nature of child pornography in that sense. Care has been taken to exclude reference to names that might identify either victims or offenders. To that extent the reader is insulated from the reality of the world from which, and in which, child pornography is created and exchanged. Academic discussion or the reasoned debate of issues that must characterise any systematic examination of a complex social issue necessarily creates a distance between the reader and the topic of examination. However, the research that this book draws on has involved continued access to and examination of child pornography, its victims and the offenders. Both authors are involved in the COPINE Project, and have drawn on their experience of forensic and clinical psychology to develop the material presented here. The pictures that are the issue of concern are of real children, and those pictures are a permanent and enduring record of at least one aspect of their lives. The children's stories are seldom told because, despite all the contemporary attention given to this topic, we have very little knowledge about the children who appear in child pornography – very few are identified.

Many of the commonly occurring pictures on the Internet are more than thirty years old. The individuals portrayed are now in their forties, perhaps in settled relationships, perhaps with children of their own. Can we imagine the effects on their family or friends of revelation of such pictures of this aspect of their childhood? Can we have any sense of the effects on these adults of these records of parts of their childhood? The pictures we are concerned with, therefore, are more than just visual representations. Even the more innocent and less offensive pictures belong in a complex context of the child's life at the time the photographs were taken, and need to be treated with the respect this implies. Ill-considered efforts at the identification of victims in such circumstances could greatly add to negative consequences for the individuals involved.

At the moment, the primary driving force in the management of child pornography is the law enforcement community. Until recently, child pornography was rarely identified as a factor in child sexual abuse, not necessarily because taking sexual photographs of children did not occur, but because, in the main, social welfare intervention with survivors of child sexual abuse has not seen it as a particularly relevant factor in treatment or counselling. The current ease of availability, and the sheer volume of child pornography on the Internet, has drawn our attention to the existence of child pornography in a very dramatic way. But we need to remember that child pornography was not invented in the 1960s when there was the first upsurge in public availability. Nor is it an invention associated with the development of photography. Child pornography (like adult pornography) is a feature of sexual activity, and has always been produced in different forms, using whatever the contemporary media of the time were. What we are grappling with now is a coming to terms with its existence and, in doing so, trying to understand what it is, what role it plays, and in consequence, developing means of at least controlling its production and distribution. To do this, we need to move understanding out of narrow law enforcement and social welfare arenas, and to develop a more systematic understanding of both child pornography, and the principal means of distribution, the Internet. The principal aspiration of the authors in writing this book is to contribute to that process.

Chapter 2

The nature of child pornography

WHAT IS THE PROBLEM?

As we noted in Chapter 1, over recent years offences related to the production, possession and distribution of child pornography have assumed great prominence. Our attention has been focused on these crimes by what at times has been intense media coverage. Paradoxically, however, because possession of child pornography is now in the main illegal and also because by its nature it is an underground activity, there is little public knowledge of what it actually is, its attributes, or even the processes involved in its creation. We might even be misled into thinking that it is a new phenomenon, something that has its origins in the late twentieth century.

In this chapter, we will explore issues related to the nature of child pornography, its features and the legal and psychological factors related to it. Our obvious starting point in examining the nature of child pornography is that it relates in some way to the sexual abuse of children – that ultimately is why we are concerned about it, and why it merits the attention it receives. Later in the chapter we will introduce and contrast some of the legal and psychological approaches that aid our understanding, but for the moment it is sufficient to note that our concerns about child pornography are grounded in the association of it with what in general we regard as inappropriate and at times illegal sexual interests in children. We can approach these qualities of child pornography in two ways: from the perspective of *production*, and from the perspective of *viewing*.

Production

We have noted in Chapter 1 that, at its worst, child pornography is a picture of a sexual assault on a child. Given this, it is relatively easy, therefore, to bring into focus our concerns about the *production* of child pornography. To produce it, someone has to assault a child, or pose a child in a sexualised way, and to make a photographic record of it. For the purpose of our discussion, in the following, unless otherwise noted, no particular distinction will be made between still photography, video and cine photography, all of which are subsumed under the general label of photograph. Although comments later in this chapter will make reference to adventitious photographs and to the complexity of deciding what actually constitutes child pornography in specific circumstances, we can confidently assert that in general child pornography is never accidental; it is constructed by the photographer, the child is posed and the actions that take place are deliberate and intentional. Sexual interests, and often sexual assault, lie at the very heart of the production of child pornography.

We can illustrate the deliberate quality of child pornography in a very simple way. A common characteristic of child pornography is that the subject is generally smiling; it is rare to see pornographic photographs of a child in distress. Smiling is important because it suggests the child is happy, even enjoying, what is happening. In terms of fantasy generation, it supports the image of the compliant sexually involved child who willingly participates in the sexual behaviour being portrayed. Comments about pictures from collectors make clear their rejection of photographs that do not meet such fantasy requirements. 'I didn't like the ones where the girls weren't pretty . . . I didn't like the ones where there were quite a lot where er . . . they you know the victims were obviously in distress' (KQ). A clearer reference to the significance of 'smiling' and 'happiness' can be seen in these quotations: 'But I made sure the pictures I had . . . the children didn't look like they were being hurt. They actually looked happy a lot' (EI). This quotation further illustrates this theme: 'the girls who appeared in these shots . . . had this air of you know enjoying themselves . . . you know . . . they were doing it because they wanted to' (MQ).

Insights into the process of production of child pornography are difficult to come by, and generally speaking, video footage, for example, either has no sound track, or simply has music recorded on it. However, from time to time, videos emerge that have sound tracks that give the voice of the photographer whilst the filming is taking place. These videos reveal the process of making video sequences, and the extent to which the photographic activities are directed. More to the point, such audio material shows how instructions to 'smile', and 'look at the camera and smile' occur frequently throughout the photographic session. The smiling image is a construction recognised as both desirable and necessary by the photographer. Instructions are not necessarily benign; occasionally, the bribes and threats made by the photographer to induce the child to do what is required can also be heard, further emphasising the ease with which a covert coercive context can change through photography to an overtly coercive environment. This can be illustrated by the following quotation from a man who was involved in producing increasingly explicit child pornography involving one young girl. 'I was quite persuasive . . . not in a violent way . . . I was using like tactics like if you do this I'll treat you to something . . . so like trying to offer her stuff to . . . because before that she hadn't really resisted to any of the activities as such apart from the oral sex, which she did not wanna do' (ES).

We can reasonably assert, therefore, that the production of child pornography is never accidental. It is a construction and its content is both deliberate and stylised to meet certain implicit and explicit requirements. To complete this brief discussion, there are two broad kinds of context that we can identify in which child pornography is produced. The first relates to private production, for the use of the producer. The photographer is almost invariably a parent, guardian of some kind, or someone from the immediate family circle of the child when young children are involved. However, for older children, especially boys, this may also be someone not immediately in the child's family circle. The second relates to production with a view to further distribution, either between a small circle of likeminded people, or perhaps with reference to some commercial context. In this case, the photographer again is most likely to be someone from the child's immediate circle of family or friends. The implications of this simple distinction will be considered later.

Viewing

We can think of viewing as including the possession, collection and distribution of child pornography. This is a more diffuse activity than production, however, and bringing into focus our concerns here is rather more complex. Indeed, use of the term 'viewing', although it describes in part what people do with child pornography, may be itself problematic. Tate (1990) has observed that paedophiles talk about 'viewing' pictures or images, and use of the term 'viewing' is also a feature of the COPINE research interviews. 'Viewing' implies some level of passive observation, but, as Tate concludes, 'pedophiles don't simply view the material they collect, they catalogue and index it as well' (112). We might add that they also sexually interact with it through masturbation and fantasy. What is significant in relation to child pornography is the way that the viewer engages with the material downloaded.

An important if obvious starting point is that there is generally no direct link between the viewer and the child photographed; the viewer is distanced in place, and time, from the person photographed. The viewer, therefore, unlike the photographer does not engage in the particular sexual behaviour portrayed, other than in imagination. We do know, of course, that viewing child pornography can be associated with sexual behaviour of the viewer, notably masturbation, and that for adults with a sexual interest in children, child pornography serves an important function in generating and sustaining masturbatory fantasy. Thus, even at this level, viewing child pornography is not a passive act, and usually involves sexual behaviour. In general, however, that behaviour is solitary, confined only to the viewer. However, in addition, child pornography can also play a part in sexual behaviour in other ways as in, for example, a part of the grooming process used by paedophiles to become close to and sexually de-sensitise children (Durkin 1997; Healy 1997). Tyler and Stone (1985) have suggested that child molesters who possess child pornography in any form use such material to facilitate the seduction of new victims. A child might be shown child pornography as part of the process of breaking down inhibitions, cementing relationships, etc. This is not uniquely related to child pornography, however, as adult pornography may also be used in the same way. (This issue is discussed in later chapters.)

Why then do we seek to control the engagement through *viewing* of child pornography? Its production in the main involves a sexual assault, but why should viewing (and possession) be a problem? Indeed, Edwards (1994) sought to establish the position that the structure of sexuality within visual imagery (in this instance nude images of children) 'is as much a social factor as a human one' (38), and that nudist images of children do not compromise the integrity of the subject. This position allowed her to argue that: 'The nudity portrayed by Sturges was, in effect, *sexualised* by the legal action of the FBI and the San Francisco police' (42) in their seizure of his photographs. It is clear that in liberal democracies the answer to this dilemma cannot lie in seeking to control inappropriate sexual fantasy amongst viewers. It is a reasonable assumption that many people have at different times many sexual fantasies that are inappropriate, or even illegal. We cannot know anyway, of course, what an individual fantasises about unless they tell us, or unless they engage in behaviour affecting others that in some way reveals the nature of that fantasy. We need more substantial reasons than inappropriate fantasy to justify viewing child pornography as a serious criminal offence.

The following are some of the reasons why we might be concerned about viewing child pornography:

1 It requires that a child be abused to produce it. The process of production requires the photographer to create a situation where a child is either directly abused, or posed in sexualised ways, and as such it is a product of an illegal and inappropriate act. The viewer is in a sense aiding and abetting that process, by providing a market for the material and for making evident (through Internet activity, private contact or through payment for commercial material) a demand.
2 A photographic record in whatever media preserves the pictures of that abuse. At worst, therefore, it is a permanent record of crime, and serves to perpetuate the images and memory of that abuse for as long as it exists. Distributing and viewing child pornography, therefore, ensures the continued and even increased availability of the pictures. The implications of this for the family of the child and the child itself may be very severe and traumatic; it also represents a violation of the child and its family's privacy, and generally a visible demonstration of abuse of position or relationship. This becomes of greater significance in the context of the Internet. Once a photograph is digitised and distributed on the Internet, it can be perfectly reproduced endlessly by anyone in possession of it. In the case of a normal photograph, destruction of the negative severely limits the likelihood of that photograph being reproduced; in the case of Internet images, the only way to control reproduction of a photograph is to destroy all copies – an impossible task once a picture has been posted to an Internet source.
3 By generating inappropriate sexual fantasy in an individual, we may be concerned about the risk of fantasy becoming reality; concerned that by watching a sexual assault, it normalises the activity and encourages the viewer

subsequently to commit such an assault. Intellectually this may seem a reasonable fear, although empirically, the evidence, such as there is, tends to discount it (Seto *et al.* 2001), at least in so far as adult pornography is concerned. On the other hand, research by Carter *et al.* (1987) examined the reported use of and exposure to pornographic materials by two groups: convicted rapists and child molesters. While both groups indicated similar prior exposure, child molesters were more likely to use such materials prior to and during the commission of an offence. This was similar to the findings of Marshall (1988) which suggested that within his sample, slightly more than one third of child molesters had at least occasionally been incited to commit an offence by exposure to pornographic material. A much clearer risk lies in pornographic material becoming the model that encourages and generates viewers to take photographs themselves – in other words, for some people it provides the stimulus (when other circumstances allow) to cross the boundary from viewing to abusing. 'I would say it fuelled my interest that I had anyway that was in me . . . but it seemed to reinforce it and . . . made me want to act on it' (DX). Whether child pornography *per se* creates that stimulus, whether the social context in which child pornography is traded (especially on the Internet) is the critical factor, or whether it facilitates and gives expression to an intention already formed is not clear. However, that there is a relationship of some kind for some individuals is quite clear. The following interview quotation makes this association very apparent: 'When I made this video tape I was copying these er movie clips . . . that I'd downloaded er . . . I wanted to be . . . doing what they were doing' (KQ).

4 Child pornography can act as a learning instrument in the 'grooming' process, whereby a child is de-sensitised to sexual demands and encouraged to normalise inappropriate activities. Burgess and Hartman (1987) suggested that 'child pornography is produced at the psychological expense of the photographed child' (248) because the use of such photography binds the victim by normalising the acts and ultimately by acting as a source of blackmail for the child. Silbert (1989) suggested that 'One of the most destructive impacts on juveniles of their participation in pornography is the silent conspiracy into which they feel bound by the offender' (227). Children who have been identified as the victims of pornography are unlikely to talk about the abuse. In their study of ten such children, Svedin and Back (1996) suggested that 'The children are filled with shame when they talk about their experiences and there is a great sense of degradation and blame and fear of the possible consequences of exposure' (64). What is especially sad is that there is evidence that very vulnerable children, particularly those from underprivileged homes or where childcare is lacking, are likely to be most at risk of being photographed (Collings 1995). Where very young children are photographed, such exploitation has largely been by their own parents or others involved in their care (Lanning and Burgess 1989). The process of de-sensitisation might also affect the viewer, who seeks to maintain arousal

by seeking out new, or more sexually extreme, material: 'it was a slippery . . . slope erm a very unhealthy slope that I was going down . . . erm I suppose in a lot of ways I was becoming de-sensitised to it . . . the more I was seeing the less it was bothering me . . . and the more I was seeing the more I was thinking this is er perfectly acceptable behaviour because . . . there's so much of it there you know it can't be that bad' (KQ).

5 A consequence of viewing sexual pictures of children is that it may sexualise other aspects of childhood and family life. However, there seems to be a broad consensus in contemporary Western society that childhood and family life should not be encroached on in this way. This is a more general issue than the specific examples given above, and makes assumptions about the nature of society, and the role of children in society. Whatever individual views on this might be, it is none the less a source of concern. Kincaid (1998) draws our attention to the social and psychological consequences associated with media and other accounts of child molesting; how much greater then is the damage done by actual photographs of a child being molested?

To summarise, what then is the problem with child pornography? For the producer, the situation is clear – they photograph offences, and maybe participate in them. Engaging with child pornography through viewing, collecting and distributing, whilst not directly abusive, nevertheless contributes to the process of abuse, and supports and nourishes the production of child pornography. This, therefore, identifies the problem; what then is child pornography?

WHAT IS CHILD PORNOGRAPHY? LEGAL AND PSYCHOLOGICAL PERSPECTIVES

Because of its emotive nature, and also because possession is in the main illegal, research into the nature and extent of child pornography is limited. Such published material that there is tends to be primarily from law enforcement perspectives, meeting rather narrow ends and tending to focus on somewhat limited evidential perspectives. In what is one of the most significant early contributions to this area, Lanning (1992) outlined a behaviour analysis of child molesters that described the role of child pornography in their offending behaviour. Unusually, in this paper he discussed the characteristics of child pornography collections, drawing attention to their importance for the collector, their constancy, the degree of organisation of the collection, their permanent qualities, and the extent to which the material they contain is both concealed and shared. Provocative as this analysis is, unfortunately a major weakness of this work is its lack of empirical verification, relying instead on the experience of the author in law enforcement work in this area.

However, Lanning (1992: 24–6) introduced the important distinction between child pornography ('the sexually explicit reproduction of a child's image') and child erotica ('any material, relating to children, that serves a sexual purpose for a given individual'). The significance of this distinction is to emphasise the potential sexual qualities of a whole range of kinds of photograph (and other material as well) not all of which may be pictures of sexual assaults. The implications of that distinction in the context of the Internet could not at that time be fully explored by Lanning, although he did, in that and later work, clearly recognise the significance of the new technologies. The operational implications for law enforcement agencies of that distinction are significant, however, and can be seen in the way in which investigative agencies frequently divide evidential material into three categories:

1 Indicative – material depicting clothed children, which suggests a sexual interest in children;
2 Indecent – material depicting naked children which suggests a sexual interest in children;
3 Obscene – material which depicts children in explicit sexual acts.

This kind of categorisation may be helpful for law enforcement agencies in the initial stages of investigating child pornography cases. But it is too broad, and because of that does little to progress our understanding. Furthermore, it adds little to our knowledge of the qualities of offenders involved in either production or possession of child pornography, or of the features of adult sexual interest in children. It also tends to deflect attention away from a more discriminating analysis of the photographs themselves, and the relationship between the child, the photographer, the photograph and the viewer. Boyle (2000) made a similar point within a larger framework related to pornography in general, suggesting that research has been over-concerned with the 'effects' of pornography, and neglects to consider the harm done to women, men and children in the production of pornography. A major weakness in contemporary work in this area is that it does not consider how individual consumers use and understand pornographic or other photographic media nor does it acknowledge their choice, responsibility and accountability for their behaviours.

A particular absence in the literature is any attempt to understand the nature of photographs of children, or their significance for the user. Indeed, simple descriptions of the content of child pornography photographs are rarely referred to. An exception to this is Tate (1990), who commented on how the material ranged from 'revealing stills of naked children, through more explicit shots of their genitalia thumbed apart to the recording of oral, anal and vaginal abuse and intercourse' (15–16). Even a more focused recent review of knowledge of awareness of the legality of images on the Internet from a legal perspective (McCabe 2000) failed to distinguish between kinds of image other than real and pseudo-images (which present particular legal problems), as we will discuss below.

A detailed account of the extent and qualities of child pornography was given by Taylor (1999). This presented an overview of the situation at that time, particularly with respect to the Internet. However, given the extensive involvement of the Internet in child pornography distribution, the account also served to summarise the more general picture of adult sexual interest in children and the Internet. More hidden areas, such as the production and distribution of child pornography videos, are much less well understood, but there are grounds for thinking that video production is the major contemporary 'primary' source of child pornography, with the Internet at the moment serving as a medium for distribution rather than production. This may well change, however, as digital photography becomes more widely available. It is important to stress that at the moment the underground *production* of video child pornography may run parallel with, but be essentially unrelated to, Internet technologies for its distribution.

Just as child pornography photographs are not accidents, so, as we noted above, collections of child pornography are not accidents; they result from deliberate choices by an individual to acquire, in some sense, sexual material. However, it is important to note that the sexual or erotic nature of the images lies both in the objective qualities of the material itself, and in the mind of the collector (Howitt 1995). Indeed, Edwards (1994) took this argument further when she asserted, 'But word – or image-based representational practices are not sexual practices, and any analysis of image based representation, must take into consideration the political, economic and cultural context of production and exchange' (39). Furthermore, it is reasonable to assume that the collecting choices made reflect in some sense the 'value' to the individual collector of the material he has access to. Tate (1990) suggested that with child pornography, 'the younger the child or the more bizarre the acts depicted, the greater its value for exchange purposes' (24). Whether or not the choices made by the offender predict or influence subsequent behaviour in any way (in terms of further collecting, making contact with others with similar interests, or seeking out children to assault) is far from clear but is deserving of further investigation. A central issue here is the better understanding of the processes of collection, the factors that influence collecting behaviour, and the relationship between collecting and the collected material. We can identify two broad perspectives, legal and psychological, that are relevant when considering this issue.

Legal perspective

The legal perspective relates to what is defined in legislation as child pornography. From this perspective, what constitutes child pornography may vary from jurisdiction to jurisdiction depending on how national legislatures have framed and expressed laws related to child pornography. A by-product of this is that the responses of law enforcement agencies dealing with the problem are necessarily limited, focused and, in the absence of international agreement, also limited by national boundaries and legislation.

When the significance of a photograph in terms of labelling child pornography is determined by legal definitions, necessarily photographs that fall outside that definition tend to be either ignored, or not evaluated, because they may be seen as secondary or incidental to the main focus of prosecution. Furthermore, as we noted above, because of jurisdictional differences, photographs that may be illegal in one jurisdiction may be legal in another and vice versa. Given the international qualities of the distribution of child pornography using the Internet, this raises amongst other things the need to improve harmonisation of laws between states in the development of common policing strategies. However, as a first step and even given jurisdictional difference, an objective means of judging the nature of collections independent of legal provision would aid understanding and give a basis for international comparison.

In Chapter 1, reference was made to the different kinds of legal emphasis applied to child pornography, reflecting the core qualities of obscenity, sexuality and sexualised, or indecency. The emphasis adopted in legal provisions can make a critical difference as to how any given putative example of child pornography is regarded. For example, a critical test of obscenity in the US relates to the 'Miller Standard', the result of a United States Supreme Court decision, *Miller* v. *California*. In order to make a judgement of obscene (not simply about child pornography, but about any written or visual media), the following test must be satisfied:

1 Whether the average person applying contemporary community standards would find that the work, taken as a whole, appeals to prurient interests;
2 Whether the work depicts or describes in a patently offensive way sexual conduct specifically defined by the applicable state law;
3 Whether the work, taken as a whole, lacks serious literary, artistic, political or scientific value.

From this we can see that, as far as the Miller test is concerned, the notion of obscenity is socially constituted, may change over time and inevitably because of this lacks objective verification and consensual agreement.

In April 2002, the US Supreme Court in *Ashcroft* v. *Free Speech Coalition*, ruled that the First Amendment protects pornography or other images that only appear to depict real children engaged in sexual behaviour. The effect of this has been to require proof that a picture was of a real child (as distinct from a potentially 'virtual' child) before proceedings related to possession of child pornography can be taken. The implications of this judgement are quite profound in terms of establishing the legal position of child pornography, and effectively mean that unless a photograph can be demonstrated to be of a real child, its possession and distribution is not an offence. This therefore places current US law in this area dramatically out of synchronisation with international developments in this area.

In other jurisdictions, such as the Republic of Ireland, reference is made in the case of child pornography to the sexual qualities of the material. In the Child Pornography and Trafficking Act 1998, child pornography is defined as any visual representation that shows a child engaged in or depicted as engaged in explicit sexual activity, witnessing any such activity, or whose dominant characteristic is the depiction, for a sexual purpose, of the genital or anal regions of a child. The

International Criminal Police Organization (Interpol) Standing Working Group on Offences against Minors defines child pornography as: 'the consequence of the exploitation or sexual abuse perpetrated against a child. It can be defined as any means of depicting or promoting sexual abuse of a child, including print and/or audio, centred on sex acts or the genital organs of children.' A similar emphasis on the sexual nature of the material can be found in the UK's Criminal Justice Protection of Children Act 1978, which was amended in 1994 to state that, 'It is an offence for a person (a) to take, or permit to be taken or to make, any indecent photographs or pseudo-photographs of a child; (b) to distribute or show such indecent photographs or pseudo-photographs.' The emphasis in the latter on indecent, however, echoes the debate about the nature of obscenity, with social and cultural factors again largely determining the attributes of 'indecency'. The Sentencing Advisory Panel (2002) present a discussion of UK sentencing guidelines related to possession of child pornography.

Legal definitions of child pornography have to be objective and expressed in terms that allow the proper application of due process. In doing so, they necessarily reduce what might be a complex definitional issue to something simple and identifiable and create what are inevitably rather blunt instruments in application.

Psychological perspectives

Moving away from a legal perspective to a psychological one is not without its problems. Svedin and Back (1996) define child pornography as 'a text or an image – i.e. photo, slide, film, video or computer program – that is intended to evoke a sexual feeling, fantasy or response in adults' (9). Expressing criteria in terms of a capacity to generate fantasy may be problematic when objective definitions are required, but does reflect the reality of people's experience with child pornography. But as we have already noted, it is not possible to control fantasy, and as will become apparent, the range of materials that might evoke fantasy include photographs that can be found in any family album or clothes catalogue. An alternative approach is to draw our sense of what we mean by child pornography from the material that adults with a sexual interest in children collect. By emphasising what is effectively a behavioural and empirical approach to pictures attractive to adults with a sexual interest in children, we focus on a range of discernibly different kinds of image (Taylor 1999) only some of which may be illegal using one or other of the criteria outlined above.

If we look at the kind of material found in collections, or we identify what adults with a sexual interest in children themselves say they like, the kinds of picture that can be identified range from pictures of clothed children, through nakedness and explicit erotic posing to pictures of a sexual assault on the child photographed. We can make some objective sense of this by thinking of them in terms of a continuum of increased deliberate sexual victimisation. Any particular example of a photograph attractive to an adult with a sexual interest in children, therefore, can be located along such a continuum of explicit or deliberate sexual victimisation. This continuum ranges from everyday and perhaps accidental pictures involving either no overt erotic content, or minimal content (such as showing a child's pants or underwear) at one extreme, to pictures showing actual rape and penetration of a child, or other gross acts of obscenity at the other. Taking this perspective focuses attention not just on illegality as a significant quality of pictures, but on the preferred type of picture selected by the collector, and the value and meaning pictures have to collectors. Given that collecting and viewing is what sustains and shapes the trade in child pornography, this seems a reasonable approach.

A grading system

A by-product of thinking about pictures in this way is that such a continuum enables the construction of a simple grading system that is of value in characterising the content of child pornography pictures, and also offers a more discriminating approach to indicate the qualities of such material. It may also contribute to improving our knowledge of the factors that enable and sustain offender behaviour as the relations between collecting behaviour and the picture material become clearer. Approaching a photographic collection of an adult with a sexual interest in children in this way may also assist in developing a more discriminating approach to the management of offences by both law enforcement agencies and the courts.

As Taylor *et al.* (2001) noted, victimisation is the central topic to focus on when analysing picture content, and when attempting to develop descriptive categories. Whether a picture is accidental or deliberate, each time a picture is accessed for sexual purposes it victimises (if only by proxy) the individual concerned through fantasy. In a sense, the function of picture collections for the offender is repeatedly to victimise the child concerned, and the victim status is exaggerated by continuing use. Relevant to this, an important purpose of child picture collections for the user is that they allow, in a sense, instant access to the child (or a child) as victim (Healy 1997). Actual abuse is much more difficult, often involving complex and lengthy engagement with the child before victimisation takes place. We might also note that knowledge of the victims of child pornography is very limited, but it must be stressed that ultimately concern about victims must play a central role in the management of child pornography.

The table below summarises a ten-point category system for the grading of both individual and serial child pornography pictures. It is based on a descriptive analysis of the extensive collection of images in the COPINE database, and the experiences of the COPINE Project team in reviewing and categorising material. This database contains examples of most of the material publicly available, and represents a very large sample of the total amount of material in public circulation at the moment, with a particular focus on newer material. It is wholly based on Internet sources. From this analysis, some ten levels of severity of photographs can be discerned based on increasing sexual victimisation. Examples of individual images can be located along this ten-point scale. The category system described here extends and develops the Platform for Internet Content Selection (PICS) and

Table 2.1 Taxonomy of different kinds of child pornography

Level	*Name*	*Description of Picture Qualities*
1	**Indicative**	Non-erotic and non-sexualised pictures showing children in their underwear, swimming costumes, etc. from either commercial sources or family albums; pictures of children playing in normal settings, in which the context or organisation of pictures by the collector indicates inappropriateness.
2	**Nudist**	Pictures of naked or semi-naked children in appropriate nudist settings, and from legitimate sources.
3	**Erotica**	Surreptitiously taken photographs of children in play areas or other safe environments showing either underwear or varying degrees of nakedness.
4	**Posing**	Deliberately posed pictures of children fully, partially clothed or naked (where the amount, context and organisation suggests sexual interest).
5	**Erotic Posing**	Deliberately posed pictures of fully, partially clothed or naked children in sexualised or provocative poses.
6	**Explicit Erotic Posing**	Emphasising genital areas where the child is either naked, partially or fully clothed.
7	**Explicit Sexual Activity**	Involves touching, mutual and self-masturbation, oral sex and intercourse by child, not involving an adult.
8	**Assault**	Pictures of children being subject to a sexual assault, involving digital touching, involving an adult
9	**Gross Assault**	Grossly obscene pictures of sexual assault, involving penetrative sex, masturbation or oral sex involving an adult.
10	**Sadistic/Bestiality**	a. Pictures showing a child being tied, bound, beaten, whipped or otherwise subject to something that implies pain. b. Pictures where an animal is involved in some form of sexual behaviour with a child.

Source: from Taylor *et al.* 2001.

the Recreational Software Advisory Council (RSACi) rating system (Akdeniz 1997), but more directly focuses on pictures related to adult sexual interest in children.

This categorising system quite deliberately includes pictures that do not fall within any legal definition of child pornography, and given this, it is important to stress that collections of photographs of children *per se* are not in themselves indicative of anything inappropriate. It is the *context* to those photographs, and the way in which they are organised, or stored, or the principal themes illustrated, which may give rise to concern. Most families have extensive and entirely appropriate pictures of their children, and such pictures are not in these terms indicative of adult sexual interest in children unless they are in some sense inappropriately held. Furthermore, in the same context depictions of children in their underwear, or naked, may well be entirely appropriate. Commercial organisations involved in the production of underwear, or children's clothing, might similarly appropriately make use of photographs of partially clothed children. Such photographs can, however, be used inappropriately by adults with a sexual interest in children. Within that inappropriate context, essentially innocent pictures can fall within the category of indicative (level 1). Level 1 may include most common pictures of children, either commercially taken or from family albums. The reasons for inclusion of these kinds of photograph within the material related to adult sexual interest in children, as noted earlier, is that the extent to which a photograph may be sexualised and fantasised over lies not so much in its objective content, but in the use to which the picture might be put. In his review of eleven case studies of paedophilic sex offenders, Howitt (1995) draws attention to the significance of this kind of relatively innocent photograph in promoting and sustaining sexual fantasy. It is the context, therefore, rather than the explicit content of such photographs that is significant, and the emphasis on context in understanding child pornography cannot be overstressed.

This general debate is also relevant to considerations of the portrayal of children and child nudity in artistic settings, as found in level 2 photographs. The qualities required to make a judgement of 'artistic' may be complex, and are undoubtedly outside the scope of this book, but there is no *a priori* reason to suppose that pictures of context-appropriate naked, or partially clothed, children are necessarily inappropriate. Of course, the motivations of the producer are significant, but more importantly the context in which such photographs are viewed represents the critical quality to focus on when making a judgement about the potential of a photograph to be sexualised for a given individual. The display of such photographs within an art gallery exhibition and in a clear artistic framework, for example, seems reasonable. The presence of such pictures within collections of more clearly pornographic material would, however, in these terms constitute *prima facie* grounds for supposing such pictures to have the capacity to be sexualised by adults with a sexual interest in children.

Most pictures will clearly fall within one category, but echoing the discussion about artistic qualities, from time to time the boundaries between categories can be somewhat blurred. The critical factor in so far as the typology is concerned is overt sexual intent and content, which may in some circumstances be difficult to identify or verify objectively. For example, some newspaper advertisements (such as those advertising Calvin Klein underwear for young men) show pictures of boys and teenagers in their underwear. Whilst having no explicit or necessarily intended sexual connotation for the producer, many of these advertisements may nevertheless be thought to emphasise and exaggerate sexual qualities inappropriately, however implicitly, as part of the advertising strategy. The sexual qualities that such pictures might have lie, of course, in the mind of the viewer rather than in objective reality, although it should be noted that the significance of using the margins of sexuality to advertise is not lost on advertising agencies which design and produce such advertisements. Kincaid (1998) discussed this at some length. A more complex example can be seen in an advertisement for a children's charity, which shows a young girl of perhaps 5 or 6 standing next to an open car door appearing to be solicited by a kerb crawler, with other obvious prostitute figures evident in shadows in the vicinity (*Independent on Sunday*, 25 June 2000). The child is wearing a normal dress, and has not been posed in a provocative or erotic way. The intention behind the advertisement was presumably to juxtapose a shocking image of an innocent young girl against a background of prostitution, with the text making the point that 'neglected as a child, it was always possible Kim would be an easy victim for pimps'. However powerful this juxtaposition of images may be (which is part of a series of similar advertisements), this particular image rather than being shocking might well act as a source of stimulation if an individual fantasises about underage prostitutes or child abduction, or if the advertisement is seen as emphasising availability, rather than as a warning.

Conceptualising picture collections and child pornography in terms of this continuum emphasises the sense in which sexualisation of pictures is a psychological process. Legal specification of child pornography in terms of obscenity or sexual content necessarily fails to capture the rich array of material that is attractive to the adult with sexual interest in children. However, pictures that are collected by adults with a sexual interest in children do not fall within a simple homogeneous category.

Legal specification and this proposed taxonomy do, of course, overlap, and in most jurisdictions, pictures that could be categorised as level 6 or greater from the above table are likely to be illegal, in that they clearly in some sense emphasise sexual victimisation. In some jurisdictions, level 2 pictures (involving pictures of naked children in nudist settings) may or may not be illegal, and unless a local law explicitly prohibits sexualisable pictures of clothed children, it is unlikely that all level 4 and 5 pictures will be illegal. This highlights a major problem. Conceptualisations of child pornography that equate it with obscenity necessarily focus on an 'end' product and ignore the children as victims. Early work by Pierce (1984) suggested that there is a blatant disregard for the dehumanising experiences encountered by children in the production of all such material, and that the abuse of children emerges out of the whole spectrum of pornographic trade, including the recruitment of subject, the production and sale of material. This is particularly relevant to the debate about the criminalisation of pictures of child nudity (see Grasz and Pfaltzgraf 1998).

In conceptualising picture qualities, level 3 pictures (surreptitiously taken photographs of children showing either underwear or various degrees of nakedness) represent a particular kind of dilemma, illustrating in part the issue raised above.

Typically, these are pictures of young children and toddlers playing at paddling pools or beaches, either fully or partially undressed, or climbing on or playing with playground equipment and showing their underwear. These photographs may not necessarily be illegal in many jurisdictions, and indeed may be indistinguishable from legitimate family photographs. Yet they can be argued to represent a very serious example of sexual victimisation through photography. This may seem a paradoxical assertion to make, for there is a sense in which there is no victim in these pictures, in that the child and its caretakers, because the pictures are surreptitiously taken, are more than likely unaware of what has happened. It is not uncommon to see pictures taken with high-powered telephoto lenses, for example, such that the photographer might be 50 or more metres away from the paddling pool or playground. Other devices used are 90° lenses that disguise the photographer's intentions (a particularly effective ploy on beaches or at swimming pools). However, whilst the child and its parents or caretakers may be unaware that they are being photographed, in many respects these pictures are particularly corrosive and offensive, because they sexualise situations that should be safe and secure environments in which children can play. Perhaps the important issue here is that lack of knowledge of victimisation does not necessarily diminish its gravity. The issues here are similar to those raised by Holmes *et al.* (1998) in their discussion of the significance of 'hidden' pictures in pornography in general.

Pictures at levels 8, 9 and 10 necessarily involve the presence of someone else in the picture, either an adult, or an animal. These can be best thought of as a picture of a sexual assault or rape in process, and clearly fall within all contemporary legal definitions of child pornography, regardless of an emphasis on obscene, sexual or indecent. The same argument applies to pictures in level 7, although the offender may not be visible in the scene. Although not necessarily visible, the adult is present as the director of poses.

The utility of this grading system can be seen when it is applied to a particular example. One large grouping of pictures widely available on the Internet involves a total of some thirty-six very young girls, aged between 1.5 and 7 years old. The total number of pictures available probably exceeds 3,000, distributed in over 100 individual picture series each containing some 30–60 individual still pictures. In all probability the still pictures are at least in part video captures. The pictures appear to have been taken over a number of years, because in some cases the same child is shown at different ages. By analysing the pictures using the grading system, a sense of the nature and extent of victimisation shown in these pictures can be illustrated. This can be seen in the Figures below.

As can be seen from Figure 2.1, most of the picture series fall within level 6 or below (explicit erotic posing). To achieve this summary, each individual picture within a series is viewed and categorised and the final series grade is based on the highest level attained by any picture within the series. However, it is also clear from the diagram that a significant number of the series show much greater levels of sexual victimisation. When the pictures are analysed with respect to the particular children involved, however, it becomes apparent that only five girls are

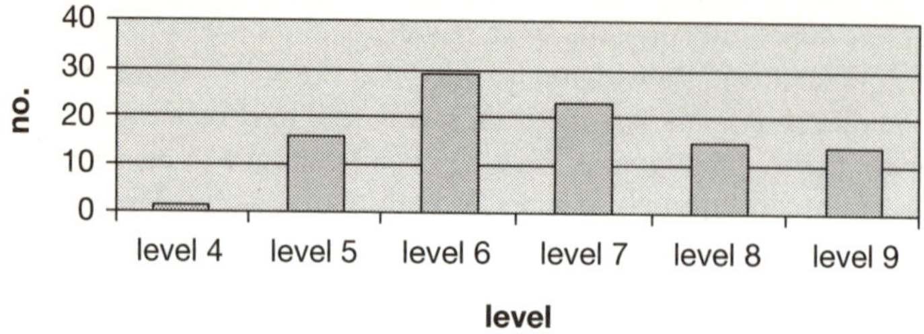

Figure 2.1 Number of series of pictures at different grading levels.

portrayed in more than two series of pictures. Grading of these picture series reveals that only these five girls are portrayed in pictures of level 7 and above (pictures showing explicit sexual activity). Figures 2.2 and 2.3 below illustrate this for the most frequently photographed child (given the name, for our purposes, of Child 1), and for the other four children (Child 2–5).

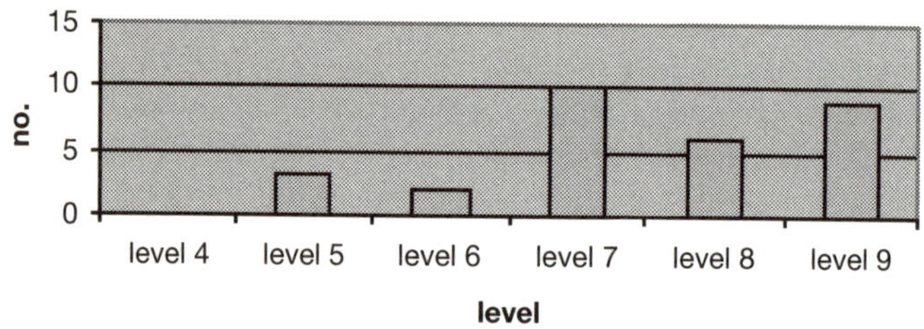

Figure 2.2 Number of series at different levels for Child 1.

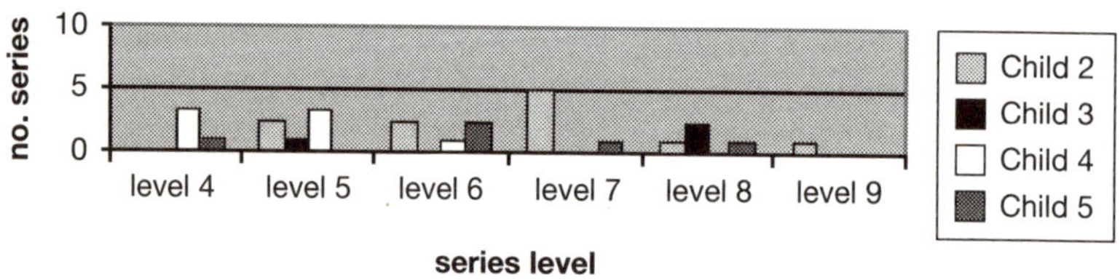

Figure 2.3 Number of series at different levels for Child 2 (3–7), Child 3 (6), Child 4 (4–6), Child 5 (1.5–3) (age range of photographs indicated in brackets).

From Figure 2.2 we can see that Child 1 has been repeatedly photographed in situations of extreme sexual abuse, and internal evidence from the pictures suggests this occurred from ages 3 to about 7. Figure 2.3 illustrates the extent of sexual victimisation illustrated for the other four children. It is noteworthy that the youngest child, Child 5, has been photographed in situations meriting a grading of 8 (pictures of children being subject to a sexual assault, involving digital touching, by an adult). These photographs represent a very serious example of serial sexual abuse and pornography production, which extends over a number of years, and embraces a number of very young girls. At the time of writing, neither these children nor the producer have been identified.

PSEUDO-PHOTOGRAPHS

Not all child pornography is what it seems. What are referred to as 'pseudo-photographs' exist, which at first sight complicate the analysis. Pseudo-photographs are constructed photographs, often very cleverly done with great technical sophistication, using digital reconstruction techniques to create an image that is not a photograph either of a real person, or of real events. Thus the head of a child might be placed on to the body of a woman, where the body features are manipulated to make it appear to be that of a child (breast reduced in size or eliminated, and pubic hair eliminated). The child's head may be someone of significance to the individual – a niece, the child of a friend – and the pseudo-photograph presumably plays a part in sexual fantasies around the child. Quite commonly, pictures of well-known child film stars are modified so that they appear either naked, or in some sexually provocative pose. Again, presumably these pictures relate to sexual fantasies involving the famous model.

Other photographs may be created for less clear motives. A picture from a well-known series of pornographic photographs of a girl was modified by the addition of an erect penis, and the girl's head was replaced by that of a boy. In technical terms, the image modifications to the genital area by the addition of the penis were very competently undertaken with no obvious signs of modification. On the other hand, the boy's head superimposed on to the original girl's was poorly done, with no effort made to hide the modification. Given such obvious attention to the genital region (in contrast to the head region) it is tempting to suggest that in this case the construction of the pseudo-image was some kind of sexual act for its producer. The amount of time involved in creating these kinds of photograph in particular is considerable, and the creators often show great technical skill and competence.

Other forms of pseudo-image superimpose different unconnected pictures; for example, a child holding a toy might be modified and superimposed on to a picture of a naked man, such that the child appears to be holding not a toy, but the man's penis. In February 2001, a Renfrewshire social worker was charged with possession of pornographic pictures made up of photographs of children's faces cut from magazines and pasted on to pornographic images downloaded from the Internet. This man was caught after fire-fighters entered his flat to put out a fire, and found the photographs amongst his possessions. For the future, it seems likely that as computer-aided animation and 3D computer graphics become easier and more accessible, then there will be a growth in animated child pornography, wholly constructed as computer images.

The person portrayed in the resultant pseudo-picture, of course, does not exist. In a sense, because these pictures are not real (that is to say the events they portray did not happen, or could not happen as the 'person' portrayed does not exist) they might be thought not to involve any victim. Legislative initiatives have, however, attempted to address this problem. In the US, the Child Pornography Prevention Act of 1996 defines child pornography as 'any visual depiction, including any photography, film, video, picture or computer generated image or picture . . . where . . . such visual depiction is, or appears to be, of a minor'. However, it seems that the *Ashcroft* v. *Free Speech Coalition* judgement has overtaken this provision and rendered it inoperable. The Irish Child Trafficking and Pornography Act 1988 embraces pseudo-images by defining child pornography as 'any visual representation . . . that shows . . . or relates to a person who is, or is depicted as being a child'.

Opponents of criminalising pseudo-child pornography have argued that this material, because no child is harmed in its production, should not be drawn within the framework of child pornography. Echoing some of the debate referred to earlier in this chapter related to why *viewing* child pornography can be problematic, they argue that because the historic purpose of criminalising production of child pornography is to prevent children from being sexually abused, and because pseudo-images do not involve actual abuse, they should not be criminalised. Indeed, opponents of these measures, such as the American Civil Liberties Union, have argued that people's thoughts are their private thoughts, and that prohibition of pseudo-child pornography is a violation of free speech rights. The *Ashcroft* v. *Free Speech Coalition* judgement seems for the moment to support this view.

The issue here is contentious. However, it can be argued that, real or not, pseudo-child pornography represents a form of victimisation just as real as child pornography, and should be treated as such. In addition, as McCabe and Gregory (1998) have indicated, abusers often use pornography to entice other children into posing for pictures or movies, and therefore whether the child or situation legally exists is in a sense irrelevant in these situations. Wasserman (1998) presented a useful review of the legal issues involved in criminalising the production of such pseudo-photographs. The psychological qualities of individuals involved in the production of these kinds of image are unknown, although it is reasonable to suppose there are complex individual motives at work.

PICTURE COLLECTIONS

The above taxonomy and grading system offers a means of categorising both series of and individual pictures. It is essential to note that an important quality of picture collections from the collectors' perspective is that it is not simply an aggregation of individual pictures. Pictures generally occur in series, and the series invariably has either some sense of implicit or explicit narrative quality, or a common thematic link. *Narrative qualities* might be a sequence of pictures showing a child undressing, or engaging in some particular act. The addition of text to pictures may serve to exaggerate their narrative qualities. Recent developments have seen the addition of text to particularly disturbing still photographs of very young children that almost include the viewer in the process, adding a disturbing new dimension to what are already worrying pictures. A characteristic of much recent child pornography on the Internet is that still photographs are in fact video captures. The process of capturing still images from videos in many ways emphasises and exaggerates the narrative qualities of the original video, and the quality of contemporary video capture technology makes the resultant photograph largely indistinguishable from still photographs. Such narrative qualities make grading of these picture series by the most extreme picture example an appropriate way of characterising picture series. In a sense the narrative generally leads to and culminates in the most extreme picture or pictures. *Thematic links* between pictures, on the other hand, might relate to particular scenes or acts. Series of pictures may focus on oral sex, sex between children, or perhaps pictures of children showing their underwear.

Both narrative and thematic linkages serve important qualities for the collector, both in terms of sustaining and generating fantasy, and in terms of personalising and engaging with the child victim. They also play an important part in structuring collecting behaviour, in that filling gaps in series may be an important factor in determining selection of material to acquire. Interviews with offenders suggest that finding pictures that fill gaps is highly reinforcing to the collector, and may add psychological value to a series.

As with all pornography, child pornographic pictures are strikingly stereotyped. In a sense, there are only a limited number of poses possible, but the poses portrayed are remarkably similar across picture series and children, to the extent that it is not always possible to tell different series apart, especially with close-up photographs where faces or other identifying qualities may not be visible. This stereotyped quality itself suggests implicit narrative properties of photographs, and some collectors seem to respond to this in terms of their efforts to complete picture series:

> you know I suppose I was deliberately going for groups . . . em . . . so you get like an idea of the full event that was going on so I suppose like I come back here it's probably more like action which is probably later on I went down to em . . . movie format . . . I you know so you get an idea of . . . the full continuation rather than just one photo . . . or like a snapshot. (TS)

There is some reason to suppose that these standardised and stereotyped poses serve a further purpose of giving structure to, and providing a sense of 'instructions' for new people to the area to copy, or to enable fantasy fulfilment. Thus, some offenders refer to imitation of poses, within preferred pictures, when accounting for their own pornographic production. Common themes evident in the photographs are also seen in text-based child pornography, and in many ways are similar to adult fantasies, only with the substitution of a child:

> Fantasies . . . it would basically run like I take the young girl on a date . . . and then we'd go home and then she'd we'd . . . you know the stuff that adults do which would lead to sex and would involve her masturbating me and then me giving her oral sex. (QH)

The central significance of a series of pictures to the collector (discussed in greater depth in Chapter 7) does not invalidate the emphasis on discriminating between individual pictures described above. In terms of the categorising process, a picture series can be characterised in terms of the highest level achieved by individual pictures within a particular series. It needs to be emphasised that the end point of a narrative series (in terms of the extent of sexual victimisation) is the most significant aspect of that series, and for the purpose of categorisation can serve to discriminate the qualities of the series. The process and features of the emergence of a picture series are also relevant factors. A similar argument may also be applied to the categorisation of video sequences.

Locating a picture, or a series of pictures, at some level in the taxonomy outlined above may not in itself always be a complete and sufficient characterisation of a particular collection of pictures. Other issues surrounding the material may also play a part in determining the sense of extent and severity of sexual victimisation. Factors that indicate greater severity within a given level may be:

1 In so far as collections are concerned, its size and the quality of its organisation. Size of collection may be indicative of the degree of involvement in the processes of collecting material, and the extent to which an individual has become absorbed within the adult sexual interest in children community. Obsessional sorting or organising of the material is also an indication of the offender's involvement with the pictures and the amount of time spent 'offline' engaging with the material. Complex categorisation systems may also be indicative of involvement with trading photographs.
2 The presence of new/private material. This may also relate to the extent to which the collector has access to producers, or to the circle around which new and valued material circulates. Again it may be indicative of the degree of involvement in the child pornography world.
3 In terms of production factors, the addition of suggestive text either indicating the availability of the child, or exaggerating the suggestive qualities of the photograph.
4 The age of the child. Recent evidence (Taylor 1999) suggests that the age of children in new child pornography is reducing. Very young children (of 5 and under) may be particularly vulnerable to involvement in child pornography, in that they may be more susceptible to what for an older child would seem inappropriate, such as requests to undress. Very young children may have little or no awareness of the sexual context to what they are being asked to do or its inappropriateness, and may be subject to sexual victimisation without the same risk of disclosure to adults. In these circumstances, there is a greater imbalance

in power between perpetrator and the victim, and the lack of language skills may reduce the child's capacity to disclose the assault. Pictures involving babies are particularly distasteful, in that they necessarily exploit situations of total dependency.

FEATURES OF CONTEMPORARY CHILD PORNOGRAPHY

There is little objective evidence about the extent and availability of child pornography. Media headlines of police seizures of collections involving 50,000 photographs may make good copy, but do little to give a sense of the scale of the problem. In any event, counting the number of photographs available is not the way to approach this issue. The number of pictures available is a rather arbitrary and fluid thing, related as much to the producer's whim as to objective qualities. For example, given that many still photographs come from videos, the number of video captures that can be made from a 30-minute video may range from two or three to many thousand, depending on the interests, energy and technical capacity of the producer.

One objective approach to understanding the extent of available material is to draw on the information contained within the COPINE archive of child pornography. This archive is drawn from pictures downloaded from newsgroup postings, and it is therefore a sample of the material that is publicly available. The archive takes two forms: first, old pictures which are known to be over 15 years old, and second, a searchable archive of new (less than 10 years old) and recent (10 to 15 years old) pictures. The second archive is made up of pictures that are collected from in excess of sixty newsgroups known to carry child pornography, which are regularly monitored. Both archives underrepresent children over the age of 12–13, when the onset of puberty makes age determination difficult from pictures. The new and recent archive focuses on levels 6–10 in the above typology and is a large, and probably representative, sample of new photographs in the public domain.

In total, the archive includes in excess of 150,000 still pictures and 400+ video clips. Of the 150,000 images, more than half are of girls. Of those pictures of girls categorised as level 7 and above, about 7 per cent are new. Approximately 26 per cent of similar level boy photographs are new (categorised as level 7 or above). In these new pictures, some 40 per cent of the girls and over 50 per cent of the boys are between the ages of 9 and 12, the rest being younger. The vast majority of both sexes of children depicted in the new pictures of level 7 and above are white Caucasian, with Asiatic children more likely to appear in posed images (levels 5 and 6). There is a marked absence of black children in any of the age groups, and as yet there is little evidence as to why this should be the case. Anecdotal information from the COPINE interviews with offenders suggested that many collectors show a preference for thin, fair children, where genitalia are clearly visible and where there are no secondary sexual characteristics.

During the year 2001, photographs of new children appeared in the newsgroups monitored by the COPINE Project at a rate of about two new children per month. This is highly variable, but there is evidence that the age of the children (particularly females) is getting younger, that there is an increase in 'domestic' production (where the settings are family rooms), and that there has been a growth in the number of photographs of Eastern European children. During the year 2002, there has also been an increase in the number of pictures whose origins appear to be commercial web sites, based in South America or Eastern Europe; these pictures tend to be in levels 5 and 6. These, and the emergence of more explicit child pornography from Eastern Europe access to which involves payment, seem to represent a new and disturbing growth in commercial exploitation of the market for child pornography.

From the photographic evidence available, it can be estimated that over 400 of the children included in the new/recent material have been subjected to serious sexual assault (being present in pictures categorised as level 7 and above). Of the 2,000 children who have been photographed while posing naked (levels 5 and 6), it is reasonable to assume that a number of these will have been sexually assaulted, either outside being photographed or without the images being publicly distributed yet. It is also reasonable to assume that the figures given here are an underestimate of the numbers of pictures in circulation as the amount of material in private circulation is unknown. However, given that new material regularly appears, it seems reasonable to assume that the underground production and distribution of child pornography is considerable.

HISTORICAL CONTEXT

As noted above, the COPINE archive consists of two parts; one archive being pictures older than about fifteen years, the other being of more recent pictures. This division is somewhat arbitrary, but is a useful rule of thumb to delineate new material from old. In pre-Internet times (and in some circumstances currently too) it can take a long time for underground pictures to circulate and be distributed, and whilst fifteen years may seem a long time, it seems to embrace the cycle of production, private distribution and eventual public dissemination. Unless videos or still photographs are seized as a result of police or Customs action, we are unaware of them as a problem until they begin to be publicly circulated. One effect of the Internet may be to reduce this cycle, with new photographs appearing much more quickly than previously.

However, around fifteen years from the year 2001 also marks something of a watershed in child pornography in another sense, because it is around then that public anxiety about child pornography first began to receive significant expression. To be precise, it is possible to put a date on an event that marked a turn in public opinion from benign disapproval to increasingly hostile action against the production of child pornography – the death of Thea Pumbroek. Thea Pumbroek died on 27 August 1984. She was aged 6, and for much of her life she had been involved in the production of child pornographic videos. She died of an overdose of cocaine in the bathroom of a room in the Holiday Inn, Amsterdam, during what appears to have been a photographic session.

Thea Pumbroek's death prompted legislative changes to the law regarding the sale and production of child pornography in Holland. More importantly, it also gave impetus to the growing pressure on Western governments to recognise the existence of child pornography, and to legislate against it. Her death marked the end of a phase of relative ease of access to commercially produced child pornography, which began in the late 1960s and early 1970s, although, as Tate (1990) notes, child pornography and the invention of photography go hand in hand. For example, in 1874, the London police raided the studio of Henry Hayler and confiscated over 130,000 photographs of children which were considered indecent (Edwards 1994). Indeed, a coherent argument could be made that changes in the technology of photography are rapidly reflected in the production of child pornography (as an aspect of a broader trade in pornography). Ease of photographic developing, the ready availability of video camera, and now digital imaging all have had an impact on the nature and availability of child pornography.

It is reasonable to assume that the requirement to use intermediaries to develop and print films serves as a limit to the production of child pornography (as with other pornography). Certainly, specialist photographic services move into niche areas such as this charging a premium for confidentiality, but for most people the production of child pornography, until the advent of cheap and anonymous means of production, was simply out of reach. Cost may have been one factor but, even when the production of child pornography was not illegal, the risk of revealing such an interest (with consequent risk of public exposure, or perhaps blackmail) would deter all but the most ardent amateur producer. Edwards (1994) dated the pornographic use of photography to the 1840s, with the production of an album of erotic photographs of children by J. T. Withe, and with photographers such as Oscar Gustav Rejlander making photographs of nude and semi-nude little girls. In addition, erotic postcards of children were in circulation in Victorian times, but these did not pass into popular culture without censure. Local home-based production of child pornography no doubt occurred from the early days of photography, but its distribution if it occurred at all was limited to private collections. However, given the evident demand, this provided a market for commercial production, where the risks could be minimised for both the producer and the purchaser.

In the late 1960s and early 1970s, most Western European countries went through a period of relaxation of censorship laws, particularly with respect to obscenity. Denmark led the way in this, in that the production of all forms of pornography was legalised in July 1969, setting the tone for what became a decade of liberalisation of obscenity laws throughout Europe. Most of the material that we now know as child pornography has its origins in this time, in terms of the cine films, and later videos, and magazines that were produced for commercial sale. The earliest film materials produced were marketed under the name 'Lolita', and Tate

(1990) suggested that at least 36 ten-minute cine films were produced under this title between 1971 and 1979. Whilst the cine filming was taking place, still photography also occurred, which resulted in parallel publishing of magazines that to a degree mirrored the content of the cine films. The Lolita films were made by a company called Color Climax, with registered offices in Copenhagen. These films exclusively involved pictures of young girls being sexually abused, primarily by men, but sometimes involving women or other children. The girls were mainly in the age range 7–11, but with some younger. Other companies and individuals also operated in Denmark at that time selling child pornographic material. Tate (1990) refers to a Danish citizen Willy Strauss as perhaps the major producer of child pornography magazines. Tate (1990) suggested that Strauss published 1,500 child pornography magazines, with titles such as *Bambina Sex*, *Anna and her Father* and *Lolita Sex*. These magazines were again primarily concerned with the abuse of young girls. Other Danish companies focused on homosexual child abuse, reflected in magazines with titles such as *Piccolo* and *Joe and his Uncles*. Parallel with these European developments, in the USA a similar commercial interest in the production and distribution of child pornography emerged. Liberal views on pornography, combined with lax law enforcement, enabled local US pornographers to produce both video and magazines. Links also developed between the European producers and US producers, such that photographs produced in the USA were sent to Europe for publication, and subsequently imported back to the USA.

These films and magazines provided the corpus of material that was exported all over the Western world. As the industry grew, and involved producers in other European countries and the USA, the primary base of distribution became Amsterdam. Dutch tolerance of the sex trade in general, and pornography in particular, provided an environment that enabled the systematic commercial exploitation of pornography, including child pornography, to flourish. Magazines with titles such as *Lollitots*, *Sweet Pattie*, *Sweet Linda*, *Lolita Color Specials*, *Children Love*, *Incestuous Love*, *Randy Lolitas*, *Nymph Lovers*, *Wonderboy*, *Joyboy*, *Prinz*, *Chicken*, *Kim*, *Mick*, *Kinde Liebe* and many others all date from this time. The pictures contained in these magazines seem to have come from various sources, including pictures sold to the publisher by parents or others who abused the children photographed. Some sense of how this operated can be seen from the testimony of Joseph Francis Henry to the Permanent Subcommittee on Governmental Affairs before the United States Senate, Ninety-Ninth Congress, 21 February 1985. Henry was involved in the sexual abuse of twenty-two young girls. In his testimony he states that

> Various motels and homes of two men were used as locations for the molestation. The children were also photographed during sessions with the men. Although I did not participate in this, one of the men, I can't be sure which, apparently sold photos to the Dutch child porn magazine *Lolita* because in the Lolita issues 29, 30, and 31, there were shots of Tammy and Yvonne in various explicit poses.

Magazines such as *Lolita* contained advertisements asking for photographs to be sent to the publishers.

The contemporary significance of this is that these magazines and videos continue to provide the core child pornography material. The magazines and videos produced in the 1970s can still be obtained, and lie at the centre of many child pornography collections. Even now, contemporary police seizures of child pornography regularly include hard copies of these magazines and videos. However, what is significant for our purposes is that this material (both magazines and videos), digitally scanned and placed on the Internet, remains by far the largest element of current child pornography available. The titles of the magazines and videos are preserved in their electronic form as the titles of the picture series – 'Sweet Pattie' becomes 'Pattie' for example – the various Lolita videos and magazines are identified as LL followed by the series number 1 to 36. A picture called LL23–30 therefore refers to the thirtieth picture scanned from *Lolita* video number 23.

Whilst this remains the core of the material available, it must be emphasised that since the 1980s, when legislative provision against child pornography became more effective, new material has continued to be produced. What has characterised this material has been its base of production. Early child pornographers often used hotel bedrooms in which to take their photographs. Increasingly, as the early forms of commercial production have diminished, home production has increased in significance. This has been possible because of changes in the technology of photography – the advent of instant cameras removed the need for still photographs to be developed by third parties, as did the growing availability of video for moving pictures. Coupled with this, however, was the emergence of a new, cheap and easily available medium for distribution: the Internet, along with the means of making photographs accessible to Internet users: cheap scanners to enable digitisation of photographs. As in other areas of life, the Internet has enabled direct communication between people, who in this case exchange pornographic photographs of children. More recently, however, this domestic material seems increasingly to be augmented by commercially produced photographs and videos, which unlike in the past now has connections with organised crime.

A further noteworthy aspect of newer child pornography is the growing involvement of third world children. Thailand, the Philippines, India and more recently South America, are locations from which child pornography production has increasingly been evident. Most notable of all, however, are the increasing number of children from Eastern European countries. The amateur producers of this material (as distinct from commercial suppliers) tend to be Westerners, who deliberately set out to establish contacts with disadvantaged children. The following quotation from a news story from *The Times of India* about the arrest of two Swiss nationals presents a recent case which illustrates this:

> The couple was arrested by the social service branch of the city police on December 9 for allegedly luring two slum children to pose for pornographic

> pictures. The couple had offered them expensive toys and gifts while allegedly luring them to a hotel room and forcing them to indulge in pornographic acts, the police alleged. A police party raided the hotel room on December 9 and found the couple and the children in the nude.
>
> . . .
>
> It is learnt that the couple had made at least 12 trips to India and are believed to be running the racket for more than a decade. The police have also asked Interpol to probe whether the couple were involved in luring minors for pornography in other countries like Sri Lanka and Thailand. [© 2001 The Times of India Group 12 January 2001].

An alarming potential development in Eastern Europe appears to be a growing involvement of organised crime in the distribution of child pornography, and presumably its production.

CONCLUDING COMMENT

Perhaps the most significant issue to emerge from our discussion of old child pornography is that the children who appear in these photographs that are so avidly collected, fantasised over and exchanged are in fact now 30- to 40-year-old women and men, in all probability married with families of their own. What their feelings might be about the photographs of them that are still in circulation is largely unknown, but for the person sexually interested in children the existence of such photographs 'ensures that there will always be an image of the child at their age of sexual preference' (Healy 1997). In photographs, if not in real life, these images preserve the child. New photographs, of course, just add to this cycle of exploitation. Perhaps this point above all others brings into focus the discussion of 'What is the problem' of child pornography that started this chapter. Preserving images of the exploitation of children effectively preserves that exploitation, and enables it to extend beyond even generations.

The broadly psychological approach developed in this chapter has a utility beyond a narrow legalistic perspective, although it is not without problems. Identifying child pornography with pictures that are attractive to adults with a sexual interest in children extends concern to photographs that are not in any sense necessarily indecent or obscene. It is not possible to legislate for this essentially fantasy use of photographs, and nor should it be even considered. But it does force our attention to the individual, and the activities of that individual that can be lost when a narrow legalistic approach is taken. Collecting and producing child pornography is a complex activity, and the following chapters will enable that complexity to be explored.

Chapter 3

Adult sexual interest in children

Sexual interest and contact between adults and children has been observed and documented over written history, and such accounts would suggest varying degrees of social acceptance (McConaghy 1998). However, the concept of child sexual abuse (CSA) as a social problem is a relatively new phenomenon and did not emerge in the academic literature until the 1980s. Its identification as a social problem led to a proliferation of studies examining the nature of the offender and their behaviour, as well as increased efforts towards documenting its prevalence and understanding the impact that such abuse might have on victims (Freeman and Morris 2001). What is also noticeable is the emergence of terminology emphasising the adult as perpetrator and the child as victim. Epidemiological studies have suggested the presence of widespread incest and child molestation, leading Finkelhor (1994) to assert that 'In every locale where it has been sought, researchers have demonstrated its existence at levels high enough to be detected through surveys of a few hundred adults in the general population' (412). In the twentieth century, within North American and European cultures, the person who engages in sexual contact with children is demonised as the least desirable member of our community, and when convicted of such a crime often requires special protection within the judicial system.

The purpose of this chapter is to examine how we currently make sense of adult sexual interest in children. This chapter does not focus on the relationship between sexual offences against children and the Internet, which is addressed in the next chapter. This chapter sets the scene to allow us to explore and evaluate critically what differences, if any, are associated with this new technology. In exploring what we mean by adult sexual interest in children it is important to note that our conceptualisations belong largely to this time, and take place alongside changes in how we think about children and childhood, and the role of mass communication. Kincaid (1998) has drawn our attention to the ways in which Western societies currently 'eroticise' children (seen most explicitly in advertising), while at the same time both denying their sexuality and overvaluing ideas of innocence. Thus we create a sexualised child whom we pretend to be protecting. This fusion of innocence and sexuality may be one of many factors that play a part in the objectification of children as sexual artifacts, and that results in younger and younger children being sought as sexual stimuli. This may be reflected in the changing nature of child pornography as it emerges on the Internet (Taylor 1999).

A further point for consideration relates to the fact that the majority of those appearing to commit sexual offences are men (Cowburn and Pringle 2000). Whether this relates to men's oppressive and abusive practices towards women and children, or an underreporting of offences committed by women and children, remains unclear. However, what we are starting to see are accounts of both women and children as offenders, and these will be considered alongside current theorising about men as abusers.

GLOBAL ACCOUNTS OF SEX OFFENDERS

Our current ideas about adults who are sexually interested in children are largely drawn from the last century, and emerged from theorising about the nature of sexual behaviour and its categorisation. Inevitably, such categorising of behaviour tends to dichotomise activities, so that we end up attaching to them labels such as normal/abnormal, moral/immoral, acceptable/deviant and so on. Such early accounts are often called 'global', because they do not have as their specific focus sexual interest in children, but are a more comprehensive account of whole groups of behaviours.

One of the most influential global accounts was provided by Freud, where sexual behaviours that were considered deviant were situated within the context of character disorders. Freud used the word perversion to describe such behaviours, and suggested that either the aim or the object of the person's sexual desire had become diverted. The location for such perversion was early childhood, and Freud (1975) emphasised that these behaviours were highly resistant to change. He noted that the sexual abuse of children was frequently found 'among school children and child attendants' (14), and that sexual impulses were amongst those least controlled by 'the higher activities of the mind'. This rather tame conclusion did little to help our understanding of such sexual behaviours and as Lanyon (1991) has suggested, the 'untreatability' aspect of Freud's account has had a profound effect on attitudes toward treatment that has only been challenged within more recent years. A subsequent analytic account was provided by Fraser (1976), which focused on unresolved Oedipal strivings on the part of the male, who, in spite of growing older, remains deeply in love with the person he was as a child. However, as Horley (2000) points out, Fraser's linking of homosexuality with child sex abuse cannot account for the number of men who are both sexually attracted to, and who engage in sexual activity with, immature females.

A further global theory that has had most influence within the therapeutic community is behavioural in its orientation. Here the problem is conceptualised as an inappropriate frequency of events such as behaviours, thoughts and feelings, and has allowed for the classification of deviant behaviours according to their stimulus and response characteristics (Langevin 1983). Within this framework it is argued that children can be exposed to contexts where they experience some early arousal to stimuli, which, when combined with inappropriate masturbatory fantasies during adolescence, leads to deviant sexual behaviour. Such inappropriate events are seen as problematic in themselves, rather than as symptomatic of some further underlying dysfunction. This is in marked contrast to biological theories, which have focused on genetic, hormonal or neuropsychological factors underpinning the deviant behaviour. For example, a recent paper by Bogaert (2001) examined the evidence for elevated non-righthandedness in sex offenders as a measure of underlying developmental or central nervous system abnormalities. While such correlational studies are interesting, they do little to move us away from models emphasising associations between a variety of biological factors and the emergence of behaviour that is socially labelled as deviant. They do not establish what 'causes' people to behave differently and reinforce the 'medicalisation' of such sexual behaviour. The latter has become one powerful way that many organisations who promote sexual contact between children justify their interest and distance themselves from taking personal responsibility for their behaviour.

Such accounts of sexual deviance have also been termed paraphilias within the medical community and entered into the classification system of the American Psychiatric Association (APA). According to the diagnostic tool DSM-IV (APA 1994), such disorders are characterised by recurrent and intense sexual urges, fantasies or behaviours involving either non-human objects, children or non-consenting adults, or the experience of suffering or humiliation. For a person to be diagnosed in this way, they have to be experiencing such urges, fantasies or behaviours for at least six months, and they must also be having a negative impact on the person's social or work activity. Paedophilia is seen as one such paraphilia, and is placed under the heading 'Sexuality and Gender Identity Disorders'. DSM-IV distinguishes between those who are attracted only to children (exclusive type) and those who are attracted to adults as well (non-exclusive type). This typology of sexual interest bears a strong resemblance to other, dynamically oriented perspectives, but is possibly of limited value because meeting the first criteria (evidence of duration of urges, fantasies or behaviours) inevitably excludes a large number of people with a sexual interest in children.

TYPOLOGIES OF SEXUAL INTEREST IN CHILDREN

Some of the earliest accounts of sexual offences against children attempted to create typologies of offenders. One of the most influential of such accounts was that of Groth (e.g. Groth *et al.* 1982). Within this psychodynamic framework, child molestation was viewed as a pseudo-sexual act, where the offending behaviour was in the service of non-sexual needs. Seen in this way, the underlying motivation to the sexual behaviour was not really sexual but a bid to resolve non-sexual needs and to deal with everyday life issues. Offenders were divided into two basic types, according to their level of psychosexual motivation, and excluded those who used violence against children. These were termed child rapists and were seen as being qualitatively different from molesters. Molesters were seen to be either regressed or fixated. The regressed offender was theorized to have developed age-appropriate sexual and interpersonal orientations, but under particular circumstances (for example, the absence of the marital partner) could regress to sexual involvement with children. The fixated offender was one whose primary sexual interest was children, and who never developed psychosexually beyond that level. Such accounts are still very influential and are evident in attempts to judge how 'dangerous' the individual is.

A more sophisticated empirical classification typology was developed by Knight *et al.* (1989) who acknowledged that child molesters were a markedly heterogeneous group, and that the development of an adequate typology would moderate decision making. Their typology, termed MTC:CM3 (Massachusetts Treatment Centre: Child Molester Typology, version 3) rated offenders along two axes. Axis I involved dichotomous decisions on two independent, crossed constructs: fixation and social competence. Fixation assessed the strength of paedophilic interest (the extent to which children had been a major focus of cognitions and fantasies) while social competence assessed the offender's success in employment, adult relationships and social responsibilities. Axis II required a hierarchical series of decisions, beginning with the amount of contact with children, both sexual and non-sexual, which would categorise the person as either a high-contact or low-contact offender. This is a behavioural measure of the amount of time that an offender spends with or near children, excluding parent-related contact. Any involvement in a job or social or recreational activities that requires regular contact with children qualifies as non-sexual contact.

The authors felt that this classification system was an important first step in design of research on the aetiology, treatment disposition and prognosis of further offending. One problem with such measures is that they rely exclusively on archival data (such as prison and programme records), as opposed to screening methods such as the Abel Screen (Abel *et al.* 1994) or plethysmographic measures. What emerges from this literature is that the classification, diagnosis and assessment of those adults who sexually engage with children are complicated by a high degree of variability among such people in terms of personal characteristics, life experiences, criminal histories and reasons for offending. Prentky *et al.* (1997) suggested that there is 'no single "profile" that accurately describes or accounts for all child molesters'. However, what we start to see emphasised is the importance of factors such as ease of access to children (also seen in Freud's account), and the presence or absence of other factors such as social skills or social isolation.

EVALUATING RISK

Such data-driven approaches to the validation of taxonomic systems for the classification of adults with a sexual interest in children remain important (e.g. Rosenberg and Knight 1988; Kalichman 1991), as they largely inform estimates of 'dangerousness' and influence decisions about both sentencing and incarceration. The question of dangerousness is closely linked with that of recidivism – whether the person will offend again. It has been suggested that the likelihood of reoffending can be predicted from a number of static or dynamic variables. Static risk factors are those which cannot change, and include a history of childhood maladjustment or prior offences. They are thought to indicate 'deviant developmental trajectories' and as such can be used to mark long-term propensities to engage in criminal behaviour (Hanson 1998). Such factors, however, are not used in determining either when or if offences will occur (for example, somebody might have benefited from treatment). Dynamic factors are thought to be those that predict whether a person will reoffend and have the potential for changing (associated with increases or decreases in recidivism). Such dynamic factors can be further divided into stable (e.g. deviant sexual preferences or alcoholism) and acute (e.g. sexual arousal or drunkenness) factors. Hanson (1998) suggested that making an evaluation about enduring changes in risk levels inevitably must rely on changes in stable risk factors.

Hanson and Harris (2000) organised dynamic risk factors identified in a previous study into a structured assessment procedure, The Sex Offender Need Assessment Rating (SONAR). This included five relatively stable factors (intimacy deficits, negative social influences, attitude tolerant of sex offending, sexual self-regulation, general self-regulation) and four acute factors (substance abuse, negative mood, anger, victim access). It was anticipated that the stable factors would have a long duration, such as weeks or months, whereas the acute factors would change over weeks or days. These scales were examined using data previously collected on sex offenders who had reoffended compared to those who had not. The scale showed a moderate ability to differentiate between those who reoffended (recidivists) and those who did not. The former showed the greatest problems in conforming to the demands of community supervision, and to a lesser extent problems in sexual self-regulation, attitudes tolerant of sex offending, and negative peer associations. Possibly one important aspect of this research is the recognition that the level of risk of an individual offender can change substantially. Without such an acknowledgement, it would be inevitable to assume that all offenders pose the same level of risk of reoffending and that they remain indefinitely at high risk to reoffend.

Assessment measures which do not rely on self-report or archival material include phallometric testing. This measures penile erection responses to stimuli depicting various sexual stimuli, based on the early assumption that such arousal is largely involuntary and therefore less likely to be influenced by faking. (What this also emphasises is the adversarial approach to assessment where clinicians are looking for 'proof' of deviant sexual arousal.) Hanson and Bussière (1996) conducted a meta-analysis of sixty-one studies reporting sexual offender recidivism. They derived a 'pedophile index' from phallometric evaluation, and this was the most powerful predictor of recidivism. Their total sample of offenders included both rapists and child molesters, but a similarly derived 'rape index' failed to predict reoffending. However, difficulties in the standardisation of such phallometric measures, paucity about the nature of the research subjects or the stimuli used and lack of information about controls for faking during assessment have led authors such as Marshall and Fernandez (2000) to urge caution in the conclusions that can be drawn. It may be that the clinical utility of phallometric assessments might suggest their use in combination with other measures in order to determine: which offenders display 'deviant' sexual arousal (and therefore need treatment); whether or not treatment has reduced 'deviant' tendencies; and estimating the likelihood of reoffending.

An alternative to phallometric assessment has been visual reaction time, which measures the amount of time participants spend looking at sexual and non-sexual stimuli. A variant of this is the Abel Assessment for Sexual Interest (AASI). As the person looks at slides that present clothed people in varying contexts, the length of the latency period required for the person to respond with a self-reported ranking of sexual interest in the slide's content is measured. It is hypothesised that the longer someone attends to a slide, the greater the level of sexual interest is in the slide. An average of responding time latency periods to all slides within the same category of sexual interest is used as a measure of sexual interest in each category. Abel *et al.* (2001) attempted to demonstrate the ability of the AASI to discriminate between non-child molesters and admitting child molesters. An important aspect of this study was to address the potential for falsifying responses (a significant problem with phallometric assessments). The authors used a group of 747 participants matched by age, race and income to develop three logistic regression equations. The models compared a group of non-child molesting subjects who were under investigation for other paraphilias to three groups of child molesters. These were a group of admitting molesters of girls under 14 years of age, a similar group whose target was boys under 14 and a group believed to be concealing or denying having molested. Their results suggested that both of the equations designed to discriminate between admitting child molesters and non-child molesters were statistically significant. The equation used to contrast those who sought to conceal their behaviour and non-child molesting subjects was also significant. However, some caution is needed in interpreting the latter results as the 'liar-denier model' was estimated on a sample of sixty-five participants who denied any child molestation but who were believed by professionals to be actual molesters. The authors also acknowledge that a probability value does not reflect certainty, no matter how high. Also, even though a person assessed using AASI may have a high probability of classification in one of the three categories, this does not mean that any current accusations being made against them are indeed correct. However, the practical and ethical advantages of using such an assessment over traditional phallometric measures are considerable.

Fisher and Thornton (1993) identified two major difficulties in risk assessment for reoffending. The first of these is the inherent problem in making assumptions about the general level of risk posed by broad classes of offender. Studer *et al.* (2000), for example, discussed how research literature has been used by professionals to justify the belief that incest offenders, as opposed to non-familial offenders, pose little chance of reoffending (e.g. Greenberg *et al.* 2000). The results of Studer's study of 328 offenders (178 of whom were classed as non-incestuous) suggested that many offenders who initially appeared incestuous were, in fact, more paedophilic in their tendencies and had acted on those preferences in the past. Therefore, caution needs to be used in predictions based on class of offender, as these in part may relate to opportunity to offend rather than preference. The second difficulty in risk assessment, according to Fisher and Thornton, is the divergence of opinion regarding relative risk levels. For example, if the offender 'denies' the offence, is this to be taken as an increasing sign of risk, or an inevitable sign of defensiveness on the part of the offender? This is further complicated by both the varying amounts of information available to the assessor and the fact that there are different motivations on the part of the offender and the assessor. The process is an adversarial one where the accused seeks to minimise the nature of the offence or may opt to be 'open' with the assessor as an indication of the way that they have changed.

Grubin and Wingate (1996) argue against the use of actuarial models, using a study by Quinsey *et al.* (1995) to highlight the fundamental problems associated with them. Quinsey *et al.*'s (1995) study was empirically driven from a population of 178 offenders treated in a maximum-security hospital. The subjects of this study were classified as either rapists (if their victim was a female over the age of 14) or child molesters (where the female had been under the age of 14 and the offender was at least five years older than the victim or where the victim was a male under 16 and at least five years younger than the offender). One hundred and twenty-four men were defined as child molesters, twenty-eight as rapists and twenty-six as both. Variables included demographic information (such as occupation, marital status and IQ), psychiatric history, non-sexual criminal history, history of sexual offences and a phallometric assessment that yielded a 'deviance differential'. The results of the study suggested that sexual recidivism was predicted by previous criminal history, with psychopathy ratings and phallometric assessment data contributing only marginally to the variance. This was somewhat surprising given earlier claims made by the same authors about the predictive value of these two variables.

There is little to suggest that the findings of this population, obtained from a maximum-security prison, can be generalised to another. In addition, what is implied is that 'human beings are entirely a function of their histories' (354) and that, regardless of treatment or maturity, the risk of reoffending should remain unaltered. The reality is that historical data do not change, regardless of treatment or personal development. Grubin and Wingate (1996) concluded that the most crucial difficulty, however, arises from the fact that actuarial prediction is about groups rather than individuals, and unless the behaviour is high frequency it can tell us little about individual differences. Actuarial models therefore indicate associations, rather than tell us about causation. As explanatory models, they tend to be circular, show little relevance to specific cases and fail to inform intervention. Krauss *et al.* (2000) have suggested that actuarial instruments are, by and large, atheoretical and do not address the causes of the behaviour that they are designed to predict. For example, past criminal behaviour is a good predictor of future criminal activity, but this offers no insight about rehabilitation or the prevention of others from committing the same act.

Much of this research has its focus on what people do that constitutes the offence, or what they did in terms of past behaviours. An area that has focused much more on how individuals think about themselves, their behaviour and that of the child or children they are interested in is that of cognition and sexual functioning. To put this very simply, it is assumed that there is something problematic in the way the person thinks that increases the likelihood of engaging sexually with children. As we will see in later chapters, those with a sexual interest in children have equally used the argument that there is something problematic in the way that 'non-paedophiles' think that makes sexual engagement with children a crime.

COGNITION AND SEXUAL FUNCTIONING

Cognition and sexual functioning has attracted interest in more recent years, although what this refers to has been conceived and operationalised in a number of different ways. Segal and Stermac (1990) have described cognitive processes as operating at four different levels. Cognitive structure (e.g. schemata) refers to how memories are organised; cognitive propositions refer to the type of information stored in memory; cognitive operations refer to the various processes by which system components operate (e.g. information processing); cognitive products refer to the actual thoughts or images that result from the other three (such as self-statements or attributions). Horley (2000) suggested that beliefs, attitudes and values are among the specific concepts that qualify as propositions, while fantasies or daydreams would be seen more in terms of products, and that much of the work in this area in relation to offences against children has a focus on processes and products. For example, Finkelhor and Araji (1986) generated a four-factor theory of child molestation, which included a number of variables, such as deviant fantasy involving children and inappropriate beliefs about children, that appear to be relevant to understanding offender behaviour. However, understanding the relationship between the factors and the role of cognitive processes is still to be explored.

'Cognitive' accounts of offending focus on factors such as empathy, social skills and cognitive processes as a way of understanding, and hopefully changing, offender behaviour. Here the implication is that there is something problematic in both the way that offenders view or interpret their social world and the ways they respond to it. What lies between individuals and their offending behaviour is a way of thinking that results from an active, but inaccurate, thinking process, rather than a lack of processing activity. As a result of this, cognitive processing is taking place, but the thinking has become in some way distorted. In the sex offender literature such 'cognitive distortions' are most often defined as attitudes and beliefs that offenders use to deny, minimise and rationalise their behaviour. Such distortions have been defined as consistent errors in thinking that occur automatically (Geer *et al.* 2000), and include beliefs such as: if children fail to resist advances, they must want sex; sexual activity with children is an appropriate means to increase the sexual knowledge of children; if children fail to report sexual activity, they must condone it; in the future, sex between adults and children will be acceptable if not encouraged; if one fondles, rather than penetrates, sex with children is acceptable; any children who ask questions about sex really desire it; and one can develop a close relationship with a child through sexual contact (Horley 2000). A fundamental assumption of such approaches is that these attitudes and beliefs play a major role in both precipitating and maintaining offending behaviour (Abel *et al.* 1994). However, it is not always clear whether distortions are thought to have aetiological status in offending behaviour or to be *post hoc* rationalisations of offending. This is an issue that we will return to later, for now, though, we will present a summary of some of the main approaches to, and findings from, studies of cognitive distortions.

One major problem with attempts to examine 'cognitive distortions' is the reliance on scales, such as the Cognitions Scale (Abel *et al.* 1989) and the MOLEST scale (Bumby 1996). Using the Cognitions Scale, Abel *et al.* (1989) found that people who commit sexual offences against children were more likely to endorse attitudes and beliefs about the acceptability of sexual acts with children, than people committing sexual offences against adults. Similar results were found by Stermac and Segal (1989) in the context of a vignette study. The results of this suggested that child molesters differed from other respondents in perceiving more benefits to the child, greater complicity on the child's part and less responsibility on the adult's part. They concluded that such cognitions might contribute to, or have a facilitative role, in offending behaviour.

However, self-rating scales often use items that are transparent and are therefore open to misrepresentation, or 'faking good'. Blumenthal *et al.* (1999) examined the cognitive distortions and blame attributions of both child and adult sex offenders on a number of separate scales: MOLEST (relating to children and their sexuality, and including statements such as 'I believe that sex with children can make the child feel closer to adults'); RAPE (items endorsing rape, including 'Women who get raped probably deserve it'); and the Revised Gudjonddon Blame Attribution Inventory (BAI) determining attribution of blame for crimes. These authors also measured 'impression management' and 'self-deception', which had been found to influence scores on other measures. Their results suggested that despite previous evidence of faking questionnaire responses, in this study there was no indication that social desirability influenced responses, although there was some evidence that those who commit sexual offences against children may have a greater investment in impression management because of the perceived seriousness of their responses. Their results supported earlier research in that people who offended against children scored higher on the MOLEST scale, but there were no differences between groups on the RAPE scale. The items on these scales are very transparent, and it is perhaps surprising that those who had committed offences against children should have scored so highly. One possible conclusion is an overall elevation in attitudes and beliefs about sexual offending, regardless of the age of the victim. Previous work by Bumby (1996) had also suggested that there are differences between rapists and child molesters in cognitive distortions. It may be that in those who commit rape, such distorted ways of thinking are linked to the actual offence context and may be thought of as 'state' distortions, which would not necessarily occur in other situations. However, those who commit sexual offences against children might be thought of as expressing distortions, which apply across all contexts ('trait' distortions). Blumenthal *et al.*'s (1999) study also suggested that those who had committed sex offences against adults also endorsed more external attributions than did those who had offended against children. For example, rapists were more likely to attribute their crime to having had too much alcohol prior to the offence.

Within much of the research in this area, there seems to be an assumption that cognitive distortions are a result of a set of internal, individualised, fairly static attitudes and beliefs rather than, say, an outcome of a particular discursive strategy in a given setting. Ward *et al.* (1997), in a review of the cognitive distortion literature, highlighted the lack of attention to the temporal component of offending. They claimed that too much attention has been focused on post-offence cognitions and called for increased attention to information processing mechanisms before and during the offence cycle. They further highlighted the fact that cognitive processes can change markedly through the offending sequence as a result of increased sexual arousal and mood states. What is not clear, however, is how one would access accounts of such cognitions. If we take as an alternative perspective the socially situated nature of cognition, making assumptions about the global or stable nature of cognitive distortions seems problematic. Accounts occur within specific contexts, and serve particular functions. Under certain circumstances non-offender populations also give accounts, which at the very least are ambiguous with regard to the acceptability of sexual behaviour, in relation to both adults and children.

Ward *et al.* (1997) suggested that stored social information, or pre-existing beliefs, can, once activated, influence all aspects of social information processing 'including attention to and interpretation of information and, consequently, inferences and judgements made from that information' (482). Chronicity and temporality are thought to influence their activation. For example, chronic beliefs are ones that are central to the perceiver's self-concept, and are easily activated. In the context of a sex offender, this may refer to sex-related thoughts. Temporality relates to context, such that some contexts will easily activate certain thoughts (sitting outside a school yard at playtime). Incoming information is then interpreted in an expectancy-consistent manner, with people taking 'short-cuts' such as using stereotypes and well-learned behavioural scripts. To some extent, such beliefs can be modified by expectancy-disconfirming information, which is often seen as the goal of therapeutic intervention. For example, an offender may believe that because the child appeared smiling and happy during the sexual contact this was equivalent to the child actually giving consent. One goal of therapy might be to explore this belief in the context of what we know about abusive situations. Such information may serve to disconfirm well-learned information and reduce the likelihood of the offender taking the usual 'short-cuts' when next interpreting a child's behaviour. However, outside the context of 'therapy', most offenders continue to tell themselves things that allow them to engage in the same offence-related way.

Murphy (1990) has suggested three ways in which sex offenders deal with incoming information that allow them to continue to offend. First, they justify their conduct by construing it as morally or psychologically permissible. Second, they distort or misperceive the consequences of their abusive behaviour by either minimising its effect on their victim, or attributing the consequences to something else. Finally, they devalue or dehumanise their victims, and attribute blame to them for the offence rather than accepting responsibility themselves. Such justifications, however, are not confined to offending populations, and possibly suggest common cultural strategies for excusing sexual aggression. For example, in a study by Back and Lips (1998), undergraduate students were asked to make attributions of responsibility to a series of vignettes depicting children and adults engaged in sexual activity. The results of the study suggested that attributions directed towards the victim and non-offending parent may be a function of victim age. The ages of the children in the vignettes ranged from 6 to 13, and greater attributions for responsibility were made as the child's age increased. This is possibly no different from general assumptions made by, for example, the popular press with regard to teenage sexual behaviour. As the person increases in age, we attribute greater responsibility to them with regard to their sexual behaviour regardless of what is actually the case in law.

Ward (2000) has argued that sexual offenders' cognitive distortions emerge from 'underlying causal theories about the nature of their victims', rather than stemming from unrelated, independent beliefs. These implicit theories are thought to function like scientific theories and are used as a way of explaining other people's actions and to make predictions about the world. Ward has suggested that these theories are made up of a number of interlocking beliefs and their component concepts and categories. Ward used the idea of implicit theories in the same way that other psychologists have used the concept of schema, and discusses the way that sex offenders' implicit theories about their victims are structured around two core sets of mental constructs, beliefs and desires. In this way, an offender's theory or model of a victim contains representations of the victim's desires, beliefs and attitudes, and these theories guide the processing of information that aids in the process of confirmation or disconfirmation. The offender, therefore, uses the implicit theories about victims to infer their mental state, to interpret their behaviour and to make predictions about their future actions and mental states. Ward hypothesised that there are levels of beliefs, starting with very general low-level beliefs about the nature of people and the world and progressing to very specific beliefs about a victim. An example given in relation to this is that at a very general level the offender may not construe beliefs and desires as representational and, therefore, fail to appreciate that people view the same situation in different ways.

At a middle level, the offender may construe women and children in an inaccurate manner (for example, seeing children as wanting sex). Finally, an offender may develop a false theory of their specific victim, claiming, for example, that this child is different to others who are not mature enough to be able to give consent.

One feature of this conceptual model is that it allows us to distinguish between different types of offender according to whether they primarily focus on the offender, the victim or the world, and can be used as an aid to clarify possible cognitive differences between offender types. However, Ward (2000) failed to account for the origin of such implicit theories and their relationship to discrete patterns of behaviour and concludes that they:

> emerge from an offender's early developmental experiences and represent their attempt to explain regularities in the family and local environment. Theories are constructed at this point because of the importance, persistence, and emotional impact of the events. Relevant events may involve close family interaction patterns, relationship with sibling, individual's own attributes and actions, or the actions of other people (e.g. sexual abuse by an uncle).
>
> (Ward 2000: 503)

We are left with yet another diathesis–stress model of offending behaviour, where early developmental experiences are seen as the basis for the creation of implicit theories which are then activated at a later stage by some form of stressor. Such experiences can only be accessed through the post-offending accounts provided by people, and there is no way of ascertaining the veracity of one account over another.

EMPATHY

A related area of research has examined 'empathy' in sex offenders. Fisher and Howells (1993) defined empathy as the ability to perceive another person's point of view, experience the emotions of another and behave compassionately. Early work with offenders led to the assumption that lack of empathy in sex offenders plays a role in the development and maintenance of sexual offending behaviour. Marshall *et al.* (1995), based on a review of the literature on empathy, claimed that studies usually involved a focus on 'cognitive abilities [perspective taking] and the vicarious matching of another person's emotional state' (100). Such studies most often relied on the 'trait' approach to understanding empathy, of which they are critical. That is, empathy is viewed as a relatively stable internal trait over time. Instead, these authors offered a multi-component staged model of empathy, with each component being needed for progression to the next step. Within this model, the first step involved accurately identifying affect or emotion in another person. The second step was being able to take that person's perspective in order fully to comprehend the emotion detected. The third step involved evocation of an emotion similar to that observed in the other person, and the fourth step involved the formulation and delivery of an appropriate response. The process also required that the individual was sensitive to the subtleties of a situation that provide feedback and result in subsequent modifications as the process unfolds.

While intuitively it seems appealing that an explanation for offending behaviour lies in the individual's inability to empathise with the victim, it has not received universal support. Geer *et al.* (2000) have argued that the evidence for clear-cut deficits within the population of sex offenders is not yet available, and are critical of the measures used to measure empathy. Common measures of empathy include: self-report measures (which tend to be non-specific), and scaled measures of non-person-specific empathy. Three such scales are: the Empathy Scale (Hogan 1969); Emotional Empathy Scale (Mehrabian and Epstein 1972); and the Interpersonal Reactivity Index (Davis 1983). All three scales are based on 'trait' assumptions about empathy, which are insensitive to contextual or temporal differences. For example, Marshall *et al.* (1993) examined the general empathy levels of incarcerated and non-incarcerated child molesters, using the Interpersonal Reactivity Index (Davis 1983). The offenders in prison did not display a general lack of empathy (as compared to normative data), whereas those offenders living in the community did. Marshall *et al.* speculated that incarcerated offenders were attempting to appear empathic in order to facilitate their release. This again highlights the transparency of such scales and the offender's ability to distort the results in a socially acceptable way. However, importantly, it led Marshall *et al.* (1993) to contend that the sex offender's empathic responsiveness may vary as a function of situation, victim characteristics and *post hoc* attempts to rationalise socially unacceptable behaviour. Of relevance here is what it means to 'learn' an empathic response through therapy. Learning appropriate 'empathic' language and response practice may seem not incompatible with the 'child-love' narrative that is also used as a means of justifying offending behaviour.

Geer *et al.* (2000) concluded that, while it is generally accepted that sex offenders 'lack empathy', research actually indicates that in reality some sex offenders are quite capable of being empathic. This is seen most clearly in the way that some sex offenders select children to abuse, and is highlighted in the following extracts from an interview with OT:

> In the past I've always targeted my victims very carefully. [mm] Am . . . picked victims who were vulnerable from one way or another [mm] Erm . . . out of a lack of love [mm] maybe even with two parents you weren't getting the attention or [mm] children who were vulnerable [mm]. I always targeted them very very carefully. [mm]. Went through a long period of getting to know the parents [mm] or parent, getting to know the child. I followed the classic pattern [mm]. Am . . . I never selected a victim without getting to know the parents. (24)

> I get the feeling his parents . . . bought his love rather than gave him their love [mm] and I think D would have probably responded to the attention.

> [okay]. Am it's the nearest I can put it, it's more than that [mm] and it's stronger than that and it's actually finding the words [mm] am . . . D is the only one I would have said would have been possibly a potential target for me in years back. (38)

> This is what I said if I'd had met him at ten [okay] there have been no contest [mm] but no he was . . . too independent you see I needed to create a dependency in my victims [mm] I needed to have them dependent on me [mm] . . . in every way that I could get them dependent. [mm] It wasn't enough just to be hey look he can teach us to draw, let's hang around him [mm] that wasn't enough [mm] that's wouldn't been enough [mm] it had to be I NEED YOU [okay] in a very real way [mm]. (39)

These extracts indicate that OT appeared to meet many of the criteria for empathy as outlined by Fisher and Howells (1993). In fact, OT was able to use this empathic response to engage with and successfully abuse children. It might be argued that his behaviour, up to the point of the abuse itself, would have been seen to be highly empathic and compassionate, if it was not in the service of his own sexual needs. Hudson *et al.* (1997) similarly suggested that men with a longstanding preference for pseudo-romantic styled relationships tend to be both generally empathic, report greater concern for others, and report having no difficulties in taking another's perspective.

What seems most problematic about research on empathy and cognitive distortions in relation to sexual offences is the model of the individual it is based on, that is the assumption of a rational information-processing individual, possessing relatively stable internal characteristics. For example, Ward *et al.* (1997) suggested that 'the crux of social cognition research is the specification of how beliefs affect the ongoing flow of social behaviour' (490). As with many mainstream approaches to understanding experience, this research seeks to explain, and treat, complex social behaviour solely in terms of the 'underlying' cognitive processes of an individual. Such assumptions tend to divorce the individual from the social interaction in which offending takes place. It is difficult to see how models of offending based solely on internal traits or an information-processing framework can make the leap to discuss sexual offending as situated in complex relational and interactional contexts. Also problematic is the assumed relationship between relatively stable cognitive traits and instances of offending behaviour, when what emerges from the literature is obviously confusion as to whether empathy or cognitive distortions are post-offence rationalisations or have an aetiological character. Finally, as highlighted by Marx *et al.* (1999), studies concerned with differences in cognition neglect to offer any explanation as to their origin. An alternative constructionist viewpoint is that both social cognitions and behaviour are emergent from ongoing interactions.

Non-offending social interactions have been the focus of much research and still inform many treatment approaches. Again, this in part reflects assumptions about those with a sexual interest in children that in fact one possible explanation for such engagement relates to an inability to engage with appropriate adults.

OFFENDING AND SOCIAL SKILLS

The ways in which offenders act and interact within social domains has largely been examined within the context of social skills or competence. Earlier work by Barlow *et al.* (1977) had compared the performance of a group of 'sexual deviates' with 'socially skilled males' during a five-minute conversation with a female confederate. The sample size was very small (ten) and the offences included sexual fetishes, rape and exhibitionism. However, the work suggested that these sex offenders were deficient in basic conversational skills, voice quality and affect. Segal and Marshall (1985) used a similar behavioural measure with a sample of rapists and child molesters. These were compared to incarcerated non-sex offenders and non-incarcerated men. The participants were asked to initiate and maintain a conversation with a female confederate and then rate how confident they were on a variety of social measures. Blind raters judged their social behaviour, and predictions of self-efficacy were compared with these ratings. Their results suggested that rapists as a group did not differ from other males of low socio-economic status on any of the measures used. However, with regard to group differences, child molesters were perceived as less socially skilled than the other subject groups. They also scored higher on measures of social anxiety and distress. Behavioural measures, physiological measures and self-reports were used by Overholser and Beck (1986) to investigate social skills and social anxiety. Their subjects were two sex offender groups (rapists and child molesters) and three non-sex offender controls, with twelve subjects in each. A behavioural role-play test suggested overall heterosexual skills deficits for both rapists and child molesters, when compared to the control groups, and child molesters reported significantly more fear of negative evaluation.

One of the difficulties in evaluating the research on social skills is that the research has been conducted in a variety of ways, and using a number of measures. Self-report measures are often linked to social desirability, and as such may be particularly problematic. Using brief role-plays in contrived and at times very artificial social situations may also create difficulties, and it is unclear as to whether results on such measures generalise across all social settings. It may also be that such behaviour is mediated by emotional arousal, and where the emotion is anxiety rather than sexual arousal, social performance may be affected. Geer *et al.* (2000) have suggested that to say that sex offenders have social skills deficits is an oversimplification of the way in which individuals interact with others in their environment. These authors suggest that a more useful way to think about skills and competence within a social domain is to examine them within the context of information processing.

McFall's (1982) information-processing model of social skills and social competence has been used as a way of exploring the hypothesis that sex offenders are deficient in their ability to process interpersonal cues. The purpose of the model was to specify the process and conditions that lead individuals to engage in sexually deviant behaviour, such as rape, rather than to simply identify and label a person as a rapist. The three stages of this model refer to decoding skills (afferent processes involved in receiving, perceiving and interpreting incoming stimulus information), decision skills (processes by which the situation is transformed into a specific behavioural programme), and execution skills (efferent processes that are involved in smoothly executing a response). Deficits in any or all of these steps can lead to decrements in observed behaviour. Using this model, Stahl and Sacco (1995) assessed the ability of child molesters, rapists and violent and non-violent sex offenders in interpreting women's affective cues and level of sexual desire in dating situations (decoding skills), using vignettes of couples on a first date. Their results suggested that child molesters had significant deficiencies in interpreting women's affective and sexual cues, which were not evidenced by rapists. Further studies have attempted to explore the roles of decision and enactment skills in social competence, which again have supported the hypothesis that child molesters appear to be the most deficient of offenders. While the model is interesting in that it provides a theoretical basis to work in this area, the empirical studies to date do not address the fact that child sex offenders are not a homogeneous group.

THEORY OF MIND

Ward *et al.* (2000) argued that empathy problems, intimacy deficits and cognitive distortions in fact all point to a lack of awareness of other people's beliefs, desires, perspectives and needs and that this can be seen as arising from deficits in one central mechanism: the ability to infer mental states. This ability has been conceptualised as a 'theory of mind' and is based on developmental research with children. It has also been used to account for the behaviour evidenced by autistic children and adults diagnosed as schizophrenic. Ward *et al.* (2000) suggested that a theory of mind includes 'knowledge about the basic elements of people's psychological functioning (mental states), how these mental states generate behaviour, and the relationship between situations and mental states' (48). Sex offenders are often described as socially isolated, lonely individuals who appear to have few close relationships, and where such relationships do exist they are often seen as superficial and lacking in intimacy (Marshall 1989). Ward *et al.* (2000) suggested that current theoretical perspectives tend to focus on individuals' underlying beliefs or internal working models of relationships. Such models contain assumptions about the mental states of both persons concerned, offender and victim, and this inability accurately to infer mental states in other people may extend to themselves as well. Such deficits are argued to be either a relatively enduring problem, caused by a lack of knowledge about mental states and their relationship to behaviour, or primarily a function of particular psychological or physical states.

This theory hypothesises that there are two types of problem evident in offender understanding of mental states. The first are enduring or trait deficiencies and the second are episodic or state-induced impairments. The first type of problem has its basis in a lack of knowledge about people in certain kinds of relationship, whereas a specific theory deficit would mean that the offender lacks a theory about certain kinds of mental state in specific contexts, or is characterised by false assumptions about their victim. The authors also suggested that positive affective states can impair theory of mind functioning, making the offender reluctant to utilise their knowledge about other people's mental states in the appropriate contexts. A good example of this is sexual arousal, where offence-related cognitions change as a consequence of arousal. While Ward *et al.* (2000) used this trait state dichotomy to explain differences in empathy scores, they found it more difficult to explain why some offenders appear to show little or no empathic difficulties. These are attributed to 'subtle deficits in their theory of mind' (56). The model emphasises the developmental histories of offenders and the possibility that offenders as a group have more adverse early experiences in their childhood, particularly within the context of their family. However, this model fails adequately to explain why there are differences in the development of theory of mind and why these become apparent in adulthood, as opposed to childhood.

The link between early experience and subsequent offending behaviour is seen most strongly in the context of childhood physical and sexual abuse. For example, Briere and Runtz (1990) linked physical abuse in childhood to aggression towards others in adulthood, emotional abuse in childhood to low self-esteem in adulthood, and sexual abuse in childhood to maladaptive sexual behaviour in adulthood. A study by Dhawan and Marshall (1996) reported that 58 per cent of their sample of sex offenders had experienced sexual abuse in childhood, as opposed to 20 per cent for non-offenders. Further support for this argument was offered by Lindsay *et al.* (2001) in the context of a population of forty-six sex offenders and forty-eight non-sex offenders, all with intellectual disability. Within this sample, 38 per cent of the sex offender group and 12.7 per cent of the non-sex offender group were classified as having been sexually abused. However, the sample size was small and depended on archival data and the sample included prostitution offences (eight subjects) as part of the offender cohort. We must conclude that while it is intuitively appealing to connect childhood abuse with subsequent offending behaviour, it would be overly simplistic to see it as the only variable in what has come to be called the 'cycle of abuse'.

Early aversive experiences in childhood are often used by offenders to explain, make sense of or justify their behaviour as adults. Within the COPINE interviews, men who had gone on to engage in sexual relationships with children often talked about their own early sexual engagement with older children or adults. An example of this can be seen in the extract of an interview with EI:

> I think it was Paul's father and basically they were teaching me how to how how to I don't know what you'd call it how to do a blow job or something [mm] . . . (sigh) am . . . it's a . . . hard to describe really it's like I can feel it now I can actually feel an ache here and back of my throat is . . . I sort of like

> know it's not sore now but it feels sore almost because [mm] it's it's . . . mm . . . my stomach's going as well [mm] (97)

Clearly such experiences are not related by all people who are sexually interested in children, and equally the relationship is not causal in that not all adults abused as children go on to abuse. It is also paradoxical that accounts such as that given by EI often describe such early experiences as aversive, and yet manage to rationalise their own behaviour with children as 'child-love'. Such accounts are interesting and valuable because they give us an 'insider' perspective. They help us look at how those with a sexual interest in children talk about and present their own thoughts, feelings and experiences. Such research does not have as its focus the truthfulness of accounts, but rather what function they have, what they 'do'.

OFFENDER PERSPECTIVES

More recently a literature has emerged based on interviews or analysis of text produced by the offender that is in marked contrast to the studies based on psychometric assessments or models of faulty cognitive processing. Ward *et al.* (1998) used a qualitative analysis (grounded theory) to examine offence narratives elicited from incarcerated child molesters to identify 'overall processing style'. They identified a number of cognitive operations that they felt were distinct from content, such as describing, explaining, interpreting, evaluating, denying, minimising and planning. However, their claim that such 'cognitive operations' could be identified separately from the content of accounts seems problematic. Ward *et al.* also reported on an interesting study by Phelen (1995), who explored the different meanings incestuous fathers and daughters attached to abusive events. Phelen found that the majority of fathers claimed that the child initiated and enjoyed the sexual experience. In contrast none of the daughters described the experience in positive terms. Other themes that emerged were 'the tendency of some fathers to equate sex with love, a preoccupation with power and control, and the misperception of the child's responses as indicating acquiescence. The daughters described feeling confused and somewhat cut off from the experience during the abuse' (493).

A further qualitative study by Ivey and Simpson (1998) explored the subjective meaning of the paedophile experience for identified child molesters. The analysis was based on a series of interviews which led the authors to conclude that within this sample such offending behaviour originated from a range of non-sexual motives primarily related to unmet needs for parental affection and affirmation. Such offenders were seen to remove themselves from the dangerous world of adult sexuality, turning to children as substitute sources of emotional and physical intimacy. The conclusions drawn from this study bear a strong resemblance to earlier, psychodynamic formulations, although it is difficult to see how the authors arrive at these results, as there is little actual data presented. They do however draw on a number of interesting themes from their analysis and highlight issues often raised in paedophiles' narratives, for example accounts of critical and rejecting mothers, or the issue of being raised in an atmosphere of 'moral/religious antipathy' towards sex. However, the authors tended to make large generalisations about their data (for example, that the child's gender is unimportant as the paedophile is driven primarily by the need for affirmation and affection), which are at odds with existing empirical data.

In a similar vein, Durkin and Bryant (1999) carried out a thematic analysis of paedophiles' online accounts on Usenet. Usenet is a set of more than 10,000 newsgroups, covering almost every conceivable topic, which are distributed over the Internet, and which are so organised that they can be read like a newspaper. Data gathered from a Usenet discussion group were used to investigate how paedophiles who used the Internet account for their 'deviance'. Durkin and Bryant only used data from group participants (93 postings from 41 out of 80 participants) who were self-confessed paedophiles. While there are problems in taking such accounts at face value (the Internet is an anonymous environment where one can assume any attributes one wishes to), their study found that half of the admitted paedophiles offered accounts of their behaviour and all accounts took the form of justifications rather than excuses. Again this is perhaps not surprising given the supportive context offered by a 'boy-love' discussion group, and their accounts may have been different given another audience.

This work, however, does offer the opportunity of examining accounts from people interested in child sex who do not come from a clinical or correctional population. Durkin and Bryant argued that paedophile accounts offer a means of examining the distorted belief systems of this population (a model that underpins nearly all of the current research in this area). The function of accounts are discussed in three ways: exculpatory function; impression management; and facilitating future deviance. In their analysis Durkin and Bryant made a distinction between excuses and justification in accounts. This distinction comes from Scott and Lyman's (1968) framework for understanding accounts. Accounts that offer excuses involve an admission of the problematic nature of the behaviour in question but the individual does not take full responsibility for the act. On the other hand, justifications involve an admission of responsibility but a denial of the stigmatising quality of the act, and there may be some attempt to persuade the audience to the alternative view. Durkin and Bryant identified a number of types of justification: denial of victim, denial of injury, condemnation of condemners, appeal to loyalties, a sad tale, a claim of self-fulfilment, and basking in the reflected glory of related others. Of these, 'denial of injury' was the most commonly used justification. It is interesting to note that many of the accounts offered by the paedophiles were extremely complex, and offered multiple justifications.

Durkin and Bryant's (1999) analysis of Usenet accounts bears similarities to the classification produced by DeYoung (1989) in her study of NAMBLA texts. The North American Man/Boy Love Association (NAMBLA) is an organisation advocating adult sexual behaviour with male children. DeYoung used a content analysis to examine how, in the context of negative societal attitudes towards such behaviour, NAMBLA justifies, rationalises and normalises its objectives and its members' behaviour through their texts (newsletters, brochures, booklets). From her analysis DeYoung classified accounts in terms of: denial of injury; condemnation of the condemners; appeal to higher loyalties; and denial of the victim. Through its publications NAMBLA promotes the idea that there are advantages to children having a sexual relationship with an adult. At times they acknowledge that there may be some harm to children following a sexual encounter with an adult; however, the harm is described in terms of others (parents, law enforcement) responding inappropriately to what NAMBLA describes as adult–child sex. DeYoung discussed how much of NAMBLA's publications are taken up with sustained polemics against those who censure members' activities, for example professionals in the field of child sexual abuse, criminal justice and mental health systems. In one example a text compared experts on child sex abuse to 'conmen . . . selling snake oil', and appealed to higher loyalties in order to normalise members' activities and to liberate children from societal repression. These accounts justify the child as an active and willing participant in the sexual event, and therefore not a victim. Such a move also removes or reduces the responsibility of the adult for the sexual encounter. However, these accounts are the product of an organisation and as such are not attributable to an individual. This in itself may make generalisations difficult.

It is surprising that offender accounts are underrepresented in the published literature. It may be, at a simplistic level, that this is because it is assumed that such accounts will be a misrepresentation of an individual's thoughts, feelings or behaviour, a 'faking good' in order to minimise what has happened or what is still being considered. It may also be the case that as a society we have attempted to silence voices that talk of sexual interest in children, to distance them from the rest of 'us'. It is maybe not so surprising that in the context of the largely unsupervised world of the Internet there is a proliferation of 'voice'.

FEMALE PERPETRATORS OF CHILD SEXUAL ABUSE

Until recently, the bulk of the research on sex offenders has focused on adult males. What is now starting to emerge are accounts of women and children's sexual involvement with other children. For many years it was widely assumed, although rarely specifically stated, that women hardly ever committed acts of sexual abuse against children. There is very little published literature in this area and it is mainly composed of descriptions of clinical populations (e.g. Faller 1995). Authors such as Allen (1991) have speculated that female-perpetrated sexual abuse is greatly underreported, although it is impossible to ascertain the veracity of this. There appears to be some agreement that sexual contact between women and children forms the minority of child–adult contacts (Finkelhor and Russell 1984), although there is a suggestion of women participating in abuse (Kaufman *et al.* 1995).

Grayston and De Luca (1999), in their review of related empirical and clinical literature, outlined characteristics of women offenders, their victims and the offences they commit. Such data as exists would seem to suggest that female offenders are a heterogeneous group (Wakefield and Underwager 1991), showing a substantial age range. The information about socio-economic background is equally equivocal, depending on where the population studied has been sourced. There has been little speculation about the specific factors involved in the emergence and maintenance of female abusive behaviour, but one of the most consistent findings relates to early experiences, particularly that of previous victimisation. Travin *et al.* (1990) suggested that maltreatment (either physical, emotional or sexual) is a common factor in the histories of many female offenders. Studies by Johnson (1989), Green and Kaplan (1994) and Hunter *et al.* (1993) all reported invasive acts of sexual abuse against women who go on to abuse, and Allen (1991) suggested that severe acts of physical violence (such as being scalded or burned, threatened with a weapon or assaulted with a knife or gun) are also relatively common. However, while these results are similar to those found in male populations, they are insufficient in themselves to account for the prevalence of abuse. Similar evidence has been given for the prevalence of other psychiatric problems within this population, with again an emphasis on low self-esteem and development (Matthews *et al.* 1991).

Grayston and De Luca (1999) attempted to provide a profile of a 'typical' female sex offender. They concluded that she is likely to be a young woman in her 20s or 30s, having come from a dysfunctional family and possibly having experienced physical, emotional and/or sexual abuse as part of her developmental history. Such experiences of abuse are likely to have been severe, and may have included a female perpetrator. In addition, the typical offender is likely to be experiencing multiple problems in other areas of her life, with poor marital or peer relationships, and suffering from a range of mental health difficulties.

The literature does not give support to any particular motives for the sexual abuse, although authors such as Cooper *et al.* (1990) suggested that some women display deviant sexual fantasies, similar to those discussed in the literature on male sex offenders, and distorted perceptions regarding the appropriateness of their acts. There is some suggestion that victims are more likely to be female than male, and the relationship is likely to be familial, possibly in collusion with a male. While Grayston and De Luca's review is interesting, the studies tended to focus on incarcerated populations using very small numbers of subjects. In many areas, the results of such studies are similar to those found in male populations. These authors did not speculate why there should be so few reports of female sexual behaviour with children.

It is possible that within our particular culture, women are allowed much greater physical access to children than are men, which is seen as acceptable and sanctioned behaviour. The borderline between such behaviours and sexual activity is blurred, and female sexual arousal is not so apparent to the child. It may be that only when sexual behaviour is aggressive or physically invasive (for example, the use of an implement to penetrate a child), does it get labelled as abusive.

CHILD-ON-CHILD SEXUAL ABUSE

Sexual play between children is seen as a normal exploration of the nature of sexuality. Shaw *et al.* (2000) suggested that through play and sexual exploration with others, children begin to assimilate the elements of sexual life and establish patterns of sexual excitement and pathways to sexual gratification. Sexual play may therefore be a feature of an ongoing, mutually enjoyable relationship, in part influenced by fortuitous and opportunistic experiences. Araji (1997) talked of such sexual play as including a whole range of emotions, such as pleasure, joy and embarrassment, and as taking place with varying degrees of inhibition and disinhibition. The context for such sexual behaviour is that it usually is with children of the same age and size and is mutually consensual. The concept of consent is important both in the context of adult abuse of children and where children are seen as perpetrators. The National Task Force on Juvenile Sexual Offending (1993) defined sexually abusive behaviour as sexual acts perpetrated on another without consent, equality or as a result of coercion. Within this context, consent includes all of the following:

1 understanding what is proposed;
2 knowledge of societal standards for what is proposed;
3 awareness of potential consequences and alternatives;
4 an assumption that agreement or disagreement will be respected equally;
5 voluntary decision;
6 mental competence.

Equality refers to participants operating with the same level of power within a relationship, and coercion as an exploitation of authority, use of bribes, threats of force, or intimidation.

The highest risk for the initiation of sexually assaultive behaviour appears to occur between 15 and 16 years, although there is a suggestion that the majority commit their first sexual offence before the age of 15 (Elliott 1994; Araji 1997), and the child victims of juvenile sexual abusers are younger than those abused by adult perpetrators (Shaw *et al.* 2000). In this latter study of 194 victims of juvenile abuse, sexual behaviours included oral and vaginal intercourse and forcible penetration of the anus or vagina with fingers or other objects. It is of interest that within this study, the abuser was more likely to be female. Aylwin *et al.* (2000) examined male adolescent and adult offenders with regard to gender preference of their victims. Their results indicated differences between the two groups, with adolescents less likely to molest exclusively females and an increased willingness to take on victims of either gender, along with higher levels of very invasive sexual behaviour (such as anal penetration). The authors felt that there may be multifactorial reasons for these differences, including opportunity to offend and difficulties with self-report data. While comparisons are problematic owing to the sample populations, it is of interest that Shaw *et al.* (2000) found that males were overrepresented among the victims of juvenile offenders. Previous work by Hunter and Becker (1999) had also suggested that juveniles commit many of the sexual assaults carried out against boys.

The literature in relation to the characteristics of adolescent sex offenders suggests an elevation of psychiatric and behavioural problems and violence and dysfunction within the family (Lewis *et al.* 1981; Hsu and Starzynski 1990). There is an elevation of childhood physical and sexual abuse, which Davis and Lietenberg (1987) suggested may be associated with aggressive conduct on the part of the juvenile owing to poor parental modelling. There is also frequent reference to the fact that child molesters progress from non-violent to more serious sexual offences as adults, and that the nature of the initial offence is correlated with subsequent offending (Longo and Groth 1983). Boyd *et al.* (2000) concluded that early onset of sexually abusive behaviour and early problems with delinquency are indicators of increased likelihood of reoffending.

A recent study by Lightfoot and Evans (2000) examined the risk factors for a New Zealand sample of sexually abusive children and adolescents. A sample of twenty children (age range 7–16 years with 60 per cent boys) was examined across multiple measures, including demographic and historical variables, as well as self-perception and support and clinical ratings by others who knew the child well. The description of sexually abusive behaviours committed by the children included fondling and stimulation of the genitals over clothing, to anal and vaginal penetration with an object, and full rape. Younger children were generally responsible for less serious assaults, although one of the youngest boys was one of the four most serious offenders. The majority of victims were not related to the abusive child, but were well-known associates through either school or the community. In this study, both genders were likely to abuse children of the opposite sex, although five children molested victims of both genders. High rates of family disruption were evidenced, and in particular lack of stable, care-giving relationships. The children were interviewed in a bid by the authors to understand the contextual variables that influenced the assaultive behaviour. All children had reported experiencing an extreme emotion-arousing event in the twenty-four hours preceding the offence, and difficulties were experienced in containing their distress or feeling a disconnection between emotion and behaviour. A high percentage of the children indicated that they did have an adult whom they could talk to, but when confronted by distress their typical behaviour was to withdraw to be alone.

Lightfoot and Evans (2000) felt that their findings were consistent with that of Johnson (1996) who suggested that sexually aggressive behaviour will develop from both the experience of child abuse and neglect and abandonment/disruption to attachment, and the experience of a pairing of sex with aggression (either vicariously or directly). The consequence of these is a heightened physiological response to stress and a sensitisation to traumatic cues, such as aggression and sexual stimuli. The arousal itself becomes a conditioned response under such circumstances, which in turn generates negative cognitive effects and difficulties in regulating arousal. Such accounts have a direct link with theorising about the relationship between violent behaviour and sexual activity which children are exposed to through media such as television, video and the Internet.

THE ROLE OF PORNOGRAPHY IN SEXUAL OFFENDING

For over a quarter of a century there have been public and academic debates about the harmful effects of pornography and its relationship to violent or sexual offending. The context to the debate is the sexual victimisation of women and children. A large-scale survey by Finkelhor *et al.* (1990) in the United States suggested that approximately 27 per cent of females and 16 per cent of males have experienced some form of sexual abuse as children. While there has been much outrage voiced about these statistics, it has not stopped the growth of the pornography industry, with an increase in sales of videos, magazines, telephone sex, CD-ROMs and Internet services. The public face of our society shows disapproval of the expression of sexually aggressive or demeaning acts against women and children, yet it is supportive of an industry that represents all of these, albeit vicariously. Advances in technological sophistication have led to an increase in the amount of high-quality pornography available, along with relatively easy access. Research by Barron and Kimmel (2000), in the context of adult pornography, measured the sexually violent content in magazine, video and Usenet (Internet newsgroup) pornography. Their results indicated a consistent increase in the amount of violence from one medium to the next, although the increase between magazines and videos was not significant. Their analysis also indicated that while magazines and videos portrayed the violence as consensual, with women as 'victimisers' more frequently than men, the reverse was true for Usenet. It is perhaps not surprising that such findings have fuelled the debate about the relationship between pornography and sexual aggression.

Several theories have been put forward to elaborate on the possible relationship between the two, and these will be examined briefly. One of the most influential has been the application of behavioural (classical and operant conditioning) theories to the role of pornography in offending (Laws and Marshall 1990). It is largely based on the proposition that pornography is used as an aid to masturbation. When the viewer masturbates to ejaculation, this reinforces their sexual response to the content of the pornography. This increases the likelihood that the behaviour will be repeated. As the viewer habituates to the pornography, they seek out more 'intense' content (such intensity might be along any continuum, such as increasing violence, or decreasing the age of the child). The following extract with TS illustrates this:

> I think it was more a progression from the adult stuff . . . I think . . . it's very one dimensional you know it's just pictures there's no feedback there so I think you try I think I tried to look for more and more extreme stuff [OK] . . . you know just to get more and more . . . excited [OK] . . . or stimulated . . . trying to push the boundaries. (14)

Conditioning theories would predict that the arousing effect of pornography increases as the viewer masturbates to ejaculation, and that the explicitness and content of pornography changes over time as the viewer habituates. Within this model, it would seem that sex offenders should use more unconventional pornography than non-offenders (or more offence-related pornography). However, the results of studies that have examined the use of pornography by offenders do not lend strong support to this. Studies of identified offenders, using largely self-report measures, found that sex offenders reported less frequent exposure to pornography than comparison groups of non-offenders (e.g. Condron and Nutter 1988). However, when rapists were compared to child molesters (Carter *et al.* 1987), the latter used more pornography than rapists and were more likely to incorporate it into their sexual offending. What this does not address is the types of pornography used; rather, as does much of the literature, it treats pornography as if it was homogeneous. Howitt (1995), in relation to eleven offenders who used pornography, found that the use of commercial child pornography was rare, but that offenders created their own collections of materials. It appears likely that offenders who use pornography select material that is both available and fits their own preferred sexual script.

A related area of research comes from social learning theory, which suggests that people may learn indirectly about their social world through observing others. The strength of this learning depends on the rewards and punishments (functional determinants) received by the model (Bandura 1977) and the viewer's evaluation that they would obtain the same for performing a similar action. Such a theory would suggest that violent pornography can increase subsequent aggressive behaviour, because it portrays this behaviour as rewarding. Therefore, the more the person identifies with what he is viewing, the more likely he will go on to engage in sexually aggressive behaviour. An example from an interview with DX illustrates this:

> it made me want to do things I wanted to do. It gave me more courage to do them . . . knowing that I've seen it on there . . . they were doing it . . . I can do it. (67)

It is not such a leap from this level of theorising to more feminist approaches, where it is alleged that the sexualisation of physical, sexual and emotional harm enacted against women in pornography leads to the social subordination of women and their possible victimisation. Cowburn and Pringle (2000) talked of the exercise of power as central to pornography, not only in terms of the acts depicted but in the objectification central to the creation and use of pornography. There is then a fusion of abusive power with sexual gratification. An example of this is given from an interview with OC:

> it was just a picture . . . there was nothing to worry about . . . they couldn't talk back to you . . . they couldn't argue . . . they couldn't run away . . . it was just there . . . it wasn't a person it was just a flat image, a flat picture. (55)

It is unclear as to whether pornography negatively alters both male and female perceptions of women and children, or whether sexual arousal towards aggression as depicted in pornography occurs alongside attitudes supportive of sexual aggression towards women and children. However, where depictions of sexual aggression suggest that the victim is correspondingly aroused, this appears to increase men's beliefs in 'rape myths', particularly in those who were inclined to be more aggressive towards women (Malamuth and Check 1985). A useful review of the psychological literature pertaining to this area can be found in Seto *et al.* (2001).

Overall, there appears to be little support for the allegation of a direct causal link between viewing pornography and subsequent offending behaviour. However, the majority of the studies in this area have been in the context of adult, rather than child, pornography. There are also methodological and ethical difficulties in examining such relationships, particularly with adults who have a sexual interest in children. Laboratory studies which expose offenders to images and measure their level of physiological arousal are likely to use comparatively short exposure times, whereas pornography users (particularly in the context of the Internet) are likely to view pornography for extended periods. An example of this comes from an interview with DX:

> I would say after probably two or three hours I would say . . . about two or three hours then I would masturbate. If I hadn't found anything particular that I liked on the Internet I could always go back to me disks and feed off them. (9)

In addition, the use of such sexual stimuli is rarely matched to the idiosyncrasies of preferred sexual images by individuals, and instead involves a category of stimuli presented to offenders as a group. Seto *et al.* (2001) argued that 'individuals who are already predisposed to sexually offend are the most likely to show an effect of pornography exposure and are the most likely to show the strongest effects' (46). It is also important to note that, until recently, obtaining sexually explicit pornographic images of children was both difficult and dangerous, and therefore the use of such material as related to offending was possibly reduced by lack of opportunity.

As we have noted earlier, there is a suggestion that there is not a single 'profile' of an offender in the context of pornography use. It may be that pornography exposure may influence, but not cause, the development of sexual offending in some men (Marshall 2000). What is more likely is that having an appetite for pornography is just another manifestation of, and a way of meeting, sexual interest. Preferred content is likely to be dynamic, rather than static, reflecting both levels of habituation and the interaction of fantasy with real-life social settings.

Chapter 4

The Internet, child pornography and adult sexual interest in children

In Chapter 3 we reviewed the various views about sexual offending, and noted that there is a paucity of research on the role of child pornography in adult sexual interest in children. Other than recognising it as an element, its significance is unclear in the broader picture. In this chapter we will explore what the function of child pornography might have for adults with a sexual interest in children and relate this to a series of interviews with offenders who have used the Internet to access pictures.

CHILD PORNOGRAPHY AND CONTACT OFFENCES

A basic issue in considering the psychological functions of pictures is the relationship between child pornography and contact offences. Both the function of child pornography and its relationship to contact offences remains unclear; yet this, of course, is a critical issue in assessing the broader deviant context to child pornography collection and viewing. Authors such as Goldstein (1999) suggested that pornography is a by-product of contact offences, or used by offenders to facilitate the seduction of new victims (Tyler and Stone 1985), and an inevitable part of the process of oganised abuse (Itzin 1997). Itzin states that 'Pornography, in the form of adult and/or child pornography used to season/groom/initiate/coerce children into agreeing to be abused, or the production of child pornography (the records of children being sexually abused), is implicated in every form of child abuse, however it is organised' (192). Itzin conceptualised the organisation of child sexual abuse as a continuum, which she represents as a form of concentric circles. The inner circle represents adult and child pornography, and emphasises how all forms of abuse can, and do, involve the use of such material and the recording of the sexual abuse of the child.

Most of the literature relating to child pornography assumes that pornographic images play an important role in sexual fantasy and are used for purposes of arousal. Lanning (1992) suggested that child pornography is used in a similar way to adult pornography – to feed sexual fantasies. He goes on to assert that, 'Some pedophiles only collect and fantasise about the material without acting out the fantasies, but in most cases the arousal and fantasy fueled by the pornography is only a prelude to actual sexual activity with children' (28). This assertion is more difficult to sustain, as we know very little about the relationship between pornography (of any sort) and actual sexual activity. It is also the case that much of what we do know about sexual interest in children relates to people who have been caught. Evidence from the Internet would seem to suggest that there are many more people who fantasise about children and who use images (pornographic or erotic) to aid those sexual fantasies, but who never come to the attention of law enforcement. Lanning (1992) also suggested that child pornography may have other functions, such as to lower children's inhibitions, blackmail a child, act as a medium of exchange with other paedophiles and as a source of profit. These are similar functions to those outlined by other authors.

Goldstein (1999) differentiated between pornography and erotica, in that the objects that form erotica may, or may not be, sexually oriented or related to a given child or children involved in a sexual offence. What is erotic is peculiar to the offender, and therefore any material may be seen as erotic if it stimulates sexual arousal. Pictures of children, therefore, may be collected as part of the commission of an offence, but, as we noted in Chapter 2, the pictures in themselves may be legal. The function of such pictures may be as an aid to fantasy, but in the context of a particular child, they may also serve to:

- Symbolically keep the child close;
- Remind the offender of what the child looked like at a particular age;
- Make the child feel important, or special;
- Lower the child's inhibitions about being photographed;
- Act as a memento that might give the offender status with other people whom he associates with;
- Demonstrate propriety by convincing children that what the offender wants them to do is acceptable because he has engaged in a similar way with other children;
- Provide a vehicle for blackmail;
- Act as an aid to seduce children, by misrepresenting moral standards and by depicting activities that the offender wishes to engage the child in.

Goldstein's (1999) work was based on evidence gained from criminal investigations, and it is apparent from his study that in the main the use of such pictures related to the planned commission of an actual contact offence. Such collections may be qualitatively different from Internet-related collections of pornography, which do not necessarily relate to a child known to the offender. Tate (1990) suggested that such pornography reinforces both the paedophile's attraction to children and his self-justification process, and although empirical verification of this is lacking, these views seem at least to be common sense. Yet in relation to the new technologies, there are people involved in both accessing and distributing child pornography who have no apparent history of child molestation (Quayle *et al.* 2000). In Chapter 2 we recognised the distinction between 'collectors' and 'producers', and it is important to stress that in that context, whilst collectors may become producers, or may draw on pornographic images to fuel actual assaults (rather than fantasy), it is not clear whether child pornography necessarily is a prelude to a contact offence. Whether paedophiles use pornography more than the general population, how this relates to contact offences and the role that the Internet may play in this remains unclear.

One recent study that addressed the role of pornography in the offending process is that of Proulx *et al.* (1999). The aim of their study was to investigate specific pathways in the offending process of people committing sexual offences against children outside their family (extrafamilial). Their results suggested that within a population of child molesters, there were two distinct pathways to offending: coercive and non-coercive. People using the coercive pathway had generally used psychoactive substances (alcohol, drugs) before their offences. Of the thirty people in this group, all had molested female victims, who were not perceived to be vulnerable and who were already well known to them. These people had not planned their offence, which was usually of short duration. The offence usually involved coital activities and was achieved through some act of verbal or physical coercion. The number in the non-coercive pathway was smaller (fourteen), and these had generally used pornography and deviant sexual fantasies prior to committing their offence. All within this group had molested a male victim, whom they perceived to be vulnerable, and who was not familiar to them. These offences differed from those of the other group in that they were planned, were of longer duration and involved non-coital activities without coercion. The limitations of this study relate to the way in which some of the historical data were gathered, and the fact that the offender was categorised only with respect to the last-known victim, which may not have typified their normal offending practice. Their findings are, however, interesting and seem to suggest differences between heterosexual and homosexual offenders that may relate to the duration of their deviant behaviour, which has allowed them to acquire a greater level of sophistication. It may also be that opportunistic offenders may have not been so engaged in the paedophile community, which would give them access to child pornography.

For such people, pornography was used as part of the commission of an offence, similar to the findings of Marshall (1988) where 53 per cent of the sample of child molesters deliberately used pornographic stimuli as part of their planned preparation for offending. Carter *et al.* (1987) also examined the use of pornography in the criminal and developmental histories of sex offenders. They found that all offenders had a similar prior exposure to pornography in childhood, but child molesters were more likely to use such child pornographic material prior to and during their offences and 'employ pornography to relieve an impulse to commit offenses' (205). In contrast to other accounts, this suggests the idea that pornography for some offenders may also have a positive function in that it may prevent the commission of a contact offence. However, in contrast to the view expressed in Carter *et al.* much of the research to date about the relationship between pornographies and contact offences suggests an association between induced sexual arousal and the depiction of sexual activities. Marshall (2000), in his review of the literature relating to the use of pornography by sexual offenders, concluded that pornography exposure may influence, but not be the sole cause of, the development of sexual offending, but for most 'its use is simply one of the many manifestations of an already developed appetite for deviant sexuality' (74).

One of the difficulties with much of the research examining the relationship between child pornography and offending relates to methodology. Laboratory experiments necessarily involve relatively short exposure to such stimuli, whereas collectors of pornography spend considerable amounts of time with their collections. It is also the case that many paedophiles are highly selective in their choice of material, a factor largely ignored by experimenters (Howitt 1995). What this also highlights is that what is sexually stimulating does not necessarily relate to overt content but more to the way the offender perceives it, a point discussed at some length in Chapter 2. It may be that the congruence between pornographic content and behaviour is influenced by how much the viewer identifies in some sense with the pornography. Seto *et al.* (2001) suggested that men who are sexually deviant, such as paedophiles, may preferentially seek out pornography that depicts content that is highly arousing to them. It may be that subjective responses to pornography depend on how well the depicted content matches the individual's existing, preferred sexual scripts (Mosher 1988).

Furthermore, much of the research that has examined the functions of child pornography for the offender has focused on traditional ways of accessing material, through either magazines or videos. However, the Internet has now emerged as one of the most versatile and accessible outlets for pornography. As we have already noted, much of the child pornography available on the Internet has its origins in commercial production, but has been placed on the Internet for non-commercial purposes, and is freely available (Taylor 1999). Barron and Kimmel (2000) suggested that there has been a 'democratisation' as the cost of producing pornography has dropped and the control of production has become diffused. In the context of adult pornography, these authors found evidence of an increase in the amount of non-consensual violent material available on the Internet, suggesting that men were more likely to be depicted in dominant positions as victimiser and not victim in far greater proportions than in magazines and videos. They also suggested evidence of satiation, leading the consumer to seek out newer, more explicit and more violent forms of sexual material in order to gain arousal. It is unclear as to whether this is reflected in similar changes in child pornography on the Internet, but there is certainly a suggestion that the emergence of new photographs of children are of very young age groups and depicting more sexual victimisation (Taylor 1999).

Pierce (1984) has drawn our attention to the fact that by focusing on the finished product (the pornographic image) rather than on the harm done to the participating child, we appear to be blatantly disregarding the dehumanising experience the child or children may encounter. This can be exaggerated when such images are seen as commodities to be collected and exchanged. Lanning (1992) likened this to collecting baseball cards. What this emphasises is that child pornography has functions that go beyond that of sexual arousal and, as we will consider in Chapters 5 and 6, encompasses the importance of collecting and social cohesion. Holmes *et al.* (1998) suggested that the computer acts as a mechanism of metamorphosis in that fantasies are provided with the opportunities and resources to become more concrete. Fantasies may also take on a new realism that can be shared online with others who have similar interests. The Internet also provides anonymity, giving both pleasure from 'hiding' oneself and one's behaviour and the potential pleasure of playing another role (Chou and Hsiao 2000).

What is also evident with the Internet is that, for many people, engagement with this medium is not a passive response. It can be used by individuals to alter mood in the context of feeling down, anxious or isolated (Morahan-Martin and Schumacher 2000). For those who have difficulty in relating to others, Internet communication can lessen social risk and lower inhibitions, without the demands of traditional friendship (Turkle 1995). It can enable multiple self-representation and may provide a context where deviance can flourish (Lamb 1998). For paedophiles, online communities show strong evidence of group dynamics (Lamb 1998; Evans 2001), expressed through issues of status, expertise and apprenticeship (Linehan *et al.* 2002). They noted that within the Internet child pornography community, child pornography played a role in that status within the community was achieved through amassing a large organised collection, through distributing parts of missing series of photographs and through providing new pictures via postings. Used in this way, child pornography both validated and justified paedophile behaviour and acted as a medium of exchange within a community (Healy 1997; Durkin 1997). It is also the case that the Internet is an environment that challenges old concepts of regulation, which are reliant upon tangibility in time and space (Akdeniz 1997). Conventional hierarchies are disrupted by a distributed, decentralised network in which power is spread among various people and groups (Granic and Lamey 2000). One possible consequence of this is that those who have been traditionally marginalised within our society, such as paedophiles, may in fact be empowered by the Internet. Such empowerment is likely to be reinforced by anonymity but also by the fact that everybody's agenda can find a niche on the Internet. Such experiences may contribute to the development of personal beliefs about efficacy and control that serve to heighten disinhibition in the offline world through a blurring of fantasy and reality.

UNDERSTANDING THE FUNCTIONS OF CHILD PORNOGRAPHY

Accessing the world of child pornography is difficult. Aside from being an essentially illegal world, there are also moral issues involved in any form of research that involves participation. An alternative route, however, is to seek to explore how people who were a part of that world make sense of it and of what they did. Interviews with offenders guilty of child pornography offences offer this opportunity, and in the following we examine the accounts of a number of offenders convicted of downloading pornography in order to further our understanding of the complex relationship between those who are sexually interested in children and the Internet. What are explored are the different discourses that emerge when these respondents talk about child pornography, and the role that the Internet plays in such discourses. Above all, it recognises the central significance of meaning for the individual in understanding the role of child pornography.

The data is drawn from semi-structured interviews with thirteen men, all of whom had been convicted of possessing illegal and obscene images of children on their computers (see Taylor *et al.*, 2001 for further discussion of this). While preferences were shown for certain images over others, all participants had viewed similar images (as identified by forensic evidence). Of these men, four were also convicted of assault on children, three had been involved in assaults prior to accessing pornography on the Internet and two had produced pornographic pictures of children, which had not been traded. They came from a variety of demographic backgrounds and varied in terms of both current judicial status and engagement with treatment programmes. The respondents were accessed through Probation, Police, Social Work and Voluntary agencies. All were approached prior to the Interview, were given information about the study, and gave their consent. The data set is part of a much larger, ongoing series of interviews and was chosen because they had all used the Internet to download child pornography. The interviews, each lasting approximately two hours, were recorded using a mini-disc system and then transcribed. All identifying names were removed or changed to ensure anonymity and the transcripts were kept in a secure environment. The same individual researcher both interviewed the respondents and transcribed the data.

Both data collection and analysis were informed by the research of Hollway and Jefferson (2000) in working with defended subjects. This work suggests that defended subjects may not hear the question through the same meaning-frame as that of the interviewer or other interviewees; are invested in particular positions in discourses to protect vulnerable aspects of self; may not know why they experience or feel things in the way that they do; and are motivated, largely unconsciously, to disguise the meaning of at least some of their feelings and actions. When interviewing, open-ended rather than closed questions were used, efforts were made to elicit 'stories' in order to anchor accounts, 'why' questions were avoided, and follow-up questions used the respondent's ordering and phrasing.

Once transcribed, the Interviews were read and re-read and questions were asked in relation to talk about pornography as to what was noticed, why it was noticed and how it might be interpreted. The interviews were analysed within a discursive framework, with an emphasis on the 'function orientation' of what was said (Gill 1996). What was acknowledged in this analysis is that people use discourse in order to do things: to offer blame, to make excuses and, for example, to present themselves in a better or different light. The interviews were subsequently coded in relation to the research question and the data sorted into emerging categories. These were based on an initial search for patterns within the data, looking for instances of similarity and difference between accounts. This was followed by formulating ideas about the functions of particular features of this discourse and constantly checking these against the data. Quotations are taken from the interview transcripts to illustrate the analysis.

Six principal discourses relating to the ways that respondents used child pornography emerged during the analysis. All discourses were common across respondents, with the exception of 'Child pornography facilitating social relationships', which was largely confined to respondents who had gone on to 'chat' online with others through IRC (Internet Relay Chat). The principal emerging discourses were:

- Child pornography and sexual arousal;
- Child pornography as collectibles;
- Child pornography facilitating social relationships;
- Child pornography as a way of avoiding real life;
- Accessing child pornography as therapy;
- The Internet and child pornography.

Child pornography and sexual arousal

The most dominant discourse to emerge in the analysis was that of child pornography as a means of achieving sexual arousal. Some of the pictures that were accessed (but not all) were used for masturbatory purposes, and respondents were selective in the pictures that they used. Such selectivity might relate to specific age groups, physical types, gender of the child, or to a particular sexual activity. For example:

> developing girls . . . just starting to get pubic hair and just starting to develop breasts . . . my preference was for younger people. (OK: 43)

Such pictures were used as an aid to fantasy:

> Fantasies . . . it would basically run like I take a young girl on a date . . . and then we'd go home and then she'd we'd . . . you know the stuff that adults do which would lead to sex and would involve her masturbating me and then me giving her oral sex. (QH: 10)

and were often selected, as with QH, to fit with pre-existing fantasies, some of which related to earlier contact offences, or related to new offending fantasies. Such offending fantasies often were of children known to the participants:

> I would be interested like if . . . I found pictures of children that looked like some of the kids I knew in real life. (QH: 9)

This invariably, but not exclusively, involved masturbation to the fantasies:

> Because if I was on-line for an hour or so I actually would be masturbating on and off for an hour . . . and wanting to . . . maintain the sense of arousal . . . trying not to come. (II: 21)

and levels of masturbation seemed to increase after the respondent went online:

> while I was on the Net? I mean it was anywhere between 7 and 15 . . . simply because of what I was collecting. (EI: 9)

It is interesting that what followed after masturbation was that respondents stopped looking at the pictures and either closed the computer down or moved on to some other non-sexual topic. More than this, for some, the images themselves became almost aversive in the absence of sexual arousal:

> Actually, once I had come then I'd almost be . . . I'd find it distasteful. That what had been acceptable during a state of sexual arousal . . . afterwards wasn't acceptable. (II: 21)

> usually . . . that would be the point at which I could sort of . . . switch off. (MQ: 28)

Not all respondents masturbated, one because although he was sexually aroused was unable to ejaculate, and a second respondent because the excitement came from the fact that these pictures were taboo.

Claims were made that such masturbation to child pornography was a substitute for abuse:

> our main aim in collecting the child pornography is that we weren't involved with kids . . . it was helping . . . I didn't feel the urge as strongly as I do now to try and start something with a child . . . when I was on-line with the child porn . . . because when I felt that urge I'd look at the child porn I'd masturbate or I'd read the stories more often and masturbate . . . and it was under control. (EI: 109)

although clearly such accounts failed to acknowledge that the pictures being accessed were ones of children being abused. Responsibility for such abuse is clearly placed elsewhere.

Offending fantasies in relation to images were not always confined to looking at the pictures on screen, and, within this sample, had also acted as a blueprint both for abuse and for the production of photographs:

> the offences against me victim erm . . . were touching her breasts touching her vagina . . . erm I also used a video camera . . . I copied what I'd seen on the computer. (KQ: 2)

> but for me I wanted to abuse her . . . looking at the images I wanted to do pretty much as I've seen. (DX: 25)

Accessing the images appeared to reinforce existing fantasies and was used to give permission to act on them:

> it made me want to do the things I wanted to do. It gave me more courage to do them . . . knowing that I've seen it on there . . . they were doing it . . . I can do it. (DX: 67)

Here the account used the pictures as a form of justification, a sense that if others are engaged in this then it doesn't matter. It allowed one respondent to ignore the other cues that were presented to him, such as his victim crying or constantly covering her face with her nightdress. Such fantasies were also fuelled by the excitement that came from a sense of doing something illegal.

The selection of images for sexual purposes was also made according to some sort of 'moral' or 'ethical' code, which varied according to the individual and also according to the circumstances. The boundaries which related to the acceptability of the images are similar to those that determine sexual interest, such as age, sex, activity and were influenced by superficial cues which allowed the viewer to believe that the children in the pictures were consenting and enjoyed being photographed:

> eh . . . well there was definitely never any baby pictures believe you me . . . I would have said there's definitely nothing below ten on what I have on my system. (TS: 14)

> Oh no S and M pictures, no pictures of kids being hurt, no pictures of kids being killed. (QH: 26)

The suggestion is made that smiling faces of children in the pictures in some way legitimised them:

> just basically images of girls mainly. Girls actually having sex. And they had to look happy . . . I mean I wasn't looking for rape or anything. (EI: 40)

The extreme counter-scenario of rape minimised the actual content of the pictures used for masturbation and again managed to distance the participant from being part of an offence against a child.

These moral boundaries were fairly flexible, in that if such images were accessed adventitiously, rather than searched for purposefully, then they might be kept by some participants:

> I didn't go out of my way for new pictures because I knew where the new pictures came from. Unless they were a pose or nudist. Nudist pictures

> I was interested in... These were the only pictures where I was sure that the kids weren't being hurt or coerced or anything. These pictures I was interested in. Other pictures, if I found them great, if I didn't find them I wasn't going to go out of my way for them. (QH: 8)

Where images had a social function in that they were used for exchange, this also would overcome such boundaries. This is discussed in more detail when examining the social function of child pornography.

Such collecting of pornography was often a continuation of previous interest in pictures from magazines and videos, and while these had mainly been pornographic pictures of adults, for one offender he had been collecting legitimate 'nude art' photographs of children.

Child pornography as collectibles

The discourse of collecting and its importance for respondents overlapped with but was not subsumed by discourses of arousal. Pleasure was obtained from collecting pictures as part of a series, even when the material was not attractive or sexually arousing:

> some of them I didn't much care for at all . . . but as I say they were part of a series or they were there for other people or they were just to see what was out there . . . I mean it gets to a stage also where you're just collecting to see how many different ones you can get and this sort of thing and you're not . . . necessarily aroused or turned on by all the pictures that are coming in. (OK: 42)

Such pictures were often talked about in a very dispassionate way with no reference made to the fact that they were pictures of children. This is seen both in comparisons made to other kinds of collection and also in terms used to describe the pictures themselves:

> We were trading pictures . . . it's as much as it pains me to say . . . kinda like trading baseball cards. (QH: 6)

> and there was also the thrill in collecting them. You wanted to get complete sets so it . . . was a bit like stamp collecting as well. (EI: 47)

Comparisons between baseball cards and stamps also served to normalise the activity, and made it appear innocent in its intent. When talking about the pictures, invariably no reference was made to the content as being child pornography.

Not only was pleasure obtained from completing missing pictures in a series, but also the act of categorising the photographs offline. This categorising could be either simple or complex, depending on whether access to the photographs was for individual use or for purposes of exchange.

> I had a threefold er . . . a fourfold tier system of organising my pics. First of all in alphabetical order . . . second tier would have been sexual . . . sexual act erotic pose and nudism . . . so four tiers. (QH: 30)

> I had all the material in separate directories . . . so the directories would be . . . chosen specifically for the type of material it contained. (II: 22)

Where the material was kept only for personal use and there was no trading involved, sorting would still take place but in a much more rudimentary way.

Referring back to photographs once sorted took second place to seeking out new material:

> 'cause as I said you just you just move onto the next set next set next set. (TS: 22)

> Because there was new stuff . . . there was new stuff now so . . . (ME: 24)

For the majority of participants the photographs became an archive that they could refer back to when necessary, use for trading for new material, and have as a collection of artifacts appearing in series. Completing the series was as much an end in itself as using the photographs for sexual pleasure, although it could be associated with sexual pleasure when it enabled fantasy. This was particularly the case where there was a narrative theme to a series:

> you know I suppose I was deliberately going for groups . . . erm . . . so you like get an idea of the full event that was going on . . . you know so you get an idea of . . . the full continuation rather than just one 'photo. (TS: 19)

Collecting behaviour was not solely confined to child pornography and for many participants (even those who identified their primary sexual orientation as paedophilia) it was part of a progression through collecting other forms of pornography:

> yeah I mean its like . . . very poor analogy but it's like when you drink some beers you I mean you might like Caffreys you might love it but after a while you go off it and you go to Guinness and you might go on to something else. (TS: 38)

The majority of respondents moved through a variety of pornographies, each time accessing more extreme material. This might refer to the age of the children in the photographs or to the actual activities being portrayed:

> and er it just progressed from there . . . it would go having a look at the teenage sites and then these teenage sites would point you to younger things and then it would say like illegal site . . . you'd think oh what's that . . . you'd

have a look at the site and the girls are obviously getting younger and it was a steady . . . downward trend. (KQ: 18)

The fact that the site was flagged as illegal acted almost as a prompt. With respect to the Internet, it was also the case that responses were chained, each prompt acting as a discriminative stimulus to move on to the next site. One respondent started by accessing child pornography but quickly became bored with it when he could no longer use it for sexual purposes. At this point he moved on to other categories, again accessing more and more extreme varieties of material within these categories:

well there was like full penetration from animals erm . . . dogs, donkeys . . . think there's a zebra at one point so . . . I don't think you could actually get more extreme without changing the subject area. (TS: 33)

It is important to note that by using the Internet, not only could such materials be accessed, but access could be rapid and movement could take place across categories. The density of the material that could be downloaded in any one session was high, and there is some suggestion that with this form of collecting behaviour, where the collection was a stimulus for sexual behaviour, satiation would occur quite rapidly:

I was actually getting quite bored as it were . . . erm . . . with the sort of child pornography . . . I was becoming sort of more obsessed with bondage . . . and sort of torture . . . imagery. So . . . I'd kind of exhausted . . . the potential that it had for sexual arousal. (II: 20)

Depersonalising of the pictures was seen most strongly when reference was made to the pictures as trophies:

the idea of keeping the images was like trophies. (II: 16)

as objects that could be collected and manipulated. One function of the Internet in relation to this was that images could be downloaded and changed, to meet the needs of the collector:

I was actually manipulating the images a fair bit . . . and I was aware that these were electronic files . . . there was a sense that . . . although these represented real people . . . because they were photographs . . . that kind of material . . . was in no way really connected with the original act. (II: 19)

it wasn't a person at all it was . . . it was just a flat image . . . it was a nothing. (OC: 54)

I don't mean to be denigrating but some of the people were ugly . . . so I would actually sort of chop their head off. (OC: 35)

Here OC used the word 'people' when talking about the children in the pictures, as does II. This moved attention away from the fact that the material being downloaded and manipulated to fit with the collection was actually pornographic images of children. The notion of images as commodity was also seen when one respondent talked about their commercial value to him and his partner:

> what he was doing he was downloading loads and loads of pictures . . . putting them in folders and everything . . . putting them on CDs . . . selling the CDs. (OC: 17)

Respondents talked about accessing the Internet, downloading pornography and organising their collections as if it was part of a ritual, which for many respondents led to huge collections of photographs. Earlier research in this area has suggested that one feature of such collections is that they are permanent. Certainly all the respondents in this study had kept child pornographic images either on CDs, floppy disks or their hard disks, and this had led to their prosecution. However, the majority of them had deleted images on a regular basis, but had never been able to get rid of their collection completely:

> and I was thinking I might as well get shot of these now . . . but there's a thing at the back of your mind . . . well I'll do it tomorrow, do it tomorrow and tomorrow never comes and that sort of thing. (OK: 2)

What is different about the Internet in relation to collecting child pornography may relate to the volume of material that can be accessed and the fact that once the picture is on the Internet it will remain there, accessible as a part of somebody else's collection. Unlike hard copy images which are destroyed, it is always possible to access more of the same on the Internet.

The number of pictures within a seized collection is often focused on by the media (and sometimes law enforcement) accounts as an index of the severity of the crime, or of the degree of deviance of the person collecting. There is, of course, some logic to this, given the nature of the picture content. But if picture collections are seen from the perspective of the collecting process, then size of collections seems to be more likely a factor related to success in collecting deviant material, rather than an index of deviance itself.

Child pornography facilitating social relationships

Discourse about child pornography and social relationships were almost exclusively seen in the accounts of respondents who traded images and who used IRC (Internet Relay Chat) to communicate with others. This would not be the case with adult pornography, which was previously shared with other people, particularly men in the context of work. When online, those who traded images inevitably came into social contact with others similarly engaged, and clearly this was very important to some respondents.

> pornography was there almost as much to facilitate the on-line relationship as an end in itself. (II: 17)

Where respondents traded pictures, both the pornography and the chat that was associated with it through IRC enabled social cohesion:

> Well like I said I was very good at finding people to trade with. I was a good negotiator so to speak and I would tend to find pictures . . . I managed to find the whole series from somebody and I let the channel operators know and . . . they were deeply grateful. It's kinda like an art collector who finds a lost Picasso. (QH: 13)

What this also indicated is how rapidly respondents could build up enormous collections of pictures through trading, and that there was clearly a hierarchy that was associated both with number of images and the ability to complete series of pictures. Having child pornography was also a requisite for community membership:

> if you wanted to be a member of the group . . . you just popped into the channel and started trading and if you traded correctly . . . and if you didn't abuse other users . . . and you didn't trade crap basically . . . and you didn't trade snuff or anything that showed kids actively being hurt. (EI: 64)

Clearly such membership was reinforced by having material to trade, by behaving correctly and by following the rules for trading. Once status had been achieved through membership of the group, trading reduced and instead the social function of the online exchanges and the ability to be on the inside and obtain special photographs was more important:

> There was less and less trading going on because a lot of us by now had most of what we were interested in from each other's collections. And there were very few new people or producers. I mean Paul was one and I was one of the few people he trusted enough to give everything that he was making with his kids (EI: 67)

EI's friendship with Paul gave him status but it also allowed him to access new pictures as they were being produced as well as giving him contact with Paul's children. The latter served to enable his sexual fantasies. The notion of community in relation to the pornography was reinforced by the metaphor of club or bar with reference to virtual space:

> I mean the times when I would . . . stay up all night swapping pics with people were long gone. All I did basically I was a bar tender . . . I was serving drinks and what not. (QH: 25)

This analogy is an interesting one because it emphasised the idea of the community as a club, giving people what they wanted and ensuring that everything was running smoothly. Again, we have the idea of child pornography as having some equivalence with alcohol: a commodity to enable social exchange:

> once my collection grew past 40,000 I really didn't trade that much. I would mostly let people just take what they wanted off my FTP site . . . for want of a better word my collection site . . . my museum . . . while I was conjuring up new ways of evading law enforcement and securing the collections and what not. (QH: 7)

In a similar way to earlier references about lost Picassos, the metaphor of the museum served to highlight the value of the images and also made them into legitimate artifacts to collect. Not only was the material allocated such status, the same also applied to the group members:

> I was already you know . . . on the Usenet . . . where you don't pay anything at all . . . swapping with other people . . . by this I mean quite a select group I mean . . . it wasn't just anybody willy-nilly. (OK: 23)

Not all respondents wished to trade and be members of a community. For some the decision was bound up with ideas of doing wrong by being involved, while for others it related to fears about security.

Using child pornography to build social networks and relationships served many other complex functions. It was used as a way of confirming sexual interests to others online:

> and I could sort of back that up by giving them images . . . that supported that . . . so . . . you know you name it as a sort of sexual proclivity. (II: 15)

and it generated almost an etiquette with regard to trading relationships which meant that others would trust you:

> So I was kind of talking to people and it was exchanging images with one person and then passing that image on to someone else. So there is this kind of network and these . . . these images were currency . . . because it allowed me to maintain my relationship with the people. (II: 18)

The importance of such relationships was often prioritised over the pornography:

> We were trying to support each other . . . we were friends. (EI: 106)

and occasionally resulted in the indiscriminate saving of material in case it played a role in terms of future exchange with others.

> I think some of the really nasty stuff I . . . or what I consider to be nasty I used to get rid of but the rest of the stuff I didn't because I used to think perhaps it doesn't appeal to me but it appeals to somebody else and they might send something else that doesn't appeal to them but it appeals to other people. (OK: 10)

Decisions about the nature of the material were placed in the context of its value. Even though OK might have thought of some of the pornography as nasty, he still judged it as valuable for exchange. Nor did he make any sort of value judgements about the people he was willing to trade with. The parallels with other forms of collecting, discussed in Chapter 7, are very evident.

Child pornography as a way of avoiding real life

It is interesting that for many respondents, linking up with others on the Internet provided important social support that often replaced unsatisfactory relationships in the 'real world'.

> I wanted sex all the time . . . and you know I had a very high sex . . . and I wasn't getting as much sex as I want off me wife. (DX: 19)

Accessing child pornography on the Internet became part of a bid to create a secret and separate world:

> and it was a very private thing I was doing and I . . . didn't want to share it with anyone else. (KQ: 27)

> er it was a little fantasy world for me . . . and it was so different from the mundane existence I'd been leading. Here was something that was dangerous . . . it was exciting . . . it was new. (II: 15)

Clearly this 'cyber world' had many qualities that were unobtainable in the 'real' world and allowed escape from many unpleasant realities:

> I think it mattered to the extent that it shut out the . . . part of my life that I was finding difficult to deal with . . . it was sort of my time, it was my space . . . I got to the stage where I started to feel . . . annoyed if I felt . . . other people were intruding on that. (MQ: 33)

This could be taken in a very literal way in that MQ was able to physically remove himself into the room where they kept the computer and where he could access his own files. He was also able to emotionally shut himself off from a situation that was becoming increasingly aversive and achieve pleasure and escape through sexual arousal and masturbation.

Through the Internet the unsatisfactory elements of life that were difficult to address or change could for periods be avoided and substituted for a world that was more controllable. Sexual satisfaction could be sought and gained over which the respondent had perfect control:

> it was just a picture . . . there was nothing to worry about . . . they couldn't talk back to you . . . they couldn't argue . . . they couldn't run away . . . it was just there . . . it wasn't a person it was just a flat image a flat picture. (OC: 55)

For some respondents, this way of dealing with the unsatisfactory side of life took a more extreme form when accessing the pornographic images was referred to as a form of therapy.

Accessing child pornography as therapy

This therapeutic discourse overlapped with talk of satiation and addiction. However, some respondents made claim to actively seeking pornographic images as a way of controlling their interests:

> because I really wanted to find out about myself as well . . . in a sense I wanted to know . . . what I was about . . . what was it that I . . . that actually turned me on and . . . perhaps in the process deal with it . . . accept it and then move on. (MQ: 20)

What was prioritised were his needs, his feeling of wanting to explore the nature of the problem. The children in the pictures had a function only in so far as they were meeting this need. They are almost incidental to the process. The idea of self-exploration was also seen in talk about examining the 'dark side' of one's personality.

At its most extreme, accessing child pornography was seen as a form of personal survival:

> yeah . . . I was aroused by some of the pictures . . . some of the images I wasn't aroused by . . . erm . . . you know I was just desperate to find some way of getting out of the shit life that I was in. (KQ: 44)

> it was the only thing that was remotely keeping me alive at that point 'cause I could escape on it. I could play games and look at child porn. (EI: 77)

and a way of dealing with emotions such as anger which had no other outlet:

> I think certainly they precipitated it yeah . . . and I started downloading child pornography . . . one it was getting the anger out of my system and saying up yours to the police . . . and two it was a way of relieving the pressure. (OT: 3)

The idea of therapy extended beyond what was good for the respondent to what was good for potential victims of child abuse:

> rather than go off and offend and offend again . . . rather than go out and find a victim. (OT: 4)

Accessing pornography through the Internet as therapy is an interesting 'medical' discourse and overlapped very strongly with talk about addiction. With the latter, respondents were unclear as to whether they were addicted to the Internet or to the images, the two having become inextricably intertwined. Of course, the idea of therapy functions in many ways. It allows the respondent to present himself as someone who is 'ill' in some way and who has problems that are largely out of his control. It also allows for the respondent to appear to be behaving responsibly towards his problem by attempting both to explore and deal with it. This is used as a justification for accessing the images and becomes intertwined with ideas that it is also good for children, in that it prevents actual contact abuse. This needs to be considered alongside other talk about children as images and objects, who clearly have no rights once their photographs are on the Internet.

The Internet and child pornography

Respondents' talk about child pornography inevitably, as their crimes related to downloading, overlapped with talk about the Internet. It is clear that the Internet facilitated access to photographs, whether adventitiously or purposefully:

> it was only the children side of it came into being when I discovered this er stuff on the Internet. (KQ: 69)

Accessing such material was possible because the Internet as a medium was anonymous and because there was an enormous variety of pornography freely available:

> So I then got into this kind of regime of finding hard core porn . . . the sort that if I had . . . the nerve I would have bought a magazine that showed this kind of material in a shop, but then there'd be the problem of sneaking the magazine back into the house and then accessing that material privately. (II: 7)

What was also associated with the Internet was a chain of responses, leading to more and more extreme material, even when that material was not kept for personal collections or for trading:

> it seemed to be getting younger and younger . . . as the more I got into the sites and more I diversified the more you could . . . you know . . . the harder the pornography got . . . seemed to be getting harder and harder. (DX: 3)

What we also see here is the use of the passive voice in relation to the Internet, as if the responsibility lies with it as a medium. What is also apparent is that with the Internet access is rapid and, for those interested, child pornography can be found very quickly (which would not be the case from more conventional sources). Inevitably, the more the respondent used the computer as a means of accessing pornography, the more skilful he became in finding material and getting round any security checks.

What is also interesting in relation to this is that there appeared to be a blurring of boundaries in what constituted child pornography that was exaggerated on the Internet. In some instances this was used as a justification for downloading material, while in other instances there appeared to be confusion as to the overlap between nudist and 'art' photographs and pornography:

> Where do you draw the line . . . where does society draw the line . . . where is what is considered legal in one country illegal in another? (KQ: 58)

> that's where the trouble sets in actually . . . it's hard to explain . . . it's hard to tell somebody the difference between a pornographic image and a nude art image. (ME: 6)

> They were of children, but not of child pornography . . . It was done in a tasteful . . . you could tell by the image it wasn't . . . it wasn't anything . . . there was no sexual overtones or anything it wasn't with legs spread. (ME: 8)

All respondents made reference to the Internet and addiction when talking about the compulsive elements of downloading. This is used to make sense of a loss of control, of high rate behaviour and also as a way of distancing oneself from ideas of personal agency:

> now at one point I sort of deleted all the pornography off the machine and I tried not to get back on . . . to it. But . . . the sense of addiction, compulsion and obsession was so strong that I ended up, you know, falling back into old habits. (II: 18)

> I couldn't stop looking at these pictures . . . I was a junkie . . . a junkie par extraordinaire . . . I figured that the only way I was going to stop was if I got busted. (QH: 29)

> I was obsessed by it I really was I will definitely admit that . . . an addiction . . . mmm definitely. (DX: 9)

Such distancing was also seen in talk about the nature of sexual offences against children. The person downloading images was able to put himself into another category of offender, one who had done something illegal but who had not committed an offence against a child:

> I don't like the idea of being a sex offender 'cause to me . . . a sex offender is somebody who er . . . somebody who goes raping people . . . who's harmed somebody in a sexual manner . . . not looking at images. (ME: 13)

> the way I looked at it I'm doing no harm because at the end of the day I'm not taking the pictures I'm not setting 'em up . . . I'm not distributing them . . . all I'm doing at the end of the day is just looking at em. (TS: 30)

This is further reinforced by an appeal to common sense, using the opinion of a trusted family member as the voice of reason:

> it's like me dad . . . I mean me dad thought exactly the same as me . . . he says well it's only a bloody picture. (OC: 53)

> Me dad could understand . . . he says being male . . . you know the sex drive . . . women can't understand that . . . (ME: 46)

This blurring of boundaries in what constituted pornography, is similar to the findings of McCabe (2000) who suggested that one third of her respondents thought it was all right to download such material.

THE PSYCHOLOGICAL MEANING OF CHILD PORNOGRAPHY

What emerges from these accounts is that child pornography downloaded from the Internet does act as a means of sexual arousal and is used as an aid to masturbation both on- and offline, and that for the majority of respondents in this sample it resulted in an increase in masturbatory behaviour. This is similar to the findings of Hamman (1996) in the context of cybersex on the Internet. Respondents were highly selective in the material they chose, seeking out content that was arousing for them and which fitted with individual fantasies. This confirms the suggestions made by both Howitt (1995) and Seto *et al.* (2001) but seems to conflict with the latter's allegation that there is little evidence to support assumptions that pornography users become sexually aroused and masturbate while viewing pornography. Again, onc aspect of Internet use is that respondents could largely ensure privacy, which maybe facilitates immediate sexual behaviour. It is also a fact that given the scope and extent of child pornography available on the Internet, none of the respondents had difficulty in finding material that met their sexual proclivities.

The relationship between contact offences and pornography remains unclear, and would seem to support the suggestion by Seto *et al.* (2001) that earlier studies have not considered the possibility of interactions between individual characteristics and pornography exposure. Certainly it appears that, for some respondents, pornography was used as a substitute for actual offending, whereas for others, it acted as both blueprint and stimulus for a contact offence. Justification for viewing and downloading images revolved around ideas of the consenting child, child pornography being preferential to contact abuse and the fact that 'moral' limits were set with regard to what was downloaded. Such limits often appeared to be quite flexible, however, if the photographs themselves had value in terms of exchange.

The Internet clearly plays an important role in collecting behaviour related to child pornography, and here we see a function that overlaps with that of sexual arousal. Material is often collected even when it has no arousing properties for the individual but because it is part of completing a series or is new. Collections can be correspondingly large, because the bulk of child pornography on the Internet is free and also because respondents often acquired the technological skills to use software that allowed them to download without them having to be physically present. As Tate (1990) suggested, 'pedophiles don't simply view the material they collect, they catalogue and index it as well' (112). All respondents showed some level of cataloguing behaviour, but in the main the degree of sophistication shown in relation to this was largely a function of the use to which the photographs were to be put. Those who traded also organised their collections systematically and spent a great deal of time offline cataloguing and indexing their photographs. Such collecting behaviour emphasises the role of pornography as both trophies and commodities, distancing the downloader from the content of the photographs.

Discourse about child pornography and social relationships is almost exclusively seen in the context of trading and using IRC in the sample referred to above. Such social relationships are bound by rules and have all the qualities of 'community' outlined by Linehan *et al.* (2002). Pornography played a role in such communities because status was reflected in volume, having parts of missing series and distributing these and new images through the Internet. Social relationships also allowed respondents to normalise their activities, consolidating a body of accounts that allowed others to justify or legitimise their orientation and behaviour (Durkin and Bryant 1999). Such legitimising activity was also heightened by the metaphor of the Internet as a physical space, a bar or a museum, where the commodity is pornography rather than alcohol or art.

Morahan-Martin and Schumacher (2000) talked about the Internet as providing an attractive alternative to a mundane or unhappy life. Certainly, for these respondents, accessing child pornography on the Internet was often used as a way of creating a private and intensely arousing world, where it was possible to go beyond normal limits. Such a world was often associated initially with feelings of regaining control, but this quickly changed and was followed by frequent reference to loss of control and addiction. Such discourses of addiction are not confined to those who access child pornography on the Internet. Kennedy-Souza (1998) suggested that what we are seeing is merely the continuation of a trend of people spending increasingly more time with technology than with other human beings. What is often achieved through prolonged engagement with the Internet is an alteration in mood, resulting in what Kennedy-Souza (1998) argued is Internet addiction. Griffiths (2000) has suggested that excessive use of the Internet for sexual purposes appears in the majority of cases to be purely symptomatic, but for what appears to be a small minority, the Internet may be functionally addictive. Why such addiction should take the form of collecting child pornography is more difficult to ascertain, especially when, as for some respondents, this appears to occur in the absence of any prior interest in such material.

At its most benign, the Internet facilitates access to a wide variety of child pornography. Tate (1990) suggested that the particular advantage of the Internet to the paedophile is its security, as a lifetime's collection can be hidden on a small amount of electric gadgetry, stacking the odds heavily against discovery. What also seems to be the case is that the Internet functions in such a way that there are constant links to other sites, some of which are signalled by the word 'illegal' and that these in turn act as a discriminative stimulus for accessing more and more extreme material. Respondents made frequent reference to the pictures being of younger and younger children, or of more extreme activities. It may be that the progressive qualities of the quest for newness and difference and the rapidity of habituation is exaggerated on the Internet because of the sheer volume of material available and the amount of time that downloaders spend with it.

It is evident that there is some confusion about what constitutes pornography and with regard to child pornography the issue is complex, as we have noted in earlier chapters. The Internet seems to allow for a blurring of boundaries and is used by the respondents described here as a justification for downloading. This is interesting given that these were 'insider accounts' and all acknowledged that the images, regardless of whether they could be justified as 'art' or 'naturist', were sexually arousing to the viewer. While the label of 'sex offender' was accepted with varying degrees by respondents (depending on whether they had also committed a contact offence), there was clearly a distinction made between the activity of downloading and the commission of a contact offence. This was reinforced by reference to common sense judgements and was made possible by the respondent distancing himself from these photographs. Such emotional distancing is one frightening aspect of these accounts, where the child is reduced to an electronic image or, as described by one respondent, 'a nothing'. The ability to manipulate images is another feature of this.

Whilst the presence of child pornography on the Internet is recognised to be a major social problem, its management to date by law enforcement agencies has tended to focus on the development of pragmatic tools of apprehension (such as sting operations), or a focus on evidential issues rather than interventions based on coherent conceptual responses. The broad analysis presented in this book suggests that child pornography may have multiple functions, and is not only associated with sexual arousal. This seems to be of particular concern when those functions become apparent within a deviant community environment. An important issue following from this relates to the extent to which otherwise dormant interests are facilitated by the dynamics of the Internet, and the extent to which facilitation of an interest in child pornography relates to the subsequent commission of contact offences against children. Further understanding of these issues has implications not only for policy makers and the Internet industry, but also for law enforcement practice and the management of offenders in therapeutic preventive programmes. Looking for causal relationships between offending and pornography is problematic, not least because in the context of the Internet, contact offences are only one of a variety of offences committed against children in which pornography plays a central role.

Chapter 5

Metamorphosis

An often-quoted cartoon that was published in the *New Yorker* magazine shows a dog sitting at a computer and saying to another dog, 'On the Internet, nobody knows you're a dog.' Morahan-Martin and Schumacher (2000) discussed this phenomenon in the context of problematic Internet use, suggesting that the ability to self-represent from the safety of the computer screen may be part of the compulsion to go online. The lack of face-to-face communication ensures some level of anonymity, which can lessen social risk and lower inhibitions. Turkle (1995) likened this to the ability to try out new ways of relating, new roles and new identities. Such new identities might include playing with changes in gender, age and race. On the Internet the 'bandwidth' of communication is relatively narrow, and the scope for controlling the presentation of self increases. 'In cyberspace you have more control over how someone sees you. Everything begins with words. You are who you say you are. And you can make yourself sound really good' (Horn 1998: 294). These changes are not impossible in the offline world, but are potentially more difficult to sustain, and carry with them greater risk of discovery.

The relationship between identity and self-representation is complex. For example, in the offline world we make choices all the time about how we wish to present ourselves, and some of these have become very conventional. An interview for an important job influences the choices we make about what to wear and what aspects of ourselves we choose to portray. Giese *et al.* (1998) suggested that these rituals of self-representation will now be transferred to a textual mode in the context of the Internet. However, the ability to self-represent in a radically different way in the offline world is more difficult. Adopting another gender or another age is open to constant visual challenges. Sustaining identity change on the Internet may also be problematic, as the individual may not have the wealth of experience to draw on to maintain credibility, but it certainly carries with it less risk. In the main, if a person is discovered playing another persona, this may result in some sanctions within the community, but the person also has the capacity to disappear, and to reappear as another persona and in another context.

The ability to 'become' may operate at many levels, from the individual who wishes to enhance their status through purporting to have done something special, or possess something important, through to the assumption of a completely new identity. Do we view such 'becomings' as deception, or simply a unique artifact of an online world where fantasy is as important as reality? To some extent this depends on the context in which the person self-represents. According to Donath (2000), 'Identity plays a key role in virtual communities. In communication, which is the primary activity, knowing the identity of those with whom you communicate is essential for understanding and evaluating interaction' (29). We use identity cues to establish the credibility of the person and to help us decide on the believability of the information given. It may be that electronic networking opens possibility for deception because many of the cues that normally circumscribe roles and which foster or inhibit participation are not present (Boshier 1990). In offline face-to-face communication, participants are usually (although not always) known to each other, at least visually. However, on the Internet people can change the way they express themselves, challenging traditional notions of authenticity and deception. Donath (2000) uses a model of deception in the animal world as a way of thinking about identity deception in cyberspace. Within this context, we are asked to think about what makes a signal 'reliable' or believable. Assessment signals are seen to be reliable as they require that the sender possesses the relevant trait. An example of this is that of communicating strength through being seen to carry heavy loads. Such assessment signals are sometimes deceiving, and in fact have become part of a known repertoire of behaviour that makes us laugh. Clowns in circuses often look to be carrying very heavy loads, only to lift them up with one finger at the end of the act. In this instance we know that a deception is taking place and we often find it funny. On the other hand, conventional signals have become correlated with a trait by custom or convention, and are often open to deception. Excessive deception might in fact undermine the signal altogether. A few years ago, seeing somebody in sports equipment might have sent out a reliable signal that they were physically active and likely to be fit. Today, the major sports brands do not direct their advertising at athletes, but at the general public where sports wear has become something of a fashion statement. As a signal it has become 'noise' because it no longer conveys information that relates to the purported function of the clothes. However, perhaps a new signal has been established about identity, which may, for example, relate to wealth.

How do we establish identity on the Internet? In the context of, for example, newsgroups, text is not only a basic form of communication, but a primary means for self-representation (Donath 2000). Account names are a basic form of ID and such information is automatically placed in the header by the posting software. It also appears in the article list that Usenet readers skim to find postings of interest and is the data used in killfiles to identify people one wishes to exclude. 'The automatically inserted account name may be the only overt identifier in the posting; while people do not always sign their letters, all postings must have the sender's account name in the header' (Donath 2000: 35). The domain is the organisation that provides the account and may yield contextual cues about the writer. For example, staff working within a university often have a domain name that relates to that organisation. Some domains clearly carry with them prestige, and Donath suggests that 'while there are not any recognised "wealthy virtual neighborhoods", it is only probably a matter of time until exclusive online addresses become symbols of status' (36). Where the object of using the Internet is to gain information, this may be important. For example, if the reliability of the information is crucial, as in diagnosing a serious medical condition, one is more likely to believe an individual whose domain name, as well as offline address, suggests a reputable organisation or community. However, on the Usenet it is possible to post information anonymously through remailing the post through a forwarding service, which strips all identifying information from the letter and then forwards it, anonymously or under a pseudonym, to the intended recipient or newsgroup.

How else is identity established on the Internet? If we stay with the idea of text as communication, then we can tell much about a person from their written 'voice'. As we have seen in the context of communities, the language that people use can be an indicator of whether they are operating from inside or outside that group. All newsgroups share some common linguistic abbreviations (such as IMHO – in my humble opinion), but specific communities have their own idiosyncratic abbreviations. Using such phrases may express one's identification with that online community, indicating the ability to share a common voice, and giving cues about status within that social group. Identity is also established through the use of signatures, which can either anchor the online persona to the offline reality, or may be an expression of an otherwise never expressed fantasy. Wood and Smith (2001) liken the use of signatures to the 'handles' used by CB radio enthusiasts. Such handles allow for discussion with comparative anonymity, but also allow for the fashioning of a unique identity. On the Internet such signatures are often called 'nicks' (short for nicknames). Participants have a single text line to give their nickname and electronic address, and choosing a nickname that conveys something about the person's 'self' and which increases the likelihood of others wanting to 'talk' is important. Bechar-Israeli (1995) investigated participants' use of nicknames on IRC (Internet Relay Chat), taken largely from four channels. The resulting 260 nicknames were coded and categorised and examined in the light of distribution across 14 categories (for example, nicks that were self-related, such as <shydude>, <belladonna>, or ones that related to figures found in literature or the media, such as <Hagolem>, <Godot>). Across these categories, many people chose a name that represented something about the identity they wished to assume online, whereas only a small number (less than 8 per cent of the total sample) chose to use their offline names. Another finding from this study was that nicknames were fiercely guarded, such that somebody else using one's name might be met by online hostility. This suggested that consistency in the use of nicknames was also important for establishing online identity.

A further use of signature is to refer to the writer's home page on the World Wide Web. Web sites allow for the transmission of text, pictures, animation and sounds to convey an online identity. What is included is directly under the control of the author, who can decide what aspects of 'self' are to be represented. A homepage may provide a detailed portrayal of its subject and it can be argued that having a 'presence' on the Web has a depth that is not found in the environment of newsgroups. This notion of creating an identity on the Net as an ongoing process may be why so many personal Web sites contain the sign indicating 'under construction' (which literally looks like the sign seen on the roads when digging is in process) (Chandler 1997). Such research into web site homepages suggests that these pages integrate the individual, make a personal statement of identity, and show in a stable and replicable way what the individual stands for and what is deemed important (Wynn and Katz 1997).

Talamo and Ligorio (2001) extended this analysis of identity in cyberspace by examining communication through Collaborative Virtual Environments (CVEs). 'CVEs are particular environments fostering communication and interaction among *social actors* rather than the *user–computer* interaction' (110). CVEs allow users to construct their identity in the following ways:

1 by choosing a nickname, that can be very different from their real name;
2 by wearing different simulacra of possible embodiment (the avatars, which are visual representations of themselves chosen by participants);
3 by talking, discussing, and negotiating about the identity that users want to show in real time.

Avatars are a new feature of these systems, and are likened by Talamo and Ligorio (2001) to a mask worn at a party – they emphasise some visual aspects or hide others. Most CVEs are based on synchronous interactions, where identities can be 'negotiated in real time'. These authors argue that we can conceptualise identity as being socially constructed in specific interactive moments. Therefore, on the Internet people can choose to use certain relevant characteristics of their identities as strategic resources to enhance their participation and the overall effectiveness of the community. The choices made are therefore at an individual level, but also reflect and influence the context. All the interactions analysed within this study were performed within 'Euroland', a community composed of students, teachers and researchers who were working on a transnational educational project. When online, participants were personified by an avatar, which was able to walk, fly and look round the virtual world. They were also able to build and manipulate three-dimensional objects, perform virtual actions, and chat with other participants. The identities that emerged were dynamic and strongly related to the context, being created and constantly recreated. They concluded that cyber identities involve resources given by specific technological tools and by community, rather than a static characteristic of participants.

The concept of the Internet as both changing and being changed by the individual is important, and moves us beyond static and stable notions of identity. Turkle (1995) has argued that the Internet acts as a postmodern 'object-to-think-with', which may profoundly change participants' belief systems, values and cognitive styles. Granic and Lamey (2000) suggested that 'these changes may be due to the reciprocal, self-organizing relationship between the interactive medium of literacy in our age and the minds of individuals who are embedded in it' (100). They suggest that at the very least people who use the Internet will become increasingly aware of the diverse approaches to any given problem or issue, and at most this may engender a new awareness of, and appreciation for, the malleability of subjective knowledge or truth. Riva and Galimberti (1998) have suggested that this postmodern notion of perspectivism and multiplicity applies not only to the representation of knowledge, but also to representations of the self. Turkle's (1995) research on participation in MUDs suggested that their attraction lies in participants' ability to cycle through and continuously change various identities.

Granic and Lamey (2000) speculated about what new mode of thought might arise from experiencing a multiplicity of self, suggesting that it may allow for a meta-cognitive representation of self as a network of many selves. At its most simplistic, it may be that by acting out various aspects of self on the Internet, we may reflect the complex nature of self in all its dimensions. Rather than a fracturing into multiple and ever-changing perceptions and projections of self, it may be that such identities and selves are perceived as 'integral and continuous' (Kendall 1999: 61). Rather than the persona being divorced from the 'real self', it may be an expression of an aspect of the self that has not been possible before. Horn (1998: 6) concluded that 'much as we might dearly love to sometimes, we can't leave ourselves behind when we get online. Even when someone is just playing around or in disguise, something true is revealed, it is never completely invented.'

Changes in the way that we think that may result from online participation may also be a result of the decentralised nature of the Internet. There is no central authority on the Internet and as a system it continues to evolve through the participation of its members. There is no official body that controls what people can or cannot do on the Internet, and for many people this will provide a first experience of operating outside a conventional hierarchy. 'But in cyberspace, authority takes on a different meaning. Conventional hierarchies are disrupted by a distributed, decentralised network in which power is spread among various people and groups and one voice does not dominate or pre-empt others' (Granic and Lamey 2000: 104). These authors suggested that such experiences may empower some people who have felt marginalised in modern society and that those who have never been able to function at their optimal level in the offline world may feel that they have a chance to do so when conventional hierarchies are broken down. Therefore the Internet may provide people with life-changing experiences that they would not otherwise have had and these experiences may contribute to more general beliefs about personal efficacy and control. Holmes *et al.* (1998) discussed the computer as a mechanism of metamorphosis where deviant fantasies are provided opportunities to become more concrete. It may be, however, that metamorphosis goes beyond this, and that for some, engagement with the Internet results in changes in how they think of themselves and the world.

SEX AND THE INTERNET

There is an almost unlimited amount of information on the Internet, and much of it relates to sexual material and channels of communication. On the Internet, one can seek advice about sexual problems, look for sexually stimulating material (text, pictures, videos) and engage in romantic and sexual relationships. Griffiths (2000) lists the diverse ways in which the Internet is used for sexual purposes. These include:

1. seeking out sexually related material for educational use;
2. buying or selling sexually related goods for further use offline;
3. visiting and/or purchasing goods in online virtual sex shops;
4. seeking out material for entertainment/masturbatory purposes for use online;
5. seeking out sex therapists;
6. seeking out sexual partners for an enduring relationship;
7. seeking out sexual partners for a transitory relationship;
8. seeking out individuals who then become victims of sexually related Internet crime;
9. engaging in and maintaining online relationships via email and/ or chat rooms;
10. exploring gender and identity roles by swapping gender or creating other personas and forming online relationships;
11. digitally manipulating images on the Internet for entertainment and/or masturbatory purposes.

Using the Internet for sexual purposes is often positioned in a very black-and-white way as either pathological or adaptive (Cooper *et al.*, 1999). For example, Durkin and Bryant (1995) examined the use of the Internet to promote deviant or criminal sexual behaviour. They suggested that 'cybersex' allows individuals to operationalise deviant sexual fantasies that would otherwise have self-extinguished were it not for the immediate reinforcement provided by online communication. The pathological model tends to emphasise such Internet use as addictive or compulsive, involving a psychological dependence on the Internet that is characterised by an increasing investment of time and resources in online activities, unpleasant feelings when offline, increasing tolerance to the effect of being online, and denial that the behaviour is a problem. As we have seen, the concept of 'Internet addiction' is very persuasive for both professionals and lay people alike, and may be used by people who use the Internet to further their sexual interest in children as a justification for their behaviour.

A more adaptive perspective of Internet-related sexual behaviour is presented by Cooper and Sportolari (1997). These authors used the term 'computer mediated relating' to describe interactions that took place through the use of e-mail, and identified a number of positive aspects to this type of relating. These included a reduction in the role that physical attributes play in the initial decision to pursue a relationship. Such relationships were more likely to be based on common interests, values and emotional intimacy rather than physical attractiveness.

In the context of identity and deception, Griffiths's list of ways in which the Internet is used for sexual purposes can be reduced to behaviours that seek to establish some level of relationship (transitory or otherwise). Such relationships may be with other adults or with people who present on the Internet as children. Whether such relationships are seen as pathological or as adaptive depends largely on the context and, inevitably, on discrepancies between participants (such as age or intellectual level). It is also important to acknowledge that sexual relationships on the Internet have, as their expression, behaviours that are every bit as real as those in the offline world. Sexual activity does not take place at an abstract level 'in one's head', but largely through on- or offline masturbatory behaviour. Much of the recent research in this area has taken as its focus IRC and chat rooms, and we will consider some aspects of sexual behaviour in these contexts as they are of considerable relevance to our examination of identity and sexual interest in children.

Chat rooms are virtual rooms hosted by online servers such as America Online and CompuServe, where people may talk with other users of the same service in real time. IRC (Internet Relay Chat) networks are non-proprietary equivalents. Participating in a chat room is not so different from being a member of a specific organisation or club, where membership indicates an interest in a given area (whether it is tennis or photography). Where the focus of such chat rooms is romance or sex, there is evidence to suggest that people are more likely to misrepresent themselves than they are in the offline world. Cornwell and Lundgren (2001) suggested that misrepresentation is directly related to the likely risk of detection.

> Exaggerations of age can be made readily in cyberspace, and misrepresentations of physical attributes are difficult to disconfirm on a computer screen. False claims regarding interests, occupation, education, or other background characteristics may be more difficult to sustain as these become the topics for conversation, questioning and further exploration. (209)

These authors concluded that such misrepresentation may not directly relate to the medium of the Internet, but may be because people seeking such relationships regard them as less serious and feel less commitment towards them.

In the context of sexual, rather than romantic, relationships, Hamman (1996) has identified two forms of 'cybersex' which take place in chat rooms. These are:

1. computer-mediated interactive masturbation in real time. In this form of cybersex, participants type instructions and descriptions of what they are 'doing' to each other and to themselves while masturbating. They often type with one hand while masturbating with the other;
2. computer-mediated telling of interactive sexual stories, in real time, with the intent of arousal. Participants who take part in this form of cybersex tell each other sexual stories with the intent of arousing themselves and other users.

In addition, Hamman identifies four other forms of cybersex, not connected with chat rooms, such as: software-based cybersex (users create their own virtual partner); Virtual Reality cybersex (high-tech goggles and movement-sensitive body suits); electronic pornography; e-mail cybersex (trading sexual stories by e-mail); and MUD-based cybersex. A further area involves the use of video-conferencing protocols.

Hamman (1996) presented an ethnographic study of sexual behaviour in chat rooms and concluded that users of online chat rooms experience loss of inhibition owing to the anonymity of the medium. This loss of inhibition allowed users to experiment more freely with their online selves and express multiple aspects of self. Such aspects may be positive (such as freeing the person to explore different ways of enjoying their sexuality) or may be negative, where anonymity is used to allow for the expression of sexual aggression. One subject in Hamman's study presented himself online as a female to allow him sexually, emotionally and mentally to abuse other men. This study examined cybersex in the context of 'cyborg' theory and concluded that those who engaged in such sexual activity became cyborgs, using the computer as a prosthetic to supplement human capabilities. Becoming a cyborg therefore allows people to use online chat to experiment with multiple selves, many of which 'real-life' society suppresses. This idea, although it may seem fanciful, has considerable relevance to the ways in which those with a sexual interest in children use computers.

So far, we have suggested that cybersex is sexual activity that relates only to Internet use. It may take place in real time (both parties masturbating while sharing fantasies) or may generate fantasies and arousal that are acted upon after disconnecting from the Internet. However, there is also evidence emerging, largely in the context of studies of gay men who use the Internet, that relationships formed through this medium may be seen as a stepping-stone to relationships in the offline world. In the context of IRC, Shaw (1997) concluded that for gay men participating in computer-mediated communication (CMC), 'the virtual experiences of IRC and real-life experience share a symbiotic relationship; that is, relationships formed within the exterior gay community lead the users to the interior CMC gay community, where they, in turn, develop new relationships which are nurtured and developed outside the bounds of CMC' (143). The role of IRC is thus to allow gay men to try on different personalities, and 'presents an opportunity for gay men, who often go through life hiding this most vital aspect of their identity, to try on this real identity' (144). Similarly Tikkanen and Ross (2000) found in their study of Swedish gay men who use chat rooms, that it was common for younger men in particular to have experiences of physically meeting sexual partners. So online sexuality is inextricably linked with the offline world, either through the physical expression of sexual behaviour with the computer acting as prosthesis, or through online relationships taking on physical embodiment in the real world.

VIRTUAL IDENTITIES AND SEXUAL INTEREST IN CHILDREN

According to Mahoney and Faulkner (1997), the Internet allows paedophiles:

- instant access to other predators worldwide;
- open discussion of their sexual desires;
- shared ideas about ways to lure victims;
- mutual support of their adult–child sex philosophies;
- instant access to potential child victims worldwide;
- disguised identities for approaching children, even to the point of presenting as a member of teen groups;
- ready access to 'teen chat rooms' to find out how and who to target as potential victims;
- means to identify and track down home contact information;
- ability to build a long-term 'Internet' relationship with a potential victim, prior to attempting to engage the child in physical contact.

But it would be simplistic to think that the Internet is only another vehicle for paedophile activity. The evidence that we have examined so far suggests that the Internet facilitates change in the individual, which in turn affects the way in which the Internet (or that section related to the individual) develops. People who use the Internet as a way of meeting their sexual needs may come to it from a variety of backgrounds. Some are curious and find that they are both interested in and aroused by child pornography. Some are aware of their sexual interest and see the Internet as a means of meeting that interest without recourse to contact with children. Others wish to find children to engage with, both at a virtual and at a face-to-face level. What seems to be the case for many individuals is that, once engaged with the Internet for the purposes of sexual gratification, that very engagement changes the way they think about themselves and others. This may be nothing more than a sense of 'coming home', of finding that there are many like-minded others, of finding a niche. For some, communication on the Internet offers a way of presenting oneself in a positive light, without the barriers of physical presence, and possibly with the added status associated with a 'good' collection of child pornography. The very process of acquiring Internet skills may leave the person feeling positive about themselves, in a way that they have never experienced before. Such changes may be thought of as passive: the by-products of engagement. However, for others, as we have seen in the context of cybersex, such change is more considered and intentional. In the final section of this chapter, we are going to examine in some detail two people who selected 'persona' in order to facilitate very specific sexual goals.

CHILD SEDUCTION ON THE INTERNET

Durkin (1997) suggested that there are four ways in which people with a sexual interest in children may misuse the Internet: to traffic child pornography; to locate children to molest; to engage in inappropriate sexual communication with children; and to communicate with other paedophiles. The following case study illustrates all of these occurring within the repertoire of one individual and facilitated by the ability to self-represent in multiple ways on the Internet (Quayle and Taylor 2001). For this individual, the means to communicate with others largely took place through chat rooms, where anonymity allowed him to assume first the persona of a child, and later an adult.

Lamb (1998) provided the first systematic study of how such chat rooms may be used by paedophiles. He sought to catalogue the types of identity and the verbal behaviours of visitors to chat rooms that specifically targeted young gay males. For the purpose of the study, the author assumed personas of young males. His analysis suggested that those who contacted the author's personas could be divided into three broad categories: browsers; cruisers; and pornographers. Browsers were genuinely curious people exploring the medium and expecting to meet real people. Their language and general knowledge was congruent with adolescence and they avoided both personal and sexual chat. They were also the smallest group represented. The largest group was the cruisers, who, while listing themselves as students, displayed little knowledge of the culture or language that would be appropriate to this group. They did, however, possess an extensive knowledge of gay sexual practices, which they wished to discuss at length. The talk was highly sexualised and focused on either their own experiences or fantasies about sexual activities with others in the chat room. Approximately half of this group also looked for contact outside the chat room. The third group, pornographers, revealed little about themselves in conversations, were seen as highly skilled users of the medium, and focused more on trading photographs. Lamb concluded, 'Most visitors to youthful sexually oriented chat rooms are apparently not as described' (133). In addition, it appeared that very few of the people in this study showed any restraints in what they wanted to say or do, engaging others whom they assumed to be young people in fantasies and mutual masturbation.

Two issues central to such a misuse of the Internet are: what aspects of the Internet allow for such a high occurrence of 'unrestrained' sexual behaviour, and how and why do people self-represent as someone other than who they really are in the offline world? Central to our understanding of the individual in relation to the Internet is awareness that there is an overlap between the online and the offline world. The importance lies in the connection between 'life online and its meaning in relationship to life offline' (Jones 1999: 23). For those with a sexual interest in children, life online operates in the context of the abuse of children both online and offline, either in the production and exchange of pornographic images, or in attempted sexual engagement. Talamo and Ligorio (2001) have emphasised that, 'whenever cyberspace is used within a real and meaningful context, the boundaries between real and virtual are blurred. Furthermore, activities in cyberspace produce outputs for real life and vice versa' (111).

Consideration of the factors that allow people to engage in highly disinhibited sexual behaviour on the Internet tends to focus on accessibility, affordability and anonymity (Cooper *et al.*, 2000a). These authors suggested that sexual relationships on the Internet can foster superficial erotic contacts and ways of relating that can have destructive results, such as people acting on or over-indulging in an accelerated, eroticised pseudo-intimacy. The Internet also offers the opportunity for the formation of online communities, in which isolated individuals can communicate with each other around sexual topics of shared interest (Linehan *et al.*, 2002). The availability of erotica (including child pornography) allows for the objectification of others, the ability to fragment one's own sexuality, and the possible emergence of otherwise dormant antisocial inclinations (Quayle *et al.*, 2000). Danet (1998) has suggested that the anonymity and playful quality of the Internet have a powerful and disinhibiting effect on behaviour. People are more likely to allow themselves to behave in ways that are different from ordinary, everyday life, and to express previously unexplored aspects of their personalities. Where in the context of adult sexual behaviour this may be seen as liberating (Palandri and Green 2000), this would not be seen to be the case where the target of this behaviour is a child (Taylor *et al.*, 2001).

The expression of sexual interest is also facilitated by the ability to represent oneself in whatever way one wants, in the apparent safety of anonymity. Cyberspace is an interactive arena, where tools such as chat rooms are used to offer new interacting resources. If we consider identity to be socially constructed rather than fixed, then playing different identities can be seen as a resource that participants use, and choice about what possible self to show is driven by strategic moves that participants can make within that situation (Widdicome 1998). The context also shapes how people represent themselves. Identities constructed during the social interaction depend on what each person decides to show about her or himself in that context, and on the impact of the context in guiding and modelling the possible choices. Self-representation on the Internet is largely achieved through verbal exchange, although people can and do use images such as photographs (Tikkanen and Ross 2000). If the purpose of self-representation is specifically sexual, as in the online seduction of children or adults, the absence of non-verbal cues makes the process of first-impression formation take on new forms. This is expressed largely through the language chosen, the style of writing, the timing of the response, speed of writing, use of punctuation and use of emoticons (Mantovani 2001). Wherc self-representation or persona is manipulated to achieve a certain goal, then such factors will be important in establishing credibility and sustaining online relationships. As already seen in the study by Lamb (1998), such cues can also be seen to undermine credibility where they are incongruent with the assumed persona. The Internet offers a unique opportunity for multiple representations of identity that need bear no relationship with other social cues that are normally so salient in the offline world.

The function of online resources, such as child pornography, serve to both heighten sexual arousal and disinhibition and are used as an aid in seduction of children through fantasy manipulation and masturbation. Such images also remain in the offline world as permanent products that can be manipulated, changed, viewed and exchanged as can any other commodity. The objectification of such images distances the user from the fact that they are photographs of sexual abuse, and this is seen most strongly when they are used as a means of social currency. What is of relevance, too, is that the use of pornography, like engagement with the Internet, is not a static process, but has a function within a range of offending activities. This might be conceptualised as a more dynamic model of problematic Internet use by individuals with a sexual interest in children (Quayle and Taylor 2002a).

QX is a man convicted of downloading child pornography. He progressed from downloading and trading pornography to communicating with others through chat rooms. Having discovered chat rooms, QX quite quickly decided to represent himself as a child persona. He described this in the context of increasing the possibility of accessing other children, and also as a measure of personal security:

> as I then perceived the children in the Chat room would more probably be likely to chat to another someone their own age.

Having tried out several child personas, QX self-represented as 'Joe', a persona that he maintained for twelve months without anyone challenging its authenticity. At the start, Joe was 11 years old, with blue eyes and blond hair. This was very similar to how QX would have looked at the same age and closely fitted his fantasy of a child he would like to have as a lover.

It was relatively easy for him to do this, as Joe's everyday experiences were anchored in the very real offline world of QX as a teacher. They shared the same interests in sports, shared a similar geographical space (an adjoining town and school), had the same birthday and had a similar 'timetable' with regard to everyday activities. QX had long had an interest in creative writing and assuming this persona was relatively easy:

> Er . . . now I talk about him in the third person but at the time I was really getting into the character . . . it's like I was script writer . . . actor . . . all in one.

This persona also allowed QX to live out fantasies that had been active since he was an adolescent:

> although I was pretending to be Joe, it was like Joe was part of me erm . . . in terms of that's what I wanted . . . so therefore I created it and portrayed it to the outside world . . . and lived out the fantasies I would have had . . . and did have under the guise of Joe.

This persona was given credibility by assigning it a 'real' identity through a photograph. Initially QX used one that he had obtained from one of the newsgroups, but this was recognised as such by other people, and censored within the community. He then sent a Polaroid picture of a boy from his cricket team to a man he had been in contact with and who lived in America. This man scanned the image and made it available to others in the chat room. The same man also took on a protective role towards Joe for the duration of his existence.

Initial contact in the chat rooms was with adult males, and involved a variety of conversations and activities:

> you name it it probably happened . . . really in terms of the range of different types of conversations and the cybersex I engaged in . . . erm but that was quite early on.

QX categorised these males according to their behaviour towards him:

> Yeah we'd have cybersex and there wouldn't be hardly any conversation erm . . . there were different types of abusers though I mean . . . there were ones that were straight direct they just wanted to meet Joe er wanted his telephone number . . . others were just happy with the cybersex and there were the ones that said how are you Joe what have you been up to recently?
>
> . . . you could label them in terms of there was the predators . . . the masturbators . . . and the befrienders.

Much of the sexual activity involved masturbation by both parties, and the descriptions and instructions given were often very explicit and involved third parties as part of the fantasy building. For example, early on QX gave Joe a brother (which was later dropped) and others in the chat room would ask Joe to get his brother out of bed and involve him in a sexual script, while supposedly engaging in sex with another young person. The setting was given reality by descriptions, for example, of what kinds of clothes Joe was wearing. Unlike offline relationships (which for QX had never involved explicit sexual activity), when online the contact would quickly move into sexual engagement:

> You can't go up to a boy in the street and say . . . do you fancy having sex erm . . . whereas you could online . . .
>
> We'd describe what we were doing on each side of the computer . . . you know what they were doing what I was doing . . . erm . . . so it was very sexualised very graphic.

Not all the relationships with men were immediately sexual, and his preferred contacts were with men who would befriend him prior to attempting to engage in any sexual activity. Playing the role of a young boy also meant that others were willing to help him build up his own computer skills, for example by coaching him in the use of mIRC (a communication programme used to access IRC).

QX as Joe then started to talk more frequently to other boys in the chat room, and as a consequence engaged less and less with sexual activities with other men:

> although Joe was having cyber sex with these other lads er . . . he wouldn't really do it with the other adults.

It is odd that although QX showed a preference for talking to other boys, he was not able to distinguish between them and adults in terms of content. Forming an attachment with one of the boys became public knowledge within the main chat room, and for a while would have precluded other sexual behaviour. Such relationships were also moved into a public area within the chat room community by, for example, imitating offline relationship behaviour:

> and erm we ended up getting married in a public room . . . because well . . . because there was a priest in there at the time.

One major difference between the offline and the online world is, of course, that in the latter there was a formal sanctioning of deviant behaviour and that this relationship moved from a chat room encounter to marriage within a matter of weeks. There was an equally rapid falling out when QX discovered that his partner (based in the US) had strong 'racist' views, which did not fit with QX's 'moral' position. During the time that this relationship was in existence, there was frequent sexual activity, and this was satisfying because it fitted with a romantic fantasy of sex with a boy that was part of QX's preferred sexual script:

> Erm . . . it would be . . . rubbing my back . . . kissing nipples erm . . . erm . . . french kissing . . . that tender side to love making . . . erm . . . really taking care that your partner is getting as much pleasure from it as you.

The move from mIRC to ICQ further enhanced the erotic nature of the exchanges:

> and I found that quite erotic because you can actually see the person typing at the same time.

The offline world merged into online activity with the exchange of gifts. In the context of the boy he had 'married' this included rings. The compressed and at times exaggerated nature of these relationships was also evidenced in what happened when they 'fell out':

> classic camp you know erm . . . almost comical gay scenario you'd see on er a sit com you know . . . throwing camp temper tantrums. (2: 17)

The element of fantasy was important in these relationships. With the men he encountered, he fantasised that they might have boys whom he could contact in real life. With the first relationship with a 13-year-old boy, the fantasy was of two boys falling in love and having sex. The notion of consensuality within the relationship was important:

> and even the fantasy of two boys falling in love and having sex . . . I found that an attraction . . . probably in the respect that I just . . . that that justifies my abuse. (2: 18)

This relationship was quickly replaced 'on the rebound' by one with Zak. The intensity and reality of these online relationships can be seen in the following:

> It really was like living out a life . . . online . . . erm . . . although it's all digital numbers and zeros and ones . . . it felt so strong so real . . . and it . . . and then especially the relationship with Zak that Joe had . . . it was almost that then that activity was then beginning to control the activity outside.

QX believed that Zak was 13, even though there were a lot of cues that might have suggested otherwise. For example, Zak's knowledge of sexual practices was extensive:

> because he did go into a lot of detail . . . erm . . . erm . . . about . . . things like . . . oh butterfly kisses and things like that . . . which I didn't know what they meant . . . erm . . . and it was extremely tender . . . an extremely romanticised view of sex. (2: 22)

Zak had also sent QX lots of gifts, many of which would have suggested that the person he was talking to was adult rather than child:

> Zak had sent me quite a few things in the post. Erm . . . during the summer holidays . . . he'd sent me I think it was 18 yellow roses . . . from a local florist erm . . . obviously done via debit card . . . he'd sent me clothes . . . he'd sent me a $100 bill.

While QX acknowledged that he should have realised that Zak was not a child, he was so involved with and enjoying the fantasy that these cues were ignored:

> I felt . . . this is what I want . . . this is where I wan to be . . . this is how life . . . how I want my life to go . . . erm . . . because my life is sad, crap and boring . . . full of emptiness . . . and here . . . is a relationship which is full. But that was a strange way . . . because you're getting that as soon as you switch off . . . log off . . . back to that again. But that feels more empty . . . more hollow and not worth living any more . . . so that . . . that is almost like a

> downward spiral . . . because you were getting so much from something that wasn't real . . . you go back to reality and reality feels even worse than it was before. (2: 25)

During the time that QX was involved with Zak, his contact with the real world was reducing, such that he was cancelling cricket matches and coaching sessions. Paradoxically, this meant that he was engaged in fewer relationships with boys during the time that he was involved with the Internet. Finally, QX was confronted by a confession from Zak that he was not 13 but was in fact an adult male. This in turn was seen as a betrayal and a source of huge emotional distress, but coupled with this were confusing ambiguous feelings, because in part QX was having to acknowledge that what had been done to him was exactly the same as he had done to Zak. QX was subsequently persuaded to move to another server, where, after a week, he met Noah. Noah again was 13 and living in the USA, and his presentation was at first as someone quite reticent who had to be won round in order to engage him in a sexual relationship.

The relationship with Noah was a very intense one, in part because he had a more complete 'personality' than in the previous relationships. This building up of his character was achieved through supplying minute details about his life:

> far more details about his judo, his friends, his brother . . . his adopted brother . . . his parents . . . his house . . . his ranch. (2: 36)

When Noah revealed that he was an adult rather than a child, QX was devastated, 'I wanted to smash something'. This anger found expression through increasing his alcohol intake. The betrayal by Noah marked the end of the persona of Joe. This was accompanied not by feelings of loss, which might have been expected, as QX had been online as Joe for over twelve months, but by a sense of relief:

> to me it was good to be me . . . online . . . er . . . from the end of February onwards . . . it was actually . . . it was actually a relief to say . . . well actually it's what . . . I'm 33.

This was followed by a decision that nothing about his sexual orientation was going to change and that his feelings of depression would be more likely to go away if he 'came out . . . as me'. The coming out and going back online was in some ways liberating:

> Because then I could have cybersex as an adult with other boys in the room . . . which is what I wanted in the first place really.

It also opened up the possibility of finding someone to abuse. His previous child persona had precluded this, because to risk meeting somebody would result in the validity of his persona being undermined. He went back into another sexually explicit chat room, and on assuming an adult role became 'Much more of a predator'. In the chat room he talked with other men both about themselves and about the types of boy that they would like to meet. The exchanges of fantasies also included swapping pornography:

> I think that's when the pornography started up quite a lot then . . . this time swapping a lot more . . . more proactively looking for film clips erm . . . erm . . . that we started talking about . . . we used to talk about the boys that would arrive erm . . . in the room. About how real they were. Have you tried chatting him up and how far did you get. Do you think he's real that sort of thing . . . Ah . . . that felt good . . . to be *me* . . . with amongst what I would then consider to be the only people that would really understand me. The only people I can be me with . . . they won't judge me. They feel the same way. We've got so much in common. I can feel . . . I fit in here . . . erm.

His role within this community was important to him and allowed him to express aspects of himself that he had not previously disclosed to others:

> so here I'm not lonely because people do know the real me and I can be open and honest. Erm and then we started talking about oh where can you go looking for boys . . . online stuff.

This actively seeking boys to meet, both online and offline 'it was far more aggressive . . . it became far more aggressive', and this was reflected in the way that he talked when online.

The bid to access boys was supported by information from other adults within the community:

> more times I would get what I would call leads from other adults . . . about boys they know, they'd abused or . . . had contact with. I was working on that one.

In spite of pursuing these avenues, through e-mail addresses and telephone numbers, over a six-month period he was not successful in making contact with anyone that resulted in a physical meeting. With one boy he engaged in telephone sex, which QX described as being initiated by the child. He arranged to meet this boy but failed to turn up as he had been drinking heavily the night before and did not wake in time. A further contact was made with another boy:

> The sequence of events was that in June or July . . . of 2000 . . . I'd given my telephone number and picture . . . photograph of myself . . . to an individual who was pretending to be 12 years old. Er they went to the police with a track they'd obviously printed out from a conversation we'd had in a chat room er . . . that obviously kicked off events. The police came round a month later.

Their online conversation had included references to QX taking photographs of the boy with a digital camera, although he subsequently said that he had had no intention of doing that, but wished to abuse the boy. It turned out that the boy in question was not 13 but was 18 and the chat room had been dedicated to young homosexuals. QX blurred his intentions with regard to this contact, saying that he was not sure that he was a child and wanted to give him the opportunity to come out as an adult who liked boys.

This case study provides evidence of how one individual used the Internet to further his sexual interest in children. This was achieved through initially accessing child pornography, which intensified his levels of sexual arousal and behaviour, and fuelled his desire to engage in a relationship with a child. His move to chat rooms allowed him to engage initially as a child persona in 'cybersex' with people presenting as both adults and boys, and then as an adult in order to access boys offline. We can see a progression in offending that moved him closer to behaviour that was clearly sanctioned online: that of the sexual predator. This is paralleled in changes in his sexual behaviour and language. Pornography was an important feature in that through it he accessed a like-minded community, secured a role in that community, and was provided with a vehicle that allowed both solitary and mutual sexual expression. Pornography cemented both adult and child relationships, giving him status through the size and quality of his collection.

This case study bears similarities with that of Lamb (1998), in that it is apparent that many people in sexually oriented chat rooms, particularly those dedicated to young gay males, are really adult men looking for cybersex. Döring (2000) drew our attention to the fact that cybersex is not a conversation about sex, but is a form of sexual encounter in itself. Her definition of cybersex is 'a computer-mediated interpersonal interaction in which the participants are sexually motivated, meaning they are seeking sexual arousal and satisfaction' (864). In the context of child seduction, personas are assumed which allow for the engagement of individuals, sometimes in apparently 'caring' relationships, to facilitate sexual contact. Lamb talked of browsers, cruisers and pornographers in relation to the people in his study. QX, however, likened these people to predators, masturbators and befrienders, all of whom would have used pornography as part of their social exchange. Lamb was able to distinguish between 'real' youths and adults pretending to be such. With QX this seems to have been much more difficult, as his assumed persona as Joe was so firmly embedded in his offline world as a teacher, that his vocabulary and immediate circumstances were congruent with a child of 13. What is also of interest is the overlap between the persona of Joe and fantasies that QX would have had as a child of that age. This merging of boundaries between the offline world and the online one made sustaining his role a relatively easy, if emotionally taxing, task.

This overlap of online and offline behaviour was also clearly seen both in the actual sexual behaviour and in the assumption of many of the ways of relating that we see offline, such as exchanging rings and getting married. Sexual activity, although largely taking place next to the computer, was not something that took place 'in the mind'. What was involved, particularly when the need was to establish a loving relationship, as opposed to providing only explicit sexual instructions or cues, was a detailed vocabulary. Such a written expression of sexual sensations has been noted by other authors as being very different from what is normally required in 'face-to-face' relationships. This overlap into the 'real' world was also evidenced in the exchange of gifts and telephone numbers, and at the end of this process, the attempt to make contact physically with children.

While QX and Joe are one and the same, his account of his child persona was often presented in the third person and he moved through talking of 'him', 'I' and 'we'. What is also evident is the idea of Joe as an idealised sense of what it could have been like at that age if he had been able overtly to express his sexuality in a safe world. The choice of Joe as a nickname is interesting as QX was adamant that it did not relate to any individual that he actually knew in the offline world. Talamo and Ligorio (2001) suggested that the choice of a nickname is the first strategic move that users do inside the community, since it exposes some characteristics of the self (even if unreal). In keeping Joe apart from other known identities, QX was able to keep ownership for himself and in himself.

ADOPTING MULTIPLE PERSONAS

Quayle *et al.* (2000) presented a case history of a man (II) convicted of downloading child pornography who adopted multiple personas on the Internet. His discovery of IRC and the capacity to talk to others about a variety of sexual topics resulted in him giving expression to aspects of his self that he had previously not explored:

> It felt as if erm there was some sort of facet of my personality that was becoming er erm more . . . it was emerging . . . which I thought well this is part of me . . . this is kind of as much part of me as any other part of my personality . . . so therefore it's a valid . . . part of my personality.

This emerging self grew out of contact with other people who were more sexually adventurous and disinhibited than he was, and was initially facilitated by the anonymous environment of the Internet. However, in order to achieve a sexual exchange with others, he explicitly adopted a persona based on an interest in more 'deviant' sexual areas and used the exchange of pornography to give this credibility:

> you see because for some people to get them to respond I'd say oh you know, I'm into that erm . . . and I could sort of back that up by giving them images . . . that supported that . . . so . . . you know you name it as a sort of sexual proclivity and I sort of manage to get the material and say like well you know I like looking at women being fucked by dogs and that sort of thing.

The choices that he made to secure access to this alternative social world were very much influenced by the context in which the communication took place, but resulted in a very real perception of 'becoming':

> Yes. Exactly. Exactly. Erm . . . and . . . what clearly had been happening was that erm I was sort of moving from over the counter porn through stuff which was more unusual to stuff which was really hard core. And talking to people you know who had a real interest in that kind of thing. And . . . erm . . . what . . . was essentially happening was that a new personality was being generated . . . I was generating a new personality . . . it was a personality which erm . . . existed on the Net . . . because I was telling people I liked what they did . . . because I was finding their discussion of those activities really stimulating . . .

II clearly differentiates the person he can be while on the Internet from the person expressed in the offline world. On the Internet there was nobody telling him who he could be, and the communities that he accessed reinforced a sense of excitement and danger:

> Yeah oh yeah . . . and . . . also no sense of censorship. There was kind of no . . . there was no . . . sort of moral guardian there . . . erm . . . I was descending into a kind of culture . . . subculture . . . of erm . . . er . . . of danger, sexual excitement . . . erm . . . where . . . pretty much everyone I chose to talk to . . . was it's OK . . . we're into this . . . erm . . . and . . . I was . . . talking to people who I . . . took to be took to be real . . .

Unlike many other people who engage in sexual relationships online, II believed in the reality of the people he communicated with. In part this was achieved through the exchange of materials such as pornography, but also through the giving and sending of more mundane things, such as Valentine cards:

> Yeah to some extent . . . it kind of legitimized my . . . sort of personality that existed on the Net . . . in that I can show you I liked this . . . you can talk to me about this because I can show I like this material. But there wasn't a concentration purely to do with child pornography because I was very much interested in the whole sort of genre.

II enjoyed a wide range of sexual experiences on the Internet, not all of which related to child pornography, and he moved through a variety of ways of expressing aspects of himself in order to secure more and more extreme forms of cybersex:

> and they were into sploshing and . . . erm . . . we'd sort of exchange images to do with sploshing and they'd sort of tell me what they done and then we'd have virtual sessions where they'd say we've got this food in . . . you tell us

> what to put on each other . . . which is what I would do . . . so again I'd sort of make appointments where I'd say I'll see you on Tuesday night, half past seven and you know we'll have this session . . . erm . . . and I never discovered whether they were real or not . . . erm but erm . . . I was really into that I was very much into things to do with group sex. I was very much into bondage . . . and in fact . . . there was a particular . . . they . . . they were . . . these women who appeared under the same nickname online . . . and . . . they said they were slaves of this dominatrix who lived somewhere in C.

II made some attempts to contact this woman, and eventually exchanged e-mails with her. Again, in order to sustain the legitimacy of his interest, he had to 'fine-tune' the aspects of himself that he wished to reveal:

> Because that was something that you know . . . was kind of sexually arousing . . . so . . . there was this whole sort of plethora of . . . sort of tuning my online identity . . . to the people that I spoke to.

There was often a convergence of largely unexplored aspects of self that were evident in the offline world, but which he had been too afraid to act upon. For example, II was aware that he had often wondered what it must be like to be a woman, as this would bring with it some means of controlling a sexual relationship. He had even gone so far as to try on female underwear, but had had neither the opportunity nor the confidence to take this further. While there is no evidence that he assumed a female persona online, he did fantasise about being a woman and would use lesbian pornography as part of this.

> Erm . . . whereas the idea of being a woman . . . and also all the material I was looking at to begin with was women on their own or women together . . . so I was kind of thinking . . . oh yeah . . . I'd love to be a woman.

II also moved from online to offline relationships. In part this was because he felt the need to prove to himself that the people he was talking to were 'real', rather than because he wished to engage in any sexual relationship with them.

> And there wasn't really any real further need to go much further because I'd met this person and they were a real person and they didn't seem much different than the . . . and that was almost enough. So there was a sense that wanting to meet these people just to see what they were like . . . just to see images of them . . . just to see what they looked like . . . to kind of build up a complete picture of this person.

This overlap between online and offline worlds influenced the choice of people he communicated with, actively looking for individuals who lived close to him geographically. Yet what was important was the difference of this online world, and while he played with the idea of importing it (through meeting people, or by introducing his wife to a sexual event), the latter never happened:

> It was . . . it was mainly that I was allowing myself to inhabit a different world . . . and assuming a different exciting identity . . . [Mmm] . . . Which wasn't being satisfied in the real world.

An important aspect of this world was a sense of control that II had over his identity and over the activities that he was engaging in. However, in order to sustain his persona he was having to engage in a process of validation through exchanging pornography, often saving and collecting material that was more and more extreme, such as pictures of babies being sexually abused. What had started as a liberating and exciting experience, where he could make choices, took on elements of compulsive behaviour when it became an activity that was all-consuming and which excluded other social contacts offline:

> Well . . . yeah . . . erm . . . then it was the case of . . . well, the whole world just sort of fell to pieces . . . because I was then completely out of . . . I was . . . I'd lost control . . . completely . . . of the situation . . . there was nothing I could do . . . to take control back again . . . [Mmm] . . . Whereas before I'd almost been in complete control . . . I was controlling the computer.

Hammon's metaphor of the cyborg is very evident in II,'s account, where he describes the role that the computer had for him:

> I'd essentially been having a sexual relationship with a computer . . . rather than with real people.

The computer had become a prosthesis, a way of sexually relating that was dependent on the machine. By this time, all sexual activity with his partner had stopped and been replaced by cybersex. Such relationships were again given reality by anchoring them to personal information, gleaned through exchanges on IRC, but in the offline world, kept as written information:

> Yeah. I had a little black book as it were . . . a profile of all these people. And . . . because I'd talk to so many people . . . sometimes a name would pop up and I'd think Oh right, there's this person and who the hell is this . . . [OK] . . . I'll have a quick look. Oh yeah, oh right, I remember . . . and start chatting to them as if I was a real friend of theirs . . . [Mmm] . . . So I might have been maintaining . . . concurrently . . . about . . . 20 friendships.

Such information not only gave credibility to the people he was communicating with, but also allowed him to go through a process of relationship building, similar to that seen with QX, based on building up personas. For this man it also enabled him to adjust the aspects of self that he wished to present to others, changing what was revealed according to the context in which the communication was taking place.

Both QX and II were changed by their engagement with the Internet, and illustrate some of the ways in which such changes can be either incidental or purposeful. Communicating with others allowed for the representation of aspects of self that had previously been suppressed or had lain dormant. It also allowed for the enactment of fantasies with others and an escalation of highly sexualised behaviour, at odds with behaviour offline. Both of these people experienced a heightening of emotions, a sense of extreme excitement, which was otherwise absent in their lives. What this also served to do was to emphasise the bleakness of the real world, where relationships, or their realisation, were problematic. It may be inevitable that this sense of being 'real' and 'alive' on the Internet led to a rejection of the offline world and an absorption with life online. For II this was problematic, because in presenting aspects of himself he chose to download and exchange child pornography, seeing this as a legitimate way of exploring his own sexuality. For QX, who had an existing sexual interest in boys before going online, the Internet allowed him to role-play fantasies, presenting himself as both child and adult in order to engage others in cybersex. For both people, the aspects of self that were presented were not separate from how they idealised self in the offline world, but gave it expression. Unfortunately, in doing so they engaged with others in ways that would prove detrimental to children.

Chapter 6

A virtual community

As the Internet has developed, and as our knowledge of how people relate to the Internet and use its facilities has grown, so we begin to see the effect of the Internet on the user as something potentially greater than a passive means of quickly and cheaply transmitting information between points. Communication on the Internet can go beyond the simple passivity that receipt of information implies to embrace emotional and social factors more usually associated with real-life communication. Even though for the moment person-to-person communication on the Internet is largely text-based, and therefore apparently limited in comparison with more usual face-to-face communication, there is a sense in which the process of passage of that information can generate a sense of group membership, the development of social networks, and the generation of a sense of community. Thus communication using Internet structures can go beyond the instrumentality implied by information exchange. The creation of social space, groups and communities are terms we use to refer to the consequences of going beyond information exchange to embrace social and emotional factors.

The term 'virtual' is used to refer to network-based communication, and related consequent communities. Rheingold's (1993) definition of a virtual community was that 'Virtual communities are social aggregations that emerge from the Net when enough people carry on public discourses long enough, with sufficient human feeling, to form webs of personal relationships in cyberspace' (5). The term 'virtual' is sometimes contrasted with actual, as if a virtual entity were not a real entity. Watson (1998) argued that the distinction between virtual community and real community is unwarranted. The entailment of calling online communities 'virtual' includes spreading and reinforcing a belief that what happens online is like a community, but isn't really a community. This can be a misleading comparison, however, for in the sense used in respect of networked communication, virtual has a rather different meaning (Lévy 1998). To illustrate this, Lévy used the example of the virtualisation of a company. He noted that a conventional organisation brings its employees together into a location, a building or buildings of some form. An employee has a location in that space (an office, a workbench, etc.), and generally a schedule indicates the hours he or she will work. Such a schedule is necessary if the various individuals who need to work together have to be organised to appear in a real space distant from their home or preferred location all at the same time. The physical presence of the building and its facilities necessarily therefore imposes a particular form of structure to the organisation. A virtual company, on the other hand, locates individual workers on an electronic communications network, and software resources of various kinds promote and enable co-operation. 'The virtualisation of the corporation consists primarily in transforming the spatiotemporal co-ordinates of work into a continuously renewed problem rather than a stable solution' (Lévy 1998: 26). The 'renewed problem' he refered to related to the organisation's centre of gravity no longer being 'a group of buildings, workstations and schedules' which are by definition fixed and permanent (referred to as 'a stable solution'), 'but a process of co-ordination' which necessarily implies a much more fluid and changing environment.

Thus, an individual can participate in a virtual organisation simply by joining its network. Where the individual is located at that time is irrelevant, provided he or she has access to the network, and has the computer resources to perform the necessary tasks. Because participation in the network does not require physical presence in a building, the temporal arrangements of work can be much more fluid. Work can be completed at any time that the appropriate people who need to be interacted with are online or can access whatever is necessary in some storage medium. However, given that in many cases the resources necessary to complete tasks are themselves already stored on network-accessible media, so the temporal parameters of work can be very fluid indeed, and the time constraints necessary to ensure people come together no longer need dominate working life. Communication between people is mediated, therefore, not by a building and structures, but by networked software resources and network access. Not all work can function in this way, of course, but many office jobs, sales work, accounting and back office activities, and creative work can be conducted in such a manner.

Work, of course, is not the only form of group or community to which we belong; many people belong to recreational groups, activity groups, interest groups, and school groups of all kinds. Many of these other groups are not so readily made virtual. Some groups necessarily have to come together physically to do something (a swimming club for example) that requires a location (a swimming pool) and presumably shared and agreed meeting times (to enable competition or coaching). Other groups that focus on information sharing, discussion, etc. do more readily lend themselves as potential virtual groups. Some recreational organisations, therefore, as distinct from work groups, can also have a virtual existence. Indeed, these kinds of group can flourish in a networked environment, because they can access many more people than those found in any given physical location.

Kollock and Smith (1999) identified at least five forms of online interaction that can mediate the emergence of virtual groups:

1 E-mail and discussion lists. E-mail allows a user to send a message directly to someone, rather than in the form of a traditional letter. Discussion lists extend this concept, however, by automatically sending the message to a group

of people on an e-mail list, rather than to an individual. The direction of a series of messages, and their responses, to the list generates a form of group discussion, which can extend across hundreds, and even thousands, of individuals. Typically, the list is 'owned' by one individual because the messages must pass through a single point. The 'owner', therefore, has the capacity to monitor and exclude or edit material flowing through the discussion list. On a large list, this may take a considerable amount of time and energy, so a more manageable format is to keep the list 'open' and without detailed editing. Even so, disruptive, inappropriate or malicious material can still be excluded without detailed monitoring.

2 Usenet and BBSs. Bulletin board systems (BBSs) are a form of asynchronous communication that allows participants to create topical groups in which a series of messages can be listed, one after another. Well-known systems of this type include the Usenet, the WELL, ECHO and BBSs run on commercial services, such as AOL and Microsoft Network. For each there is a wide collection of discussion topics and communication between participants. Kollock and Smith (1999) contrasted the 'push' media of e-mail (messages are sent to people without them necessarily doing anything) and the 'pull' media of BBSs, where people must select groups and messages that they want to read and actively request them. The Usenet is the largest of these conferencing systems and carries thousands of newsgroups. A new site joins the Usenet simply by finding any existing site that is willing to pass along a copy of the collection of messages it receives. No one owns Usenet newsgroups in most cases, and they have no central authority. Almost anyone can read the contents of a Usenet newsgroup, create new newsgroups or contribute to an existing one. This in turn makes the Usenet a different social space from that which is possible in the offline world. In the sense in which we are interested here, E-groups are similar proprietary structures, although access may be limited to 'members'.

3 Chat rooms. These differ from e-mail and BBSs in that they allow for synchronous communication. People can chat in real time by sending text messages to one another. Such chat on the Internet is organised around 'channels', which are also referred to as rooms. The majority of chat systems support a great number of these channels dedicated to a wide array of topics. Text chat uses a centralised server that gives the server owner control over access to the system and to particular channels. Commercial systems are often 'policed' by staff or appointed volunteers. Non-commercial systems, such as IRC (Internet Relay Chat), have owners who can eject people from the channel, control who enters it and restrict membership. Chat rooms may also have 'owners' or more commonly one or more operators, who can monitor and control chat room activity. However, chat networks also allow for private one-to-one communication, which is both unmonitored and uncontrollable by external agents. Chat rooms may also include visual imagery through video-conferencing protocols, such as CuSeeMe. A real-time moving image from a camera on one computer

is transmitted via a server to other computers on the same network. As in IRC channels, communication can also be private, with direct communication between computers without the use of an intermediary server. Using these protocols, visual communication may be supplemented by either voice or text transmissions. In effect, video-conferencing protocols such as CuSeeMe and networks such as ICII are effectively visual versions of tex-chat protocols, with similar capacities, although bandwidth constraints limit the numbers on any one server channel, and also visual quality.

4 MUDs. Multi-User Domains or Dungeons (MUDs) attempt to combine a sense of physical place with face-to-face interaction. This is achieved through 'rooms', which are textually constructed but which are detailed enough to provide a real sense of physical space. Wood and Smith (2001) suggested that MUDs are an effort towards text-based virtual realities in which participants interact with an environment, objects and other participants. Everything about the MUD is invented, although it is rule-governed by the administering program. Curtis (1997) suggested that the virtual reality of MUDs is a social phenomenon, and he identified three factors that distinguish MUDs from other simulations:

(a) they do not have a predetermined end goal. MUDs are ongoing adventures unlike video games that have a final goal;
(b) MUDs allow users to add to the richness of the environment by contributing new spaces and artifacts that become an ongoing part of the administrating program;
(c) they typically have more than one user connected at any given time, and all communication is synchronous, in real time.

MUDs are typically owned by the individual or group that provides the hardware, software and technical know-how to maintain the system. Such owners are often referred to as 'Gods'. They can delegate power to other selected people (Wizards) and grant other users greater access to the system, allowing them to build larger and more elaborate virtual spaces and objects.

5 World Wide Web. Often abbreviated to WWW or 'the Web', this is increasingly becoming an access point for other forms of computer-mediated communication. People can access their e-mails, look up newsgroup messages or enter a chat room through the World Wide Web. Access is through a browser, which is a program that downloads instructions taken from the Internet and displays them on the desktop computer as text, images, animation and sounds. Typical examples of such browsers are Netscape Navigator™ and Microsoft® Internet Explorer. Wood and Smith (2001) suggested that, 'the Web also possesses communicative properties based on its technological abilities and the social practices that have emerged through the use of it. One of the rhetorical effects of the Web has been the ways in which the globally accessible messages posted to it address particular audiences' (14). Different audiences can be targeted in different ways, and because it can integrate images and sounds, it can be a

> more intuitive and a potentially richer context for communication on the Internet. BBSs and various forms of chat facility (including video conferencing) can all be accessed through web browsers.

All of these are predominantly text-based media, but there is a growing potential for richer forms of sound and visual communication through the various forms of video conferencing, and other visual and auditory media formats.

THE DEBATE ABOUT COMMUNITY

While there is evidence that a strong sense of 'groupness' does emerge regularly on the Internet, there is continuing debate as to whether these aggregations of people can be called communities. McLaughlin *et al.* (1998) suggested that such virtual collectives might be more properly characterised as 'pseudo-communities', as they are not networks of primary interpersonal relationships but rather of impersonal associations integrated via a mass medium. In part, the debate is influenced by traditional definitions of community, which are based on the sense of relatedness and shared experiences among people living in the same locality. Such definitions require shared proximity as well as a degree of common experience and interests. However, spatial or temporal proximity of communicants is almost never part of computer-mediated communication over the Internet. Wood and Smith (2001) questioned the assumption that community is geographically bound and that the people who share a community must interact face to face,

> In more recent times, chatting is still a popular pastime, but many people's conception of what makes a community has changed. A community might now consist of a data laden Information Superhighway; pharmaceutical advice is dispensed on an electronic bulletin board; and the neighbour you feel closest to could be half a world away in Australia. (109)

Watson (1998) has suggested that instead of emphasising geographical proximity, we should look to preserve the connection between communication and community, as without ongoing communication amongst its participants, a community dissolves. Neighbourhood and kinship ties are only a portion of people's overall community networks, because cars, planes and 'phones can maintain relationships over long distances. Again, the emphasis is on a move from defining community in terms of space to defining it in terms of social networks (Wellman *et al.*, 1988). Watson (1998) suggested that 'We should begin thinking of community as a product not of shared space, but of shared *relationships* among people' (120).

Within a more traditional definition of community, relationships among people carry with them a sense of stake or obligation to that community (Postman 1993). A criticism of the term 'virtual community' is that online collectives do not contain the stake that exists in offline or real communities, and lack the consequences of not meeting or participating in the common obligation of that community. For example, Postman suggests that community involves living amongst people with whom we may disagree strongly, but with whom we continue to communicate for the purposes of meeting our common obligations. However, Internet groups are mainly formed out of common interest, not obligation. From this point of view, therefore, at the heart of the concept of community is the concept of commonality (Fernback 1999). Wood and Smith (2001) therefore argued that 'Virtual communities thus allow people to transcend geographic boundaries and unite with others who share their common interests, whether that's watching a particular television series or buying plastic figures of Charlie Brown and Bugs Bunny' (110).

Rothaermel and Sugiyama (2001) have equally argued that a virtual community is similar to a community of mind described by Tönnies (1967), except 'that it forms through an electronic communication medium and is not bound by space and time' (299). In this it is similar to an organisational community in that it allows for social interaction among its members using a variety of Internet tools, and demonstrates certain community standards and rules. Rothaermael and Sugiyama (2001) concluded that

> Combining content and communication, a virtual community allows people to engage in the exchange of information, and learn from each other and about each other. In the end, communities are not solely about aggregating information or resources, but about bringing people together to meet some of their social, and commercial needs. (299)

Hagel and Armstrong (1997) talked of online communities in terms of their function and how they meet consumer needs. Within this context, they identified four such needs:

1. Communities of interest are formed by individuals with a shared interest, expertise and passion for a wide variety of subjects (anything from rock stars to teapots);
2. Communities of relationships are formed by individuals who express a need to meet and engage with others who have shared similar experiences. Such experiences may often be intense, life-changing events, such as the death of a partner through a particular illness;
3. Communities of transaction have as their focus the exchange of information to facilitate an economic process;
4. Communities of fantasy provide people with the opportunity to explore new identities through enacting fantasy games and exchanges.

The emergence of community online goes hand in hand with the development of the medium itself and in some ways parallels the 'imagined' communities that emerged with the invention of mediated communication. For example, newspapers and television news unite people in a sense of community around a given cause, even when such people are not linked by any geographical location. The terrorist attacks in the United States, on 11 September 2001, were widely reported in all media and brought together very disparate people in a sense of community over what had happened. This included a stake in the protection of that community, which went beyond geographical boundaries. According to Jones (1997), virtual communities distinguish themselves from a simple online gathering when they feature:

1 A minimum level of interactivity – in order for a virtual community to exist, there must be a flow of messages among the participants. If one person were to post a web site and no one were to comment on it, there would be no basis for a virtual community. The community comes from interactivity amongst participants.
2 A variety of communicators – more than two contributors need to join the conversation for a community to arise. Virtual communities are enhanced by the variety of people who participate and the contribution they make.
3 Common public space – virtual communities still need to identify with a cyberplace. Jones (1997) suggested that these are the forums in which the community participants most regularly engage in communication. In the early days of computer-mediated communication, BBSs were the place where individuals went to post and read messages. Today, chat rooms serve the same purpose, but allow people to interact in real time rather than in delayed messages.
4 A minimum level of sustained membership – one visit or a simple exchange does not constitute membership in a virtual community. Rather, those who form the community have relationships to one another that are perpetuated through time.

The sense of community brings with it privileges and responsibilities if it is to be maintained. In some ways, this is similar to the concept of Postman's (1993) obligation or stake. However, people access the Internet at all sorts of different levels, and it may be better to relate some engagement to the notion of gain with minimum of expenditure or commitment. For example, most of us have used the Internet as a source of information, be it about flight times or a rare disease. McLaughlin *et al.* (1998) argued that hyper-linking technology facilitates the search for resources such that consumers may prefer to hop from site to site rather than incur any interpersonal expense. Where consumers can gain benefits without expenditure, there may be little or no incentive to reciprocate communication.

> even those who do take a moment to sign a 'guestbook' (an electronic form soliciting information from the visitor) or answer a questionnaire may be engaging in an act more closely akin to tossing a quarter in a box marked 'donations' next to a stack of free newspapers than contributing to the store of community resources. (148)

Therefore, for a community to exist there have to be sufficient people who engage with each other, who occupy a common space and who are prepared to expend energy to sustain relationships. Hauben (1997) talked of such people as 'netizens', and suggested that true netizens distinguish themselves through active contributions to the development of a sustained community.

> Netizens are the people who actively contribute online towards the development of the Net. These people understand the value of collective work and the public aspects of public communications. These are the people who actively discuss and debate topics in a constructive manner, who e-mail answers to people and provide help to new-comers, who maintain FAQ files and other public information repositories, who maintain mailing lists and so on. These are the people who discuss the nature and role of this new communications medium . . . Netizens are people who decide to make the Net a regenerative and vibrant community and resource.

Clearly, not everyone who visits a virtual community is a netizen. Wood and Smith (2001) cited some specific terminology to designate non-participants, who clearly do not fulfil the requirements for netizen status. These include the surfer (an infrequent and detached visitor); lurkers (who are present but offer no comment or contribution); and privateers (people who use the net for profit). They do not qualify because of their selfish, rather than selfless, use of technology.

Wellman and Gulia (2000) suggested that virtual communities may resemble real-life communities in the sense that support is available to its members, often in specialised relationships. Netizens are, however, distinctive in that they provide information, support, companionship and a sense of belonging to people that they hardly know offline, or who are total strangers. Such relationships online are similar to those developed in real-life communities, in that they are intermittent, specialised and varying in strength. They differ from real-life communities, however, in the basis upon which participants perceive their relationships to be intimate. As we considered earlier, such relationships are much more likely to be premised on shared interests, rather than on the basis of shared social characteristics such as age, social class, ethnicity, life-cycle stage, and other aspects of social background. However, the bag and baggage of the latter are part of the offline world that inevitably leaks into the online. Wellman and Gulia (2000) conceptualised virtual communities as 'glocalised', in that they are simultaneously more global and more local. Global connectivity de-emphasises the importance of locality for community, but at the same time people using the Internet are usually based at their own home, 'the most local environment imaginable, when they connect with their virtual communities' (187).

However, not all virtual collectives survive as communities. Falk (1998) distinguished between robust and ephemeral Internet communities. A robust community is composed of a stable membership that shares common ideals, experiences and a sense of interrelatedness. These members also believe that membership of their community will allow them to move towards achieving their objectives to a greater extent than through membership of another community. Members will gain emotional and intellectual support from the community, associate it with their ideals and aspirations, and will make an investment in terms of personal resources. This is in contrast to an ephemeral community which is seen to be transitory, changes rapidly and allows only for the formation of partial relationships, which fail to satisfy most of the members. Interaction is chaotic, and there is conflict in views about where they fit within the larger, historical perspective.

MANAGING A COMMUNITY

Even with the anarchy that is the Internet, communities that survive are bound by strategies that aid their management. McLaughlin *et al.* (1995) located community in the emergence of standards of conduct, many of which are peculiarly applicable to the electronic medium and which are aimed towards the preservation of the group. As suggested by Ostrom (1990), the problem relates to how a group of people can organise and govern themselves to obtain collective benefits, when the temptation to 'free ride and break commitments are substantial'. McLaughlin *et al.* (1995) suggested that concern for community is evidenced in reproachful communication to participants who behave in ways that threaten the well-being of the community. Strategies for management of virtual spaces with respect to issues of power and control, authority, dominance and submission have evolved. These include human and non-human agents, such as moderators and Webmasters, list-servers and cancelbots, which serve as gatekeepers, adjudicators, and imposers of sanctions for misconduct (Donath 2000). In part, managing such a community is aided by overtly giving information to both new and old members of a community about what are the standards of that community. In a way, this comes as no surprise as the subtle social cues available in the offline world are rarely present on the Internet. Wallace (2001) discussed this in the context of 'newbies' (those new to a given community or cyberplace), 'When you enter a chat channel with an ambiguous but intriguing name like #Elysium, you may not realize that the group is actually a vampire role-play and you will be kicked and banned if you violate the masquerade' (65). To help such newcomers avoid the embarrassment of misreading the community, many Internet sites offer guides about appropriate behaviour on the Net (netiquette), which are remarkably similar to the rules of etiquette seen in most conventional societies. Sometimes special information is offered that applies to specific groups or communities. For example, many Usenet newsgroups have FAQs (frequently asked questions) that explain the purpose of the group and the rules for participating. In some locations these are very explicit, and infringement of such rules may result in being banned from that channel by the channel operator. 'The owners of many chat channels, for example, warn in their titles that you will be kicked out if you are simultaneously chatting on some channel they find reprehensible, such as #snuffsex or #incest' (Wallace 2001: 65). Because common interests largely drive online communities, they are often polarised in the way agreement or dissent is expressed. Such group polarisation may be a function of the fact that on the Internet you will be able to find people with common interests, who think the way that you do, no matter what it is that you have in common. Such polarisation inevitably gives rise on occasion to conflict.

Smith (2000) discussed features of Internet communities that make conflict more likely and more difficult to manage than in real communities. These include wide cultural diversity; disparate interests, needs and expectations; the nature of electronic participation (anonymity, multiple avenues of entry, poor reliability of connections, and so forth); text-based communication; and power asymmetry. For those who behave in a way that is unacceptable to the community's standards, regulations have evolved to counter, curb or simply eliminate the offender. Maltz (1996) discussed the ways in which offenders can be sanctioned. These include chiding the offender through harassing responses; obstructing the offender's access to information; interfering with that person's ability to use the medium effectively. Donath (2000), in the context of identity and deception, gave an example of how software can be used to sanction a person who has been behaving inappropriately within a community by posting offending or defamatory messages. Killfiles are filters that allow a person to skip unwanted postings, such that if a person is put on a killfile, that individual will not see their postings again. Those using a killfile no longer see the offending messages and are not tempted to respond, thus lowering the number of angry or off-topic postings. To the person who has been killfiled, 'Usenet becomes a corridor of frustratingly shut doors: one can shout, but cannot be heard' (52). The killfile program looks for the account name in the header, which is usually inserted automatically by the posting software.

Central to the notion of community and its management, is trust. Ba (2001) defined trust in terms of three central characteristics: reliability, predictability and fairness.

1 The exchange partner is expected to be credible in such a way that their word or promise can be relied on;
2 The exchange partner will behave in ways that equitably protect the welfare of both parties;
3 The exchange partners are dedicated to reciprocating the obligations and commitments between them under an environment of uncertainty and vulnerability.

While Ba's (2001) theoretical analysis is in the context of commercial exchange, it remains valuable when considering the importance of trust in paedophile communities. While such communities are not driven by commercial considerations, the nature of the products that are exchanged (both text and pictures) requires a high level of trust between parties.

CREATING A COMMUNITY

Communities arise spontaneously on the Internet when a group of likeminded people share a commitment to set standards about their communication which is maintained over time. However, communities can also be artificially created. Wood and Smith (2001) gave an example of one company who have gone to considerable lengths to appeal to people's desire to feel that they are part of a community when online: 'GeoCities (http://www.geocities.com/), who provides subscribers with free computer storage space for their personal web pages in exchange for displaying advertising banners, uses the community metaphor in both its language and imagery' (116). People who register with GeoCities are called 'homesteaders', and when registering for space to post their pages, are asked to choose from over forty different 'neighbourhoods'. Such neighbourhoods are designed to match people with similar interests. Early on in its creation, GeoCities attempted to use visual cues to create a sense of proximity. People registering would tour a virtual suburb, looking for properties that were marked 'vacant'. GeoCities has its own community rules to help in managing conflict and to promote a sense of peaceableness. Wood and Smith (2001) suggested that this has been achieved through a sort of virtual community watch, where community members are seen as guardians of their content guidelines. Members are encouraged to use a standardised form (GeoCities Content Violation Reporting Form) to report offences such as pornography, piracy and profanity, so that the offending sites can be disciplined and, where it becomes necessary, shut down. The sense of community has been purposefully enhanced by GeoCities through the appointment of individuals to act as community leaders. Such people are responsible for assisting newcomers in the production of their pages, organising communal events, and offering awards for outstanding design skills. GeoCities works very hard to 'make people feel at home', no doubt because this meets people's need to belong, increases the likelihood of commitment and sustained engagement and through this offers the perfect medium for promoting advertisements.

VIRTUAL PAEDOPHILE COMMUNITIES

We will now turn our attention to some of the ways in which people with a sexual interest in children form communities on the Internet. To this end, we will consider in some detail one study arising out of the COPINE project which sought to examine the evidence of community in the context of one bulletin board (BBS2), which is dedicated to child pornography and/or child sex interests (Linehan *et al.*, 2002). The study focused on the process through which people learn different ways of participating in a virtual community, and how virtual space offers multiple shifting identity positions rather than static roles. The data reported in this study were gathered from two sources, but we will focus on the first of these. The first source was an Internet bulletin board site (BBS2), which was logged onto, monitored, and from which the ensuing discussions between participants were downloaded. A total of 120 hours of interaction on the bulletin board were analysed discursively (Wetherell 1998). The second strand of data was gathered through interviews with two convicted paedophiles who had used the Internet as part of their offence. This again was analysed within the same framework. The analysis involved searching for patterns, a concern with function, and openness to alternative readings and to what was not said.

One of the first issues explored was to what extent interactions on BBS2 constituted a 'virtual community'. Two patterns emerged from the data that would support the notion that participation on BBS2 could be usefully described as a 'virtual community'. The first of these related to evidence of group dynamics, and there were two particular themes that were associated with this. These related to differing member status on BBS2, and member concerns with protecting both themselves and the board from infiltrators. Both from the evidence of progressing status within the group, and from the distinction made between 'us' and 'them' (possible infiltrators), there emerged the sense that this group, at least for some of its members, represented a community to which they belong.

Members posting to the board often referred to different types of participant, reflected in terms such as newbies (new members), wise ones, or regulars. These terms are frequently seen in other contexts on the Internet. In relation to this particular study, the aim was to examine the kinds of knowledge or activity that members associated with high or low status. As Linehan *et al.* (2002) suggested, the distinction between high and low status is a rather gross one and in reality there is a fluid, rather than simple, dichotomy. The theme of member status was often linked to interactions involving challenges to, or attempts to establish, credibility. It was also linked to information-seeking activities. For example, showing respect to a wise one may be a good way of getting information while at the same time acknowledging their higher status.

In the following extract, 'Icarus' (all members use an alias or nickname when interacting on the board) expressed dissatisfaction with the board and recommended that it be closed down:

> All the regs are gone. All here is left is 'wannabe members of Pu even I have never posted anything'. Board is full of newbies who don't know anything and certainly will not post anything. I've been around years and seems that this is the end of this board. Only technical chat, newbies and spammers left. Don't bother to ask what i had posted just try to remember.

'Icarus' accounted for his dissatisfaction in terms of absence of regulars and the predominance of newbies on the board. Newbies have low value or status because of their lack of knowledge and posting activity. This theme of newbies and low status was echoed in many other contributions to the board. In the following example, 'Sleeper' supports the board through reference to the 'wise ones from the past', who presumably add to the status of the board:

> *Sleeper>icarus: Abit Harsh don't you Think? There's Always Hope. And there are Still 'Wise Ones' from the Past Here (Different Nick's) if you would Look>Take Care.

From contributions across the data in this study a sense was gained of different status accorded to participants within the community. Members were given value on the basis of:

1 Their frequency and quality of 'on-topic' postings. Members often made requests either for new child pornography or for a particular picture to fill a gap in an existing collection. Those members who could provide either new pictures or 'fills' gained status among participants on BBS2.
2 Having technical and/or security expertise. Many of the discussions on BBS2 involved technical or security topics. Members often gave or requested information on the latest hardware or on good encryption devices. Status was gained through sharing information, thus demonstrating expertise on the technical aspects of accessing, downloading and storing child pornography. Given the nature of their activities, concerns about security were also prevalent in their discussions, and knowing how to evade detection was also a route to gaining status.
3 Finally, credibility was gained through the duration of the participation on the board.

The further pattern that emerged from the data related to concerns about security. This was not surprising given the illegal nature of the board's activities. A common theme in relation to this was how to protect the board from infiltrators. There were different types of infiltrator: those who erased sites; the police; and other watchdog types who may lurk on BBS or seek to catch members in the 'real' world. The following posting from 'Gandalf' highlights some of the commonly expressed concerns about safety and security, in particular the degree to which posts through proxy servers could be traced:

> *Gandalf: If I post the url to a site here using a proxy server what likelihood is there of the cops requesting the logs of a company in the Far East or a European university to see who I really am?! The site I put up I did at an Internet café so even if the proxy-stuff fails nobody could prove it was me (I didn't notice any cctv cameras!). But if I put the url here how much effort will be made to trace the real me down and destroy me?

'Gandalf' saw the police as a problem, and he was afraid of being exposed. His concern with maintaining anonymity and the consequences of being caught was shared by many members of the board, and can be seen in the following:

> *Pirra8>I really feel that the fact that we don't post much is because we have a lot of diligent 'observers' that watch what we put up, and quickly tell the

> servers to pull the site. It is tough spending 2–5 hours posting, only to have it pulled in 10 minutes. What is the solution? Where is there a site that will allow posts? Do we need a secret 'club' that will allow you to get files? News is very easy to post and download from. Maybe we should concentrate on using news, and leave web sites go to h*ell? This board can still be useful in that case. But, a revision of policy has to be done gradually. I really see no alternative. Pirra8- the number 8 pirate.

'Pirra8's contribution was in the context of a discussion about the status of the board and the problem identified was the speed at which pornography pictures are pulled from sites. While many security concerns reflected personal identity, here there is evidence about the importance of the material posted and the amount of time and effort involved. Associated with this was the suspicion that some of the extreme pictures posted (for example, rape or torture images) were really posted by the police to alienate members. An example of this can be seen in the following posting:

> *flatgirls>Torture? Can anyone else (besides dark lurker) see the techniques of LE on this board? The idea is to spread doubt about the morality of this hobby of ours . . . anyone who asks for l*litorture, etc is looking to dissuade casual visitors with the impression that we are a bunch of child killers . . . I'm with you dark lurker . . . and Smile . . . this won't work on anyone who has taken Psych101 . . . change your nick and try something else!!!

The posting from 'flatgirls' appeared to fulfil a number of functions: it warned members about possible infiltrators on BBS2; it attempted to set boundaries and what was acceptable material for posting; and it functioned to portray the group as having morals.

A second strand of data supported the idea of BBS2's being a psychologically salient community for its members. Many of the messages posted made explicit reference both to the status of the board and to the kind of learning environment it provided for its members. Both of these themes suggested that some members at least were sufficiently engaged with the board activities for it to constitute a community for them. Members actively reflected on the board, what it was doing and how it could be improved. 'Icarus's message about closing down the board prompted a number of replies. The following posting came from 'Necrolord':

> *Necrolord>Close this board down?! What are you nuts, icarus?! This board is the best place for all us pervs to communicate with each other and share thoughts, opinions and information on the subject we all luv! (but are afraid to admit!) And I'm sure all the regulars are still lurking around, cuz theres no better place other than the newsgroups. And like Sleeper says 'theres still hope' that this board will be back better than ever! Only time will tell . . . So please icarus, don't be so pessimistic and hope for the best!!!

'Necrolord' supported the continuation of the board, describing its utility in terms of the opportunity to communicate around a topic of importance. The board also derived status from still having regular members 'lurking around', as these were people who were more likely to have technical expertise and pornography collections.

Overall, the criteria used by members to assess the value of the board included:

1 the presence of regulars or wise ones (who could post child pornography or who gave advice);
2 the quality and frequency of on-topic postings;
3 the development of newbies to ensure further secure postings.

While the quality and security of posts was linked to the presence of regulars, there was also evidence that new members could profit from BBS2 as a learning or apprenticeship environment. Such an environment then stresses the importance of teaching newcomers and is illustrated in the following statement by 'HeLLioN':

> *HeLLioN>Hey Icarus, thanx for the contributions but think about even you get something or other from this board, the newbies will get their share, will collect the oldies pix and get knowledge about how to protect themselves this is the main reason for this board make the newbies grows wise and increase our community then this seed will return in for of new posts like the ones you do, that's the way.

This notion of apprenticeship is seen in a number of ways, such as asking advice from the 'wise ones', who were of higher status:

> Is there a way I can crack/recover omega zip disk which I read/write protected with a password. Any help from the wise ones? Thank you in advance.

Examples were also seen in participants referring to themselves as a 'stupid ignorant newbie like me' or by making explicit reference to their newness, 'am very new to this and need advice'. Such requests usually were answered, and often information would be posted by other participants directing newcomers to specific sites where they might obtain useful information. This information was not only directed towards newcomers, but also served to heighten security awareness and knowledge within the group.

Linehan *et al.* went on to examine how, given their 'deviant' status within society, members of BBS2 legitimised their interest in child pornography and their own identities as paedophiles. The most common ways of accounting for and legitimising members' interests and identities included making comparisons with groups outside the BBS2 community and justifying activities in terms of promoting the maintenance and development of the group. Members positioned themselves as being the victims of oppression and intolerance, with others (such as police, general public, and Internet Service Providers) all attempting to oppress members' rights to pursue their interest in child pornography. This was given emphasis by comparisons between their situation and that of the civil or gay rights movements. This clearly attempted to place the rights of paedophiles alongside more socially acceptable movements, and to suggest that over time their rights will be acknowledged and accepted. A similar ploy is seen when participants drew on discourses of citizenship and rights to justify their activities:

> *Fresca>Gandalf>Normally, you have to bring attention to yourself. Millions surf the Net in all types of content. ISP's or Mr.LEA are only interested in those who originate illegal material. The 2nd amendment is what keeps the InterNet going. Just abide by the limits. Good luck.

Other research, in the context of the Internet and adult sexual interest in children, has supported this notion of community. Jenkins (2001) talked of those who use Internet child pornography as being members of a subculture, as they possess a huge corpus of specialised knowledge, but in this context without direct face-to-face contact. Jenkins suggested that such communities are made up of highly deviant individuals who in most cases operate as loners, never having personal contact with another deviant. He gives evidence to show that such people communicate through nicknames, concealing identity and location, and that any suggestion of contact is usually met with derision. Jenkins (2001) gave an example of postings to support this:

> *Stupid>what the hell . . . sure why not. We could start a club, maybe next door to the Girl Scouts? Nice neon sign in the window: 'Pedo Trade Meeting Every Friday at 5pm – bring the kids, we have on-site child care'??!! Why would you *want* to meet anyone? Enjoy the anonymous camaraderie . . . don't push your luck.

He emphasised that members do have intense associations, but that these take place electronically. He also suggested that 'child porn networks really do not demonstrate the sort of hierarchy or division of labor required for teams and formal organizations' (90). However, there is evidence from the COPINE interviews that in fact some members do move from electronic contacts to offline contacts, and that there is indeed a hierarchy of relationships (as demonstrated above), although these may not exactly replicate those seen in the 'real world'. These are issues that we will discuss in more detail later in this chapter.

Jenkins's (2001) research on BBS postings suggested clear evidence that such communities maintain unity and solidarity through shared interests and passions, rather than any commercial 'nexus', with some participants maintaining boards out of their own pocket, as a public service to the community. He suggested that, in a similar way to other subcultures, this world is characterised by a specialised knowledge and language that sets it apart from the mainstream. Again, the emphasis is on the acquisition of knowledge and skills which will allow for the search for newer and more desirable pictures and videos, but which will also ensure some basic security for board members. The issue of a specialist language is a feature of computer newsgroups and BBSs, with words such as 'lurker' and 'newbie', but as Jenkins indicated, the community interested in child pornography has its own special terms. For example, boards will often discuss whether material is on-topic or off-topic, which makes reference to whether the pictures are images of a child (sometimes referred to, in the case of girls, as loli) or pornographic pictures of adult women. As well as having shared interests, knowledge, language and codes of behaviour, such communities also demonstrate structure. Linehan *et al.*'s study (2002) demonstrated how respect is accorded to knowledgeable and experienced individuals, who have either operated and survived for many years or who have gained respect through posting the 'best' pictures. Jenkins (2001) gave a quote from one of the boards which clearly demonstrated this hierarchy, '"Logical progression is: newbie, lurker, regular, chat member, poster, newsgroup poster, trader, wise one. Takes about a year to get to be a wise one. After that you might get to be Admin, create your own paysite, or become an underworld guru"' (94). Clearly there not only exists a hierarchy, but there is opportunity for progression through the hierarchy that is dependent not on attributes such as education or social position (although having the financial means to buy sufficiently good hardware and software is relevant), but through acquisition of specialised knowledge and pictures.

COMMUNITIES WITHIN COMMUNITIES

It would appear that for those with a sexual interest in children, the Internet provides a sense of community that can be related to on multiple levels. For some people, the Internet is a resource, a means of obtaining desired objects (pictures, fantasy stories, videos) from other likeminded people. The illicit nature of such material means that the person has to take one step inside that community to find the right language and skills to gain access, but need not communicate in any other way. This is demonstrated in the following extract from the COPINE interviews (initials refer to individual respondents; numbers to transcript location):

> Yeah but I didn't want to get caught . . . at it. I know people get prosecuted for trading pictures and I didn't want to get prosecuted for that . . . I keep it within my own four walls . . . and I'm quite happy looking. (DX: 16)

But even looking required some level of skill and knowledge:

> and he says well what you have to use you have to use this programme called turnpike and I says well how do you use it so . . . because the turnpike was his programme it logged onto his . . . his his server that he'd got . . . so I used

> we I used his programme to log onto his server with his passwords and everything then he was showing me that the pictures weren't downloaded off . . . off websites none of none of the pictures were sort of I didn't go searching through the web looking for different sites on the web they were all off newsgroups. (OC: 16)

Such passive community membership clearly does not qualify the person to be a 'netizen'. While there is passion about the products, and possibly about the process of engagement with the Internet, it does not carry with it 'sufficient human feeling, to form webs of personal relationships in cyberspace' (Rheingold 1993). In fact, for many people the fears about safety and the feelings of social discomfort about meeting others on the Internet appear to be sufficient reasons to stop further communication:

> the more people tend to be there the less I tend to be myself and the more I tend to be the clown so that's like you know basically the mask you put on rather than be you know thinking you know you're in any kind of danger stick a mask on so I think cos so when you're in a chat room or something you know I mean OK there might only be a hundred people logged on but a hundred people is a lot of people. (TS: 29)

What then moves people from being passive participants to being active communicators within these communities? The ability to trade material, as opposed to simply downloading from BBSs or Web pages, means that the person has more control over the material available to them, and ultimately this is reflected in the quality of their collection:

> the channel flourished . . . we had a fairly large group of people that met with each other to trade pictures. (QH: 16)

However, trading images for some participants was not the sole function of the community but became a vehicle for new friendships:

> I mean it wasn't all just sex. You didn't just come on and say 'are you trading'. I mean some people did . . . some people didn't want to be your friend. (EI: 106)

The importance of such friendships must be emphasised, for in a tightly knit community there is a need to be able to trust the other individuals. Members of such communities may not expose themselves through face-to-face introductions, but they reveal a lot about themselves through: their collections; asking and giving advice; sharing personal information; sharing fantasies and 'real-life' accounts; and through the very medium by which they communicate – text. Communities clearly exist within communities, with ever more secret and complex layers of security to protect the respective members. As previously discussed, such communities have many of the qualities seen in the offline world. One example of such a community is that of wØnderland, which received such extensive coverage in the press. wØnderland was composed of a group of people, many of whom called themselves paedophiles, who were interested in trading pornographic images of children. They came from a wide range of countries and were equally diverse in terms of age and socio-economic background. They communicated with each other through IRC (Internet Relay Chat), and Jenkins (2001) suggested that there were approximately two hundred members in over forty countries. The following quotations are drawn from interviews with two senior members of this community, and are used to illustrate how wØnderland can be conceived of as a community within a community.

wØnderland demonstrated a clear hierarchy, in that there was an identifiable figure associated with its founding, and a number of 'ops' (operators) who were responsible for policing the channel:

> a guy called Harry Mudd who was one of the . . . [mm] what we call senior ops he was there right not right from the beginning but from early days [mm] he he's sort a like seniority cos he'd been there longer than most most people [mm] an some people had been what we called founders had actually founded the channel [mm] right when the Internet first started and [mm] IRC first started. They'd actually left an of course he'd ended up in charge. (EI: 63)

The community had a clear set of rules (not always adhered to or enforced) about the purpose of the channel, its 'moral boundaries', and who was allowed to join. QH, as a senior member of the community, was self-appointed in determining the 'ideology' or 'philosophy' of the group:

> one not law enforcement and two not hurting the not hurting any kids [mm]. That was like the underlying rule in the channels that I would lay there for them and run so to speak was a [mm] nobody that came in was . . . hurting their kids or hurting any kids [mm]. That we were all just looking and that's it [mm]. It was a it was a voyeur a voyeur [mm] philosophy type of thing [mm]. (QH: 8)

> The whole philosophy that I had was let's meet with each other or one paedo to another we can socialise with each other, we can get the pics that are already freely available we can trade them we can look at them but we don't touch any kids [mm] ever. (QH: 8)

> Well when we were actually running the channels if you wanted to be a member of the group you you just popped into the channel an [mm] started trading and if you traded correctly [mm] n you didn't F-Serve [mm] and you

> didn't abuse other users [mm] an you didn't trade crap basically [mm] an you didn't trade snuff or anything that showed kids actively being hurt [mm] then eventually we we'd end up voicing him more or less? [okay] as a trustworthy trader an that was pretty much how you joined the group but when we went into the secret channels we only invited the best traders there [mm] people we knew were trustworthy we knew weren't [mm] weren't cops or anything [mm] and we knew had collections. (El: 65)

While trading pictures of children was seen as the core activity of the group, the relationships formed online were also important, both because they allowed for the acquisition of other desirable goods (new computer stuff), and also because they fostered a sense of fellowship:

> I got almost I got . . . more satisfaction from actually just interacting with my fellow paedoph fellow paedophiles [mm] and just finding new new computer stuff to putz around with [mm] thaaan that I did actually looking at the pictures [mm]. (QH: 12)

The importance of being liked and having prestige within the community is clearly evident, and was one of the motives for moving the community to a more secure setting:

> I wanted people to like me. I've always been like that I've always wanted people to like me . . . Anyway I got to know the channel ops [mm]. Eventually . . . they made me an operator of the channel but right after they made me an operator there was part of the culture in the online paedophile community is that there might always be a bust so to speak [mm] and some of the more unstable people in our community they start bust rumours just to get everybody crazy [mm] so to speak. And (coughs) . . . they . . . started a rumour that the whole channel a a on the net was being monitored by the Dutch police [mm]. A rumour that later turned out to be completely untrue [mm]. Am so they moved the channel over to Downnet under a different name and right after that one of the original channels found there's a guy named Zipper came back and asked me if I wanted to start another channel [mm]. I said yes cos I jumped at the chance cos it would give me prestige in this new found so called community that I had that was there. (QH: 13)

Securing the channel required a greater level of technological sophistication, and correspondingly a higher level of investment in the community. The acquisition of knowledge came through socialising with other members of the community, many of whom (like Zipper) appeared to have a very fluid relationship with the channel:

> the thing that was more important to me was the actual socialising [mm] that was the important thing to me [mm]. He said do you want to start a channel

> with me. I said yes. Aaa we tried keeping the channel and then this third person aaa became known as ZZZ Z E E [mm] aaa came and said listen I have a a robot user that will hold the channel down for you [mm] You may have heard the term egg drop bots [mm] which is basically a program that when you run a a it looks like a user name on IRC [mm]. Well it's actually a robot that can hold the channel down for you and do all [mm] sorts of stuff and what not. Am we brought we bought the the robot in and then Zipper disappeared leaving me to run the channel. (QH: 14)

The people who sought to be members of the inner circle that was wØnderland had already been identified by themselves and others as being sexually interested in children. Moving from the periphery only took place when the person had proved themselves to be trustworthy:

> People would join the channel if they hung out for awhile we got to talking [mm] and they would eventually become quote unquote part of the circle [mm]. Again this wasn't a group like a group that would meet in real life and that would produce pictures and whatnot [mm] this was just am (tapping the desk) . . . people that were already into it. It's kind of like you don't become gay by going in a gay bar. You already are [mm] you just go into the bar so to speak. [mm] (QH: 16)

Central to this community was the ability to protect its members from law enforcement agencies, and it achieved this by moving from a channel identified with paedophile material to one that allowed them effectively to remain hidden:

> It was tight it was very strong am the channel flourished a eventually we started noticing that this would be like the beginning 96 we started realising that law enforcement was starting to notice us cos this I think was about the time that the Orchid Club [mm] nonsense started am . . . weeee . . . moved the channel first to a non paedo, cos this channel had a paedo name [mm] to a non paedo named channel. [what was the channel name?] Kid and pre sex pics [mm]. Am . . . This was am we moved it to a non paedo named channel called LOL. [mm] Still on Undernet [mm] Erm we stayed there. [Was the LOL?] Laughing Out Loud [okay]. LOL was also the name [mm] one of the more faa was also short for Lolita. [The Lolita series?] The Lolita the Lolita magazines. [okay] Actually there was actually a magazine called Lolita that was out in the seventies [mm]. Am . . . and . . . then for awhile we moved to this non descript am IRC net called aa Web Chat [mm] which was like very . . . This this was one my quote unquote more brilliant a manoeuvres because a Web Chat dot org was actually a very very how shall we say Christian . . . IRC net and I figure what better place to hide it. (17)

Protecting the community meant that it became increasingly closed to new members, as access was through a complex layer of passwords.

> Then we moved the channel to this IRC server [mm] and I was able to implement even tighter security measures and whatnot. I mean nested levels of passwords that you would need [mm] and we started implementing encrypted hard drives very heavily and strongly encrypted hard drives. (QH: 18)

The rules that protected this closed community also became more complex, starting with general rules about not physically meeting other people and rules about behaviours that related to the content of the pictures:

> I never met anybody [mm] on the internet in real life [mm] ever. That was another one that my first that was one of like my very deep rules on internet relay chat the first rule being don't hurt any kids [mm] in any way shape or form no kid is to be harmed [mm]. Rule number two was that this was to remain anonymous. We were never to meet in real life [mm]. Because at that that can lead to that could possibly lead to child molestation's [mm] . . . (QH: 15)

These rules were also positioned within a moral framework – downloading, trading and looking at child pornography was seen as a lesser crime than physically abusing children, and was even presented as a way of preventing child abuse:

> I did have other people write rules and I would amend them [mm]. But again the rules were more for cohesive community. My I I I knew that the community was built around committing a felony [mm] but my philosophy was that hopefully we would commit [a] the lesser sin of transmitting the pics rather than the greater the sin of going out and [mm] molesting children. (QH: 21)

Indeed, should these rules be infringed by, for example, somebody trying to trade pictures of babies or sado-masochistic pictures, then they might be banned from the channel:

> I would warn the user about it. We would give them a three strikes and you were out that means if we caught them a third time they were gone. (QH: 26)

As the community became more secretive and more exclusive, the rules for the channel became increasingly complex and ultimately resulted in a fracturing of the community:

> Well yea he he . . . he had he brought up this weird text file called Da-Constitution? Which had all these rules written down that [mm] people wouldn't be new users wouldn't be invited by anyone but IRC ops [mm] if

> you wanted to invite one [mm] talk to an IRC op it [mm] d the person you want to invite must have at least 10,000 images [mm] and very few duplications and so on [mm] or be a producer an there were all these hundreds of rules an I was like saying 'you're cutting us off from our news base' [mm] and yet there was no talking of vetting [okay] it was like . . . if you wanted to invite someone the IRC op would got and talk to them and that would be it [mm] they would then be invited if they enough images and that that wasn't even secure [okay] an I part partly I blame Harry for us all being arrested simply because of that when we eventually did have another bust up and I I quit I just couldn't take any of the of Harry's shit anymore [mm] an I quit an all of the channel came with me which . . . surprised me [mm]. Amm . . . it shouldn't have really looking back but it did it always surprised me when everyone supported me an [mm] and sided with me in an argument like this an Harry was left on his own [mm] and he blamed me for that afterwards but he set up his own channel he nicked an another close friend of mine called Gary. (EI: 65)

Arguments such as these were a feature of this community and seemed to emphasise the tension between freedom and control within the group. QH uses the metaphor of the channel representing his home, and other individuals choosing to dictate the way things should be within that home:

> what happened was we ended up having a bitch fight in the channel where he kept changing the channel topic to Harry has to apologise to Plato [mm] and I kept changing the channel back and finally I banned him from the channel saying 'this is my house' [mm]. You know it's kind of like you have guests in your house and one of them tells you 'oh you have to move your fireplace to the other side' [mm] you tell them to go to hell [mm] cos it's your house. Whether you're right or wrong is moot point it is your house. Amm the friends that I had the four core friends took his side [mm] and this was despite the fact that I had been a friend to these people. (QH: 20)

The result of this argument was profound and effectively the community fractured, with the oldest member being excluded.

> And basically what they did was one day I went to the server and I found the channel empty. What they had done basically was that they had made another server and secretly without my knowledge moved everybody there . . . leaving me. (QH: 22)

This, however, was not the end of wØnderland, but the beginning of two new but related communities:

> Am . . . and I built another group up [mm] a very even larger and more flourishing one than the last one, the only difference was this one was more

> towards my philosophy of lets just trade pics and that's it [mm]. We might occasionally talk about fantasies that we had but that was it. (QH: 25)

> You know like the community of people the friends that I built up and destroyed and and once again I'm going to keep repeating this I'm not saying it was right or wrong. I'm saying this is what happened [mm]. We found a few and we made more stronger security measures and we got together we formed a little channel one little robot and we I started getting pictures off the newsgroups [mm] and we sort of started trading again. (QH: 29)

In part the community broke up because not all members agreed with the ground rules, and also because there was a jockeying for power within the group. Examples of rule breaking included members of the community meeting each other offline:

> And I ended up telling all my close friends secretly am . . . on am . . . the IRC op notice thing we had which none of the other users could read [mm] we knew that. I said look this guy's talked himself into this, this Caesar he's talked himself into meeting me an [mm] if I if I go off line or start doing funny stuff (short laugh) in the next few minutes then it's not it's a set up it's the cops an you'd better run [okay] for it (laughs). So all my friends were very scared and they were monitoring me al all all the ops were monitoring me. (EI: 69)

In this instance there is a suggestion of a coerced meeting and that there were also fears with regard to the safety of the person involved. However, some meetings appeared to be a product of the relationship moving to new levels of closeness and intimacy:

> And he wanted to m he desperately wanted to meet me [mm] so he invited me up there an he even he was sending the money as well cos it would cost sixty quid on the train [mm] an he sent me sixty quid to get up there [mm]. (EI: 69)

A further example of rule breaking included the production of material, as this clearly involved the actual and current abuse of a child. At least one such member of wØnderland became involved in production and made his photographs available to selected members of the community:

> There was less and less trading going on because a lot of us by now had most of what we were interested in from each [okay] other's collections. And there were very few new people am or producers. I mean Paul was one [mm] and I was one of the few people that he trusted enough to give *everything* that he was making with his kids. (EI: 67)

Within this community, trading reduced as members reached saturation point within their collections. However, the desire for new material remained and gave power and status to people like Paul who were able to make and distribute videos that were of good quality and highly pornographic. Shirky (1995) has suggested that synchronous communication on the Internet promotes a greater sense of community than asynchronicity can: ‘When people use real time chat, they are usually less interested in what’s being discussed than in who is doing the discussing, less interested in text than in the community’ (92). This is clearly demonstrated in wØnderland, where as trading reduced, communication and intensity of relationship increased. This was the case whether or not members went on to meet each other offline:

> It was to me cos I never had that many friends, real friends amm [mm] and suddenly I had hundreds of em [mm] as it were. It was . . . a lot of people who were a a at the very least friends and in some cases *really really* close friends [mm] like brothers, we we called each other brothers cos we felt like we’d we’d been born to be brothers [mm] because we shared such a close view [right] We we seemed plugged into each other’s minds sometimes [mm] we we’d like speak with one voice I mean if somebody was going to say something and they saw that one the other one was speaking [mm] they would stop because they’d know that whatever they wanted to say was being said. (EI: 59)

> They were am . . . it was hard to say them there wasn’t that much of a distinction between an an average normal friend to me and a really close one a brother [mm] but . . . if I had to put a figure on it I’d say there was like 15 or so [mm] an . . . I had a special affection for most of the people in this country [okay] . . . (EI: 62)

> [And were you trading material at that point?]
> On and off but as I got more into running the channels I had less and less opportunity to trade because more and more often I was sorting people’s problems. (EI: 54)

What seems different about these friendships to those achieved offline was a sense of being in control. In part this was a function of anonymity – you can disappear whenever you want to, and there is only a physical presence if you wish there to be. It was also a function of status that was acquired through one’s position on the channel:

> The important part was that I couldn’t be hurt on line [mm]. See on line aa because of my computer knowledge I’m like a God [mm] . . . it it’s kind of like in this room if I wanted to ignore you I can type a command then I won’t

> hear or see you [sure]. On line I can do that [mm]. And one of the reasons why I formed the groups that I formed was because I could selectively get rid of people that I didn't want around. (QH: 66)

> The Internet was basically a way of my building a community to my specifications that I could somewhat control [mm] without actually having any any physical contact with anybody [okay mm]. Just how much I control I had is extremely questionable. (QH: 72)

This semblance of control features in other aspects of community behaviour. The status accorded to operators meant that they could effectively control what was happening within the channel, which went beyond the basic rules of the immediate group and extended to the whole IRC community:

> An then that was IRC war basically. We we . . . three times we got the whole of the Undernet IRC network slow to such a crawl the operators of the network came to us and they cleared out what ever channel we were fighting up they cleared it. (EI: 53)

Control also included the right to include, as well as exclude, people:

> I had a command on the net I could . . . a . . . perform certain commands on them say if there was a a particular trader who we'd discovered a new guy . . . That we could prove that he was worthy . . . of being traded with, he was trustworthy . . . we could actually voice him as well. (EI: 54)

Decisions were also made about the nature of activity in other groups with regard to their appropriateness and aspects of this community almost took on vigilante status, policing the channels and disrupting activity that they saw as immoral.

> It it we had to become organised to survive [mm] and not only that es especially when we were on Undernet we ran the entire paedophile scene [mm] people did not start channels that were talking *openly* about [mm] *actively* abducting an raping an murdering kids [mm] or torturing them [mm] I mean there was some kiddy torture channels an we constantly went into those channels and monitored the conversation under false identities [mm] of those spoofing our IP so that we could we could not be traced back to our own channel [mm] Am . . . we specifically did that so we could check up that these people were were indeed just fantasising. (EI: 64)

What brought this community to an end?

Jenkins (2001) suggested that wØnderland came to an end because 'police found some illegal activity largely through chance and put pressure on accused individuals to act as informants until a wider and much more serious network was identified and wound up' (152). As with other cases, the discovery partly emerged through the identification of a child who was being abused. However, it is also the case that the end of the wØnderland community may simply have marked a transition point for the emergence of another version of the same community. By the time that arrests had been made and the channel had been closed, wØnderland had already been through several cycles of creation. It is unlikely that all the members have been apprehended and there is little evidence to suggest that those who have 'gone underground' are not still actively engaged in similar communities. The nicknames of those who were caught have also entered into the folklore of Internet child pornographers, and such names are now emerging in the newsgroups, presumably borrowed by new traders.

It may be that instability is an inherent feature of communities such as wØnderland. Reid (1998) has argued that some of the reasons that online communities break down are related to the singularity and flexibility of the online personas. In the offline world, people have the capacity to change what aspects of self they choose to present to suit the context in which they are operating. However, there is continuity and coherence in these self-representations that is possibly different to the singularity that is seen online.

> It has been all too easy for virtual communities to encourage multiplicity but not coherence, with each individual persona having a limited, undiversified social range; this cultural schizophrenia makes the virtual community brittle and ill-equipped to evolve with the demand of circumstance. The human body cannot sustain increased growth of undiversified cells: that is cancer. The cultural body also demands diversity and adaptability; all too often these qualities are absent in online communities and thus they fail. (30)

wØnderland adapted to change by becoming increasingly restrictive and by attempting to enforce a hierarchy that was every bit as oppressive as anything in the offline world. The emotional tone of the exchanges in this community were often disinhibited and aggressive, and we can see evidence of this in members 'ganging up against' each other and colluding in the exclusion of the community's most senior member. Reid (1998) used the metaphor of 'Charivari' as a way of understanding the public punishment of members of virtual communities. Charivari was a medieval way of controlling errant members of a community through public ridicule and physical taunting. Yet, as Reid pointed out, such community members invariably had to stay within that community and therefore the sanctions produced some level of individual change. This is not the case on the Internet, where the 'chief concern is to protect the community by reconfirming the solidarity of the remaining members and to expel transgressors' (34). In part the difficulty in managing the community lies in the anonymity of its members. People choose the aspects of themselves that they wish to present, and can manifest themselves as multiple characters or personas. It is possible that this very flexibility reduces the complexity and depth of the people within the community and leads to a fragmentation of the self. The context in which communication takes place encourages serial presentations, a potential cycling through of personas, but in a very superficial way. Such personas have a very limited range, and in the context of wØnderland, made it difficult for the community to adapt to the demands that were made on it. Reid (1998) has suggested that for online communities to survive there has to be flexibility, accountability and persistence. Where communities are built around the exchange and production of illegal products, and the representation of self is part of fantasy, such coherence is unlikely. What is more probable, as we have seen with wØnderland, is that these communities cope with change by splitting and reforming themselves. One possible consequence of this is a succession of communities such as wØnderland.

Chapter 7

The process of collecting

The word 'collecting' is often used to refer to the process through which an individual with a sexual interest in children acquires child pornography material. That same individual is often referred to as a 'collector' of child pornography. We see reference to seized collections in newspapers after an individual has been arrested for possession of child pornography, and the size or qualities of that collection are often emphasised. Sometimes the term collection is used to refer to that which an individual has, which may be little more than an aggregation of items. On other occasions, however, we use the term collection in a more sophisticated way to refer to something more than a simple aggregation, focusing on organised and structured quantities.

This chapter will explore what we mean by collecting generally, and with particular reference to child pornography. As in the case of our discussion of virtual community, collecting refers to a broad concept that goes beyond the confines of the child pornography world. However, an understanding of that broad context will help us to bring into better focus the process of collecting related to child pornography. As part of that exploration, we will identify psychological and social qualities of collecting that are of particular relevance to our understanding of the dynamics of collecting child pornography, both in itself and with reference to the Internet.

WHAT IS COLLECTING

At a very general level, we can define collecting as the selecting, gathering and keeping of objects of subjective value (Muensterberger 1994). This definition emphasises the subjective aspects of collecting, primarily because the intensity of the feelings often attached to what is collected is not always commensurate with its monetary or commercial value. The emotional intensity that is part of collecting behaviour is also seen in the definition given by Belk (1995a), 'the process of actively, selectively, and passionately acquiring and possessing things removed from ordinary use and perceived as part of a set of non-identical objects and experiences'. This is a useful starting-point for our discussion of the role of collecting in child pornography, for it emphasises a number of features of collecting:

1 collecting is a *process*. Its development depends upon what has gone before, and the availability of items to be collected in the future;
2 that process involves *active* and *selective* qualities, in that generally a collection involves some definite and identifiable objects;
3 collections are held in *sets* of related but different items;
4 the objects collected share common qualities but are *non-identical*;
5 there is a driven quality to collecting, characterised by Belk (1995a) as *passionate*.

We might add to this two further central factors:

6 there is a *social context* to collecting, whereby the collector interacts with others who share his or her interests to acquire and develop a collection;
7 related to this, the notion of *competition* in having a bigger, better and more comprehensive collection than other collectors is relevant. This competitive quality need not necessarily be socially expressed, but may be a personal factor not revealed or expressed to others.

Other authors, whilst offering different definitions of collecting, broadly concur with the general outline above. They tend to identify the notion of process as a central element, that collections have specific qualities, and that collections are not necessarily related to intrinsic value, but acquire value through their qualities, selectivity and context for the collector. Kron (1983) suggested,

> To qualify as a collection, the items collected must have some similarity and interrelationship. By being part of a collection each piece is transformed from its original function of toy, icon, bowl, picture, whatever, into an object with new meaning – a member of an assemblage that is greater than the sum of its parts. (193–4)

Another important aspect of collecting and collections is that they have personal, as well as public, meaning. Each item within a collection has a distinct meaning for the collector, which is determined by a variety of both external and internal or intrapersonal factors. As suggested by Muensterberger (1994), while two collectors may crave the same object (seen, for example, in intense and competitive bidding in a salesroom), their causal reason for desiring it, and their way of going about obtaining it, may be very different. The collected objects are seen, therefore, to have a use or a function for the collector. Belk and Wallendorf (1997) have argued that collections are a reflection of an individual's identity, in that they offer the opportunity to express personal qualities and reflect individual experiences. Within a loose psychodynamic oriented context, these authors present a number of ethnographic case studies that focus on gender and identity qualities of collections to illustrate how collections reflect past experiences, and relate to fundamental identity qualities of the collector. Muensterberger (1994) goes beyond this to suggest that collectors assign power and value to objects because their presence and possession seem to have a modifying function in the owner's mental state, such as keeping anxiety and uncertainty under control. Collecting then becomes more than the experience of pleasure from having obtained yet another object. Collectors are never satisfied with the acquisition of one object, but make repeated acquisitions. Within a psychodynamic framework, such acquisitiveness is seen as a vehicle to cope with inner anxiety and to distance oneself from the future anxieties, with all the confusing problems of need and longing.

In the normal course of events, everyone acquires objects. Even the most non-materialistic person can experience the shock of discovery of items when moving house, when objects from the past, such as discarded, forgotten and unused clothes, suddenly come to light in the process of packing. In affluent Western societies, where there is an emphasis on consumption, the acquisition of unnecessary objects, be they items of clothing, toys, kitchen utensils, or whatever, marks the passage of life. Items, although perhaps only used once, provide entertainment and diversion, and perhaps give an added interest to an otherwise dull event or occasion. Acquisition of items in itself is, therefore, neither unusual nor inappropriate, nor is the continued retention of such items after any sense of utility is passed. But this is not collecting in the sense we mean here, and is rather better characterised as accumulation.

We can therefore distinguish between accumulation and collecting. Accumulation lacks the specificity of collecting, and also its selectivity. It is essentially a passive refusal to dispose of items, rather than an active acquisition of specific items. We can also distinguish between collecting and hoarding. Hoarding refers to largely utilitarian items, retained for future need. The items hoarded may all be the same, and a quality of a 'hoard' is not that individual items are unique, but rather it acquires value in relation to some future need (even if illusory or unlikely). Hoarding, therefore, can be seen as having a functional quality, in that the items hoarded can at some date be consumed or used when need arises. Of course, hoarding can become separated from utility, and become a process in its own right. The miser, for example, hoards money not because of the future utility of his or her money, but because an essential quality of the miser is that the hoarded money is not spent, even in extreme situations of great need. But the sense of specificity and selectivity that characterises the collection is missing in the hoard. It is also the case that the word 'hoarding' carries with it very different attributions to those of collecting. The latter tends to be associated with objects that have, or will acquire, some extrinsic value. When we talk about hoarding, we rarely make reference to the aesthetic value of the items collected. For example, people may hoard food during transport strikes, or paper clips or stamps removed from articles arriving through the post. However, hoarding in itself may have some of the qualities of collecting and can in itself become problematic. This may relate, for example, to content. While we might consider stockpiling canned food as being excessive, we are unlikely to see it as being as problematic as hoarding scraps of used paper. Hoarding often is most visibly a problem when it relates to volume.

While this might also be an issue with collecting, a house full of clocks or china cats is unlikely to have the same negative impact on the outside observer as a house full of empty cardboard boxes. Hoarding equally becomes problematic when there is an intensity of involvement in the behaviour itself, such that it excludes other more socially accepted activities, or, when the behaviour is blocked, it is the source of considerable emotional distress. Here we see an overlap with what might be called pathological aspects of hoarding, where the inability to dispose of items relates to some underlying emotional state.

In terms of the process of collecting, a further final distinction needs to be made between the collector and the dealer. Dealers acquire large numbers of items, and because they may well service collectors, the dealer in a sense holds collections. However, the critical difference is that profit rather than the intrinsic value to the dealer of the acquired items drives the acquisitive activities of the dealer. The dealer acquires collectible material to sell on to other collectors, and will dispose of the valued rare item rather than retain it. There is, of course, a more complex case where the dealer is also a collector. In these circumstances, the dealing behaviour may well support a more fundamental activity (for the individual) of collecting. The individual may deal in items to support his or her own collecting behaviour, using the process of dealing to develop his or her own collection. In this case, the rewards of both dealing and collecting are combined – an issue of some significance when we come to consider the involvement of child pornography in collecting behaviour.

Collecting, therefore, refers to a deliberate act of selection and choice where items are acquired beyond a level appropriate to necessity or need – whatever its origins, a collector makes choices to extend and acquire the items collected, according to some defining quality. Thus, a collector may collect toy soldiers, beer mats, hatpins . . . an almost endless array of objects are collected and collectible, depending on the whim and interests of the collector. Collections are not, therefore, simple aggregations; they reflect structured and deliberate choices. Such choices may be highly specific, as in a search for a particular rare item to add to a collection, or may be very general, as in collecting variations on a broad theme. Collections can be quite personal and private; they generally acquire their meaning, however, by reference to the individual, and the collections of others, either as reference points or as elements of competition. Collectors are not a homogeneous group and we have little understanding of the different ways in which the collection functions for the individual. Why should there be differences in the content of collections, such that one person amasses toy soldiers while another collects glass paperweights? It is often hard to understand the attraction of collecting some items, such as railway tickets. There are also differences in the act of collecting, such that some collectors seek to own a single example of an item within a given category, while others wish to try and collect all items within that category.

Collecting seems to be a feature of growing up, at least in Western societies. Until at least adolescence, children collect things (Newson and Newson 1968). Such collecting may serve a purpose in terms of cognitive development, and

Webley and Lea (1993) emphasised the importance of swapping collected items in the development of economic understanding of children. Collecting has been variously suggested to support in children the development of selectivity, categorisation skills, knowledge development and learning, competition, specialisation and goal-focused development. Commercial organisations recognise the importance of collecting for children, by producing items that are within the means of children to either buy or acquire for collection. The early baseball cards that were avidly collected are now replaced by Pokémon® and Digimon® cards, but the engagement of children with collecting these cards represents very clearly the process and features of collecting outlined above. On a slightly grander scale, the success of Barbie™ dolls, or the My Little Pony toys also illustrates the power that collecting can exercise over choices made by parents and others in gift purchase. Industries and businesses exist to feed collecting habits, not simply in terms of making available items that are collected, but in generating new items of interest. For adults, so-called 'collectable' items, such as commemorative coins, are explicitly marketed as being suitable for collecting; the manufacturers seeking to engage the item with collectors to ensure additional sales. What is not clear, however, is what limits an engagement at any given time with a collection. Sorting through childhood memorabilia invariably unearths a multitude of collections (cards, stamps, coins), most of which have been abandoned somewhere along the line when they ceased to have the same function for us. This may relate simply to the commercial aspects of certain objects, such that as a particular television programme went down in popularity, so did the goods that were attached to them. It may also be that developmental changes in the child mean that certain objects which were of age-appropriate interest now appear childish. There are many more abandoned collections than there are ones that have been sustained.

Belk (1995a, b) suggested that there are sex differences in items collected. He noted that men are more likely to collect automobiles, guns, stamps, antiques, books, beer cans, wines and sports-related objects. In contrast, he suggested women are likely to collect jewellery, houseware items such as dishes and silver, and animal replicas. Belk further suggested a series of dichotomies characterising male/female collecting: gigantic/tiny, strong/weak, world/home, machine/nature, extinguishing/nurture, science/art, seriousness/playful, functional/decorative, conspicuous/inconspicuous, inanimate/animate. These dichotomies look remarkably like stereotyped sex-role qualities, an issue developed further by Belk and Wallendorf (1997). If collections are assumed to be reflections of individual identity, as they argued, then collections would be expected to reveal sex-role stereotypes.

A necessary element of a collector's approach to collecting is recognition of the 'whole' to which his or her collection relates as a 'part'. The collector has a sense (however unapproachable) of the extent and nature of the possible items within the category collected, of which his or her collection is a fraction. Acquisitiveness may well be a factor in collecting behaviour, but the selectivity shown by the collector suggests that choices are strategically made in relation to a sense of the overall category of items collected. Recognition of this may help in understanding the driven qualities of collectors, in that completeness provides a powerful motivator to focus and drive collecting. Muensterberger (1994) argued that one central aspect of collecting behaviour is that there has to be a more or less continuous flow of objects to collect and that it is this flow that captivates the collector. There is, therefore, a point at which interest in a collection may change when supply diminishes beyond a certain point. Part of the thrill of collecting relates to surmounting the obstacles that get in the way of securing the desired object, but there has to be some real possibility of obtaining it.

A related feature of collecting is cataloguing. Most collections are not a random accumulation of objects, but have a structure. Collecting is not only the acquisition of objects, but also what the collector does with the object afterwards. Again there are huge variations between collectors, in part determined by the nature of the objects themselves. The collection needs to be accessible (whether or not this actually happens) and in the main, the objects need to be stored in some way that protects their physical integrity. There would be little point in the butterfly collector putting all the specimens in a cardboard box, as this would make them inaccessible and likely to lead to their deterioration. Accessibility may have a public or a private quality, such that the collection may be openly displayed or kept only for viewing by the collector. Any collection will also display some level of organisation. This may be as arbitrary as some feature of the objects (such as colour, manufacturer, species, etc.), or relate to some aesthetic quality of the item. Most children who start collections of stamps will buy large bags of unsorted stamps that they then categorise according to the country of origin. As the collection becomes more sophisticated, the stamps may be re-sorted according to particular years or special issues. One feature of such organising behaviour is that it increases the actual engagement that the collector has with the objects collected. This may be on many levels, such as sustaining the pleasure associated with the collection, or simply increasing the amount of time or money spent in meeting some perceived need in relation to the collection.

PROBLEMATIC COLLECTIONS

In the majority of cases, collecting seems to be a normal, even useful aspect of life. As a hobby or pastime it may meet many needs, and give a focus and purpose to life. Indeed, Belk (1995a) suggested that collections in many cases are maintained to compensate for lack of career success and recognition. Certainly, the personal qualities of collection referred to earlier would support this view. There is also undoubtedly a sense in which the collector through his or her collection retains and saves items that may have value. Just as entomologists maintain reference collections of insects, so collectors might be thought to be maintaining reference material of the artifacts they collect, and the creation of catalogues of collectible items has its parallel in the creation of databases of other forms of information. It is probably easier to see the significance of this with respect, for example, to the collected works of a particular artist, than to collections of beanie babies. However, even beanie babies might be argued to be representative artifacts of the late twentieth century, and have an intrinsic value in that sense, regardless of the personal value for the collector.

As we considered with hoarding, collecting can, however, be problematic. We can identify three aspects that may move it from a benign or even useful social activity to one that is associated by others, if not the collector, with problems:

1 level of engagement and rate;
2 social and financial exclusion;
3 content.

Engagement and rate

Collecting implies an active process of seeking out the items collected. In hunting for antiques, for example, travel to various auctions and viewing sales would be a normal and acceptable element of the process of collecting. It could be argued that engagement in this process had many positive features – travel, social involvement, or mental stimulation from acquiring expertise – making it an ideal hobby for the retired or the shy, and giving a sense of purpose to the individual who lacked fulfilment in their occupation and even their relationships. However, when the process of collecting becomes all-engrossing, and when it takes place to the exclusion of other activities, then we can see that it might be problematic. Clear and definitive attributes of the problematic in this sense are difficult to express in a general way. But where collecting, and the behaviour associated with it, becomes a priority over other activities, such as caring for children, engagement with work, and maintaining social relationships with partner and friends, then we can reasonably describe such behaviour as problematic. In a social and personal context, therefore, collecting may have a cost associated with it, as well as potential benefits. When the costs in either personal or social terms outweigh the benefits, then we can describe the behaviour as problematic. The issue here revolves around level of engagement, and the very high rate at which collecting behaviours may occur.

Social and financial exclusion

An associated, but not necessarily related problematic factor, can be expressed in terms of exclusion, at personal, social and financial levels. When collecting behaviour becomes so extensive that it occupies all of life, then problems can be identified at a personal level. Intensive focusing on a narrowly defined collection, to the exclusion of other interests, limits, rather than broadens, the cognitive consequences of collecting. Similarly, intense focusing, along with spending long periods of time involved in the process of collecting, might be thought seriously to diminish social opportunity. If all an individual does relates to his or her collection, and if all energies are devoted to it, then the space available for normal social interaction must necessarily decrease. The psychological and temporal space for family contacts and parenting are necessarily reduced in such circumstances. Whilst collecting may be a positive experience for an introverted or socially isolated individual in that it can provide opportunities for social contact, it can also narrow rather than expand them. A related factor concerns the financial commitment some collecting can develop. Even low-level collections of everyday items incur some cost. But if your focus is on World War II tanks, then the cost of acquisition, restoration and maintenance of your collection enormously expands. Extensive travel to auctions or exhibitions can be a broadening experience, but on a limited budget it can be crippling, with consequences not only in terms of budgets, but also in terms of social arrangements, such as parenting activities.

Content

The final problematic area relates to content of collections, an issue of obvious relevance to the concerns about child pornography. Collectors of beanie babies, for example, may or may not feel they can display their collections publicly. In any event, they can participate in public exhibitions without fear of legal sanctions, and interact openly with other collectors with similar interests. Not all collections allow this, however. Where the content of collections is illegal, then such openness is not possible. One obvious area where this might be the case relates to stolen artworks. That there is a considerable market for stolen works of art can be seen in the scale of theft of very valuable items. Some very rich people seem to be prepared to spend considerable amounts of money to acquire stolen antiques, paintings and other items. Such items cannot be disposed of on the open market (because they would immediately be recognised as stolen), and quite clearly the ultimate purchaser of stolen works is also committing a crime. Yet the trade flourishes.

This form of collecting seems not to have the same kind of social context as discussed above, presumably because of fear of exposure. Nor can the collector openly participate in social events associated with collecting, as his or her collection is illegal and private. This seems to suggest that some forms of collecting can be much more solitary than others, where the intrinsic value to the individual of the item collected itself is the principal, if not the only, factor driving collecting. Other factors may be significant here, however. Possession of a stolen 'old master' may not be something that can be flaunted and displayed; but the collector knows it is possessed. The power associated with the possession of an enormously valuable item is coupled with the power of possessing a secret. In addition, whilst possession of a stolen old master may be a totally private act, acquisition of something stolen necessarily involves interaction with the thief, or his or her agents. Successful engagement in a private world of conspiracy can also be a very important factor, especially for the very rich. It is a very clear demonstration of living outside, and perhaps above, society's rules.

In the context of concern to us, the form of problematic content of collections is pornography. Collections of adult pornography may not be illegal, but would not meet approval in all circles, which as above may limit its social context. We have no idea of the extent of collecting adult pornography, as distinct from its acquisition. However, given the strength of sales of pornographic magazines and videos, there is clearly an enormous market for it, and anecdotally reference is made to collecting. Unlike collections of beanie babies and stolen works of art, collections of pornography can have a more obvious sense of utility, in that they presumably meet the attributes of being pornographic through generating sexual arousal, and providing a focus for fantasy and sexual behaviour such as masturbation.

Child pornography represents at one level a subset of broader pornographies, but is distinguished not only by the social approbation it generates, but also by its illegality. Paradoxically, however, because it is illegal, we know rather more about collections and collectors of child pornography as a result of arrests and seizures than we do about collectors of other pornographies.

COLLECTING CHILD PORNOGRAPHY

Considering the speculation about the role of pornography in sex-related offences, there is remarkably little empirical data about collecting child pornography. Lanning (1992), from the perspective of law enforcement, suggested that one feature of paedophile behaviour is that paedophiles almost always collect child pornography or child erotica. The emphasis is on collection as it relates to saving material, rather than simply viewing it. He lists the kinds of item collected and includes: books, magazines, articles, newspapers, photographs, negatives, slides, movies, albums, drawings, audiotapes, videotapes and equipment, personal letters, diaries, clothing, sexual aids, souvenirs, toys, games, lists, paintings, ledgers, photographic equipment and so on. The defining feature of such collections is that, in some way, they all relate to children. Clearly not all paedophiles collect the same things, and such collections vary in size and scope. Within the sample of offenders interviewed for the COPINE project, materials seized from offenders while in prison typically included shoe-boxes of magazine and newspaper clippings, pictures from children's clothing catalogues pasted into home-made albums, and seemingly innocent school photographs of children known to the offender or stolen from other prisoners. Such collections were limited by access to appropriate materials, and may have appeared to a casual observer as innocuous. However, within the prison these collections had value and would be traded between people with a sexual interest in children, as well as used for fantasy and masturbatory purposes.

Lanning (1992) suggested that factors that influence the qualities of paedophile collections include socio-economic status, living arrangements and age. Until the advent of the Internet, accessing actual pornography (as opposed to erotica) was difficult, risky and expensive. The size of collections, therefore, was related to affluence. In a similar way, paedophiles who can ensure privacy, either in the context of work or domestic arrangements, would also tend to have larger collections. Collecting is also a process, and material is acquired over time. With reference to collecting more traditional forms of pornography, this often meant that older paedophiles were likely to have larger collections. The level of exclusivity of sexual interest in children is a further feature. For example, Lanning (1992) asserted that 'Situational Child Molesters might also collect pornography but not with the high degree of predictability of the Preferential Child Molester' (23). The COPINE data would suggest that where there is not an exclusive sexual interest in children, but an interest in a variety of illegal or unorthodox material, then child pornography becomes one aspect of the collection, rather than the totality. This is seen very clearly in relation to the acquisition of Internet pornography, where collectors would have categories based on some characteristic of the material saved. This is illustrated by the following extract from an interview with TS:

> I think I had three main directories towards the end which was probably something like er paedo er animal . . . and rape . . . and then the subdirectories were whatever they were . . . say if it was a group it'd be called group. (23)

Prior to the advent of the Internet, collections were likely to be limited to whatever was readily available, and certainly animal and rape pornography would not have been easily obtained.

Hartman *et al.* (1984) identified four types of collector which they called closet, isolated, cottage and commercial. The closet collector of child pornography was one who acquired material from commercial sources, kept the collection a secret and was thought not to be actively engaged in the molestation of children. The isolated collector was described as actively molesting children as well as collecting child pornography or erotica. The fear of discovery ensured that this collector used pornography either for solitary sexual behaviour or in the context of the victim. The materials collected might also include those of the victim produced by the collector, as well as those from other sources. The cottage collector was said to share his collection and sexual activity with other individuals, primarily as a means of validating his or her own behaviour and without any monetary consideration. This is similar to our earlier discussion of the exchange of erotica in prisons, as such collectors will often share, swap or trade pornography. The commercial collector sees his collection as a commercial proposition and will sell duplicates of his collection to others. Hartman *et al.* (1984) suggest that although primarily motivated by profit, such collectors are also likely to be actively engaged in the abuse of children.

There is little research that has explored why paedophiles collect child pornography and erotica. Lanning (1992) argued that collecting this material may help paedophiles satisfy, deal with or reinforce their compulsive, persistent sexual fantasies about children, and fulfil a need for validation. As we have already considered, many people with a sexual interest in children need to justify their own interest, and the availability of material to collect is one way of achieving this. This is similar to collecting articles or stories written by paedophiles, which serve the dual function of supplying information and also normalising the interest. Collections can also act as trophies, memorabilia of previous relationships with children. They fix the victim at the very age they were at when most attractive to the paedophile and this may be one of the reasons why many paedophiles carefully date and label their collections. This is considered in more detail in Chapter 4 which examines both the psychological functions of pictures and the role of community.

Lanning (1992) discussed five ways in which those with a sexual interest in children may use their collections of child pornography. He suggested that its primary use is for sexual arousal and gratification. In this context, its function is similar to adult pornography in that it enables fantasy. In Lanning's analysis, such use is described as a prelude to actual sexual activity with children, although the evidence to support this is equivocal. As we will see, in the context of the Internet, it appears that there may be offenders whose activity is limited to viewing and sharing material, rather than in sexual engagement with children (Quayle *et al.*, 2000). A second use is said to be the lowering of children's inhibitions by exposing them to pictures of other children apparently enjoying sexual activity. This form of vicarious learning can also serve to normalise the activities for the child, and increase the possibility of elevating both curiosity and arousal. A third use of such collections is blackmail. While there have been very few studies of those who are the victims of child pornography, it is agreed that such victimisation is a source of extreme shame (Svedin and Back 1996). Children are likely to assume some of the responsibility for what has taken place, and photographs are a permanent record of what has happened. Threat of disclosure of such material can be used as blackmail to ensure the child's silence. A fourth use of child pornography is as a means of exchange. Lanning talked about this exchange in the context of information. The paedophile may exchange part of his collection for information about a given child, the value of the exchange lying in the extreme qualities of the pictures. A fifth use of collections is thought to be profit, in that historically, where material was difficult to find, there was a commercial value attached to it. Even non-pornographic pictures that can function as erotica may have commercial value if used in the context of a magazine.

As we have previously considered, collections are extremely important to the collector and have a value beyond any commercial considerations. Equally, the person who collects child pornography is willing to spend time and money on the collection, although they are unlikely to make profit from their collection. In the context of hard-copy collections (such as magazines, individual photographs and videos), such collections were thought of as constant, in that the collector was unlikely ever to throw things away. This may in part reflect the difficulties experienced in acquiring the collection in the first place and the fear that once lost, such material may never be obtained again. As with other collections, child pornography tends to be organised and maintained in some way and reflects a high level of permanence. The collector will try to find a way to preserve the collection, either by hiding it or placing it in the care of another person. Hiding traditional pornography is not easy. Magazines tend to be bulky, and photographs are likely to deteriorate unless they are kept somewhere dry. The activities involved in preserving a collection of child pornography are influenced by a need for security, while at the same time leaving the collection accessible. The material is, after all, illegal, but the collection serves little purpose if the collector cannot get at it. The ways in which the collection is concealed are largely determined by the person's living circumstances and the nature of the collection. For example, if the person is living on their own and has no prior criminal history, then they may feel secure enough to keep their collection within their immediate domestic environment. Where the person lives with their family or shares accommodation with others, then the collection is likely to be hidden, for example, under floorboards or in locked trunks. Where the collection includes non-pornographic material, then the collector might feel sufficiently confident to leave some of this on display. One offender interviewed by the COPINE project had photographs of his victims framed and sitting on his dresser. To all intents and purposes they appeared to be family photographs.

Collections of child pornography on the Internet

If we consider the role of the Internet in collecting behaviour, we can see that this new technology facilitates collecting in many ways. Primarily, it increases ease of access to material that is clearly pornographic, as opposed to erotic, across a wide number of categories, including child pornography. Not only is there a wide variety of previously unobtainable material on the Internet, but access can be gained in secret without all the risks associated with attempting to purchase commercially produced items. Essentially the activity becomes as anonymous as the person wishes it to be. Pictures can be downloaded without the need to identify oneself or to communicate with another person. Equally, such activity can take place within the context of an identifiable community.

Along with ease of access comes volume. As there is little commercial exchange in relation to child pornography, most images can be obtained without any financial loss. Some of the factors that in other circumstances limit the size of collections no longer apply in connection with the Internet, and many collectors talk about the rapid acquisition of large numbers of images:

> my collection grew in the space of maybe six months from about 3,000 to about almost 40,000 pictures. (QR: 7)

> I didn't stop really until I had about 100 images and and for some reason the computer disconnected itself. (El: 40)

Such rapid acquisition is facilitated by trading images with others, or by accessing somebody else's collection:

> An I didn't have that many pictures but somebody took pity on me and let me into his collection . . . he gave 'em to me . . . 50,000 odd images in there . . . a lot of them repeated, a lot of them duplicated . . . but I mean that was where a lot of my collection came from. (EI: 49)

The ability to trade images and even to let people have free access to the collection is an important feature of the Internet. Paedophiles who use IRC (Internet Relay Chat) can make available the contents of their hard drive to other users using, for example, FTPs (File Transmission Protocols). This remains the best method of transferring large amounts of material across the Internet and can usually be accessed anonymously:

> once my collection grew past 40,000 I really didn't trade all that much. I would mostly let people take just what they wanted off my FTP site . . . for want of a better word my collection site . . . my museum . . . while I was conjuring up new ways of evading law enforcement and securing the collections. (QH: 7)

Prior to the Internet, trade had to be done either through magazines or by word of mouth, which meant a potential loss of anonymity. Equally, materials had to be sent through the post, which both restricted quantity and increased the likelihood of detection. Through the Internet, trade in pornography not only becomes easier, but carries with it anonymity.

For those who wish to communicate with likeminded others through the Internet, the sense of sharing knowledge of one's collection and the opportunity to compare collections increases. Here we have a community of collectors who can bypass many of the problems associated with the possession of illegal materials. While the collection of child pornography may remain a secret from the people who occupy the collector's immediate and 'real' social world, within the context of the Internet the collection can be as visible as the collector wishes it to be. Along with ease of access is also ease of storage. Unlike hard copies of photographs, images stored electronically, either on the hard disk, diskettes or CD-ROMs, take up very little physical space. Images can even be stored electronically at a location both anonymous and distant from the location of the collector's PC. Storage also implies some level of organisation. Whether this is simply placing all images within one file or folder, or sorting them according to some complicated system of categories, depends on the collector and the importance placed on rapid access of material. Organising material electronically means that photographs can be moved easily, so that there is a dynamic to the collection. As it increases, or the focus changes, there is a potential parallel change in the way that the collection is catalogued:

> but at some time later on I changed them to erm teen girls teen boys and then young girls young boys . . . then I split them up again the boys' ones particularly into circumcised and uncircumcised ones . . . I called it cut teens and cut boys or something. (OK: 50)

Child pornography, as it appears on the Internet, often emerges as a series of photographs. The series are identified by a name and usually a number, although the person producing or distributing the series does not necessarily release them in the production sequence. Collecting on the Internet often means looking for material that is new to the collector, or completes part of a series:

> You were hoping that someone would post something that you had a series of that had a few gaps . . . you were hoping that somebody out there would post some. (EI: 47)

The advantage to the collector of collecting series of photographs of a child, as opposed to single shots from a series, is that it adds value to the collection, both subjectively and with regard to the community. For the individual, there is satisfaction in completing a series, but there is also potential for increasing the capacity to create sexual arousal. Invariably, the series has a theme – it tells some sort of story:

> so you like get an idea of the full event that was going on . . . it's probably more like action which is probably later on I went down to erm . . . movie format erm . . . you know so you get an idea of . . . the full continuation rather than just one photo . . . or like a snapshot . . . (TS: 19)

The seeking out of new material is an important aspect of collecting *per se*, but in the context of child pornography it has a more sinister aspect. As we have noted before, many of the images available on the Internet are relatively old (in excess of twenty years). In order to supply the demand by collectors for new material, more photographs have to be taken that depict the ongoing sexual abuse of children. Within the complex social network of the Internet, accessing new or private collections requires the exchange of material that is of interest to other collectors. For some collectors, this has directly led to the production of new material through the abuse of children in the collector's immediate social network, to enable access to other material:

> The progression for me came when I started offending against my daughter . . . I was in the chat rooms . . . and obviously chatting to a lot of other people who were trading images . . . people would send lists of material that they had . . . and they were reluctant to give me access to any of that material unless I could come up with any new material . . . I was sort of left out of this sort of arena that was going on, this trading of private pictures . . . my motivation was to come up with some images that I could trade for this new material . . . it was then that I thought about steps of . . . of involving my daughter in . . . in creating video to actually trade to get the material that I wanted. (ES)

Collecting child pornography is facilitated through the acquisition of good computer skills. Using software to both access and sort photographs increases the overall number of images that can be looked at:

> well what I'd do is I'd load up PaintShopPro and look at all the thumb-nails because it shows you the file names underneath . . . and I'd split my screen and have on . . . PaintShopPro on one side and Windows Explorer on another . . . and all the images I didn't like . . . erm . . . I'd just highlight them all and I'd just delete them. And all the ones I wanted to keep I'd move into another folder. (ME: 18)

This last excerpt from an interview transcript also highlights another potential difference in collections from the Internet, as opposed to hard copies. While none of the people interviewed through the COPINE project had ever deleted all of their images, the majority of them had deleted some and were selective about what they kept. This possibly relates to the fact that photographs, once available on the Internet, are unlikely ever to go out of circulation. For the collector, the decision to delete images and remove them from the collection can be reversed very easily should the images acquire some other function or should the nature of the collection change.

One of the main difficulties in collecting child pornography through the Internet relates to the identifiers allocated to each picture. While collectors disapprove of the names or labels of each image being changed, as this makes the process of collecting more arduous and leads to the potential duplication of images within a collection, it is apparent that some collectors do alter the identifiers. This may be because the child in the series looks like a child known to the collector, or because a collector does not like the name allocated to the child. These are very personal reasons, and only become problematic to the community if the same collector allows ready access to his collection. However, there are occasions when the identifier on the photograph is changed to create the illusion that the material is new and different to what it really is, thus increasing the currency of the photographs. This clearly would not be acceptable within a tightly knit group of collectors.

When we talked earlier about collecting, we noted that a distinction needs to be made between collectors and dealers, although they are not mutually exclusive. On the Internet, while we are seeing an increase in the amount of commercially available child pornography, the vast majority of images are not commercially produced. The advent of the digital camera has meant that collectors can easily become producers of child pornography, usually in the context of domestic or institutional access to a child or children. As the move from collector to producer and distributor of such images is not commercially driven, we might assume that what motivates the individual is power. Given access to a child or a group of children with whom he or she has influence, the producer can choose what photographs to take, when to take them and when, where and to whom to distribute them. The release of new material is followed by a flurry of Internet communications demanding more images of the same child or children, release of parts of a missing series, and even requests for specific types of abuse within the images. Some new images may be privately distributed to a chosen group of people on the Internet. Such private images are invariably not for general release, although the control that the individual has over these images is illusory, as invariably they will eventually become part of a larger distribution network.

The selective release of material to enhance the status of the poster (and perhaps producer if they are the same person) can frequently be seen in the Internet child pornography environment. Incomplete series, for example, are posted to newsgroups, generating a flurry of activity and requests for more material. Subsequent postings to 'fill in' the missing pictures may follow, but perhaps with gaps of months. The attention span of avid collectors can be very long indeed, as can their patience in waiting for the material they seek.

In the context of the Internet, the qualities of an individual's collection relates largely to preference, rather than to availability, although where pictures have a currency in terms of trade, then there may be items within a given collection that have no direct appeal for the collector. Clearly there are differences between collectors that in many ways mirror the differences between collectors in general. Some people selectively collect photographs of a preferred age group, or have a preference for a particular content. For example, many with a sexual interest in children preferentially collect the soft-focus sentimentalised erotica of photographers such as David Hamilton. Other collectors are more eclectic, although still discriminating, in the pictures they choose to save. Here the focus is still on children, but may include, for example, categories of photographs that relate to pictures such as 'panty shots', or mutual fondling or masturbation. Still other collections reflect the collector's preoccupation with sexual extremes, such that a variety of pornographies are retained.

THE COLLECTOR OF PORNOGRAPHY BEFORE AND AFTER ACCESSING THE INTERNET

It may be useful to compare and contrast the different types of collection and collecting behaviour by looking at an individual who was convicted of the possession of child pornography obtained from the Internet. The same person had, however, been an avid collector of pornography prior to accessing the Internet. Our interest is not in this case *per se*, but rather in the differences and similarities evidenced in his collecting. ES is a man in his thirties who has been collecting pornography since his early teens, and the following is presented as illustrating pre and post-Internet behaviour.

Before the Internet

ES initially purchased pornography from two outlets near to his home. He lived with his family, and although he clearly had his own space within the house that ensured him some privacy, he still had to get his purchases back into the house:

> I'd smuggle them back in under my coat.

His interest was in hard-core pornography:

> I had to have all new all different ones.
>
> I was looking for the most hardcore extreme sort of stuff then.

For ES the problem was one of access, as most of the magazines did not contain sufficient extreme material to satisfy his fantasies. To meet his requirements, he would resort to sending off for them through the post. One difficulty with this was that he had to pay for this, and invariably the material he got back was no different from that which had been contained in the magazines:

> It was always a con – I don't know how many times I fell for that.

The purchase of a video recorder when he was in his twenties prompted him to switch the focus of his collecting to video tapes:

> Basically the stuff that was advertised was straight hard core sex . . . I managed to find someone who specialised in S&M films . . . and then from that I found someone who did a couple of . . . unusual stuff . . . there was combination animal . . . I found one who did sell some child tapes . . . about a half hour's worth of shorts . . . about that age so it was different so it was different so I'd have a look at it.

As earlier, his interest was always in new and more extreme material, the unifying feature of which was humiliation. His preference was for material that he could believe in as genuine, rather than role-played, and the videos of children met this criterion:

> with a young child that was being molested, that was genuine, whereas it could always be faked or consensual in adult film.

The source of tapes was largely through magazines, initially exchanging with people who liked horror films, or 'video nasties', because there would be brief segments of the films that would be 'underground'. People offering videos through specialist contact magazines would usually give a contact box and number, but ES would usually give his own address. At this stage collecting was important to him, not only because it allowed him access to preferred material which he could use to masturbate, but because the collection allowed him to exchange films with others:

> I would continue swapping with him so that I could build up my own collection and swap them for something else.

ES would collect anything at this stage that fitted with his preference for 'degradation or humiliation', and this would be the case even when the material was offensive to him. For example, he made himself look at 'scat' movies (involving faecal material), until he no longer felt physically nauseated. Collecting involved writing to people through the magazines and getting 'replies from about half of them'. He would keep in contact with an individual until he had copies of all of their tapes and then he would stop writing to them.

In spite of the difficulty in getting videos, ES had a sizeable collection:

> I think I had about 3 . . . 300 . . . probably three hour tapes . . . half a drawer of SM . . . there might be half a drawer of scat and then some amateur . . . caning . . . then there'd be a series pregnant . . . animals . . . I'd sort of divide them . . . eventually . . . once I'd got too many in the different categories.

Not all of his contacts were interested in child pornography, and the majority had a single focus to their collection:

> One person would usually have a collection of one type of film . . . you'd very rarely meet someone like myself who had different categories.

Over the course of each year, ES would regularly swap tapes with approximately twenty-five people at any one time. To do so, he would make copies of tapes to send people, never sending the original tapes:

> I would keep them for swapping and being a collector I didn't *like* throwing them away . . . if I thought they were . . . particularly well made, particularly extreme . . . particularly . . . something unusual different on them . . . I wouldn't want to get rid of them in case they were useful in the future for swapping.

Videos were seen as preferable to magazines, both in terms of their content but also because of security issues:

> Exchange and Mart was quite useful . . . I did actually through that get erm six Lolita magazines . . . which I threw away after a few years 'cause I got nervous holding them.

> Tapes you can wipe . . . magazines are harder to conceal. I threw them away. I got nervous one night and thought I don't want these anymore.

After collecting video pornography throughout his twenties, ES felt that he already had 'practically everything that was available', and finally purchased a computer and went online.

After the Internet

ES had told himself that he would use the Internet for a variety of things, including organising his collection of videos by using a spreadsheet, etc., but within a few hours of going online he was accessing child pornography.

> The aim was child pornography because it was still very rare . . . and obviously if I could get child pornography I could get anything else.

Initially, he downloaded pictures and placed them all in the same folder, but as his collection quickly grew, he needed to start sorting it:

> shoving everything into one folder and then eventually . . . after a couple of months . . . I started categorising it and putting it into different folders.

His interest was not solely child pornography, but mirrored his earlier collection:

> I didn't just collect child pornography . . . I went in there every night and had categories for practically everything . . . everything I already had on video I had a category for.

Child pornography was readily available through newsgroups, rather than web sites, and ES developed a routine of logging on every night:

> You would go through . . . you would start off with . . . you'd got the child pornography so you'd probably go for that first . . . you then probably spend . . . time looking through unusual name news groups seeing whether there was some kind of perversion or something that you'd not got before . . . trying to find out which news groups had the best supply of pictures.

As ES's collection grew, he needed more and more sophisticated software to help him manage both accessing pornography and cataloguing it:

> You have about 20 news groups eventually and collect all headers for that newsgroup . . . get all the new messages and just go through it one at a time . . . I had it set up . . . download and put into folders . . . start finding about picture viewers . . . it was recommended on the FAQ . . . you get thumbnails and everything.

His system of categorising became increasingly complex to cope with the volume of images and involved 'folder within folder within folder within folder'. This is seen most obviously in relation to the child section of his collection:

> towards the end there would be . . . you'd have . . . what did I have . . . started off by drawing, pictures, movies . . . in the pictures it would be . . . start off being boy girl . . . girl would be girl series which would be a good . . . particularly these would be the main ones where you could have . . . say a girl called Jackie or something and you'd have maybe 20 or 30 pictures and they'd be in folders . . . then there would be subfolders with different series of the same girl . . . but apart from that I'd have girl single pictures like er . . . which didn't belong to a series . . . there'd be girl solo girl masturbation . . . girl masturbating with a dildo if there was a dildo involved there'd be . . . erm girl cum shot if she was just on her own . . . if that was a girl series there'd . . . then there'd be a bizarre folder which would be if there was girl animal . . . if there was a pose with an animal . . . girl scat girl piss . . . or something like that we'd say . . . girl erm . . . there was . . . girl S&M I think if there was some kind of caning or spanking aspect to it.

Within these categories he was looking for, 'new, digital because they were good quality . . . recent, because they became more real . . . more extreme'. However, this did not stop him downloading material that he already had in order to try and improve the quality of his collection:

> if there were some reposted I'd compare them with what I had and see if I could get that picture . . . if it was a bigger picture or a better quality picture, get rid of them.

He would also look out for more pictures of a newly posted child:

> if someone posted one or two pictures of a new girl, you'd be keeping an eye open for that.

As with his prior collecting, the only limit he set with regard to what he was willing to keep was availability:

> When I started collecting any age was possible and I did have a section on babies yes . . . if there was snuff, for example . . . I would have downloaded that . . . without qualm.

He tried routes other than Usenet within the Internet in order to obtain new material, such as IRC:

> I then initially tried IRC erm . . . very slow, very cumbersome but you could get a few more rarer pictures . . . there was baby pictures, there was some . . . bondage with children.

He also accessed chat rooms, his selection being based on the extreme quality of the names used:

> You were in chat rooms . . . I'd go for the most extreme named ones possible . . . baby sex . . . child snuff or something . . . I'd go onto . . . I would click onto people who had extreme nicknames . . . Childabuser or something like that.

ES's collection of pornography from the Internet was considerable, and was much bigger than his hard-copy collection. Clearly this related in part to storage:

> I had huge collections of pornography . . . I had erm . . . on the child side . . . 10,000 girl pictures 5,000 boy pictures . . . 7 CDs of girl movies 7 CDs of boy movies . . . 3CDs of adult animal movies . . . I'd have categories of CDs of animal pictures . . . I'd have . . . not so much of scat because I had a big collection and lost them when my computer crashed and never really got back into collecting them again because it meant it meant going over old ground . . . but there were things like adult drawings cartoons of famous . . . cartoon characters in sexual situations erm . . . pregnant . . . birth pictures . . . death pictures like accident series in the grotesque group er erm . . . lesbian . . . there was a huge collection of lesbian material . . . 10,000 . . . Bukaki was probably about 5,000 . . . erm . . . Crush was about 2,000 erm.

One factor that limited ES's ability to collect pornography was the fact that he was unable to produce any new material himself. He was able to copy videos from his old collection, and some of these he used to trade, but he was not able to make new photographs:

> In the final year I had a go at er . . . since I had the video tapes I had a go at making videos and I posted the final six from the old ColorClimax films . . . I think I was more interested in how to be anonymous so it was a case of got Hack Agent . . . followed the instructions . . . you had to change lines in certain parts of the text then you had to post in a certain way . . . I was using News Scene . . . which took away where you were posting from but then those who were knowledgeable could tell where it was coming from.
>
> I didn't have anything of my own which I could swap for . . . that was personal that I could swap for anything else that was personal . . . some people would say oh I've got stuff that's not available sort of thing but I'd only swap for other stuff that's not available . . . so I couldn't get into that at all.

According to ES, the factor that made him stop downloading pornography from the Internet and which prompted him to get rid of his collection was primarily related to effort. The material that he wanted was largely in video format, and he felt that he had exhausted what was available, 'after about two years I had everything that was available on news groups', and yet there was still a desire for new, good-quality films. For example, in relation to one series of child pornography video clips posted not long before his arrest he says, 'They were British, they were new, good quality, hardcore . . . for me sort of like perfect collecting material'. But the collection of new material was becoming increasingly onerous and frustrating:

> There was one group that was just posted . . . erm I actually got rid of my collection just before I was arrested and this was the build up towards it . . . one group had just posted 20 to 25 minute long boy movies . . . erm . . . there were erm . . . er . . . 3 or 4 hundred megabytes big . . . I had an ISDN line . . . I'd download from 6 o'clock in the morning till 8 o'clock at night . . . 3 or 4 movies . . . they'd be posted in little bits of parts . . . and I'd have to download which might take an evening . . . I'd have to combine the different parts and there may be a part missing . . . you'd have to copy one part from another to duplicate this missing part . . . you'd have different systems for reassembling them . . . and it got more and more . . . I couldn't collect it all . . . and it became so frustrating that I wasn't watching telly, I wasn't reading, I wasn't doing anything . . .
>
> One evening I got rid of all the computer porn and all my children video tapes, though I did keep the other video tapes . . . but then two weeks later I got raided by the police.

CONCLUSIONS

It may be useful to revisit the features we initially identified as being important aspects of collecting, and look at what aspects of ES's behaviour meet these criteria. There is strong evidence of ES's collecting behaviour as a process, in that it was not static but dynamic, each development or stage being contingent on what and how he had collected before, and the availability of what was left to collect in the future. The process of collecting clearly had a modifying function in terms of how ES felt, and he was able to associate different emotions with different aspects of his collection. It seems that in part, what brought the process of collecting to an end was that the effort involved in securing desired objects was starting to outweigh the pleasure gained from securing them. There is some evidence, however, that the process of collecting would have started all over again.

ES's collection was quite eclectic in that, unlike many other collectors of pornography, he did not focus on one particular specific subset of subjects of pornographies but actively collected any material that related to humiliation and degradation. In the main, the focus was on visual material, because this was the most salient stimulus in evoking sexually arousing fantasies for him. Therefore the items in his collection were held in relationship to each other, but were different from each other. They shared common qualities but were not identical. ES repeatedly downloaded the same material, but selected which he was going to keep with regard to their aesthetic properties (an odd notion in the context of scat videos). There was also a driven quality to ES's collecting, both prior to and after going online. He collected to the exclusion of any other social relationships or activities, and he would negotiate his way through a variety of obstacles in order to achieve this. Indeed, outside social activities were replaced by 'inside' social activities, which related to collecting pornography. In the main, the pornography-mediated relationships were both superficial and functional. When he had exhausted the use that somebody could be to him with regard to expanding his collection, the relationship was discarded. There did not appear to be a particularly competitive element to his collecting, but he acknowledged wanting to be able to collect 'it all'.

In some respects ES's collection of pornography shared the same qualities pre- and post-Internet, but with his involvement in the Internet, became more extensive and more extreme in its content. This in part was a function of availability and ease of access. He no longer had to contact people through magazines, write to them and then wait to see if they would respond. Instead, in the course of an evening he could access large quantities of material across a variety of categories and in the safety and privacy of his own home. There was the same quasi-social aspect to these contacts, only where he had previously given out his home address he could now be more security conscious and remain largely anonymous. Ultimately, he was looking for the same format for the material in his collection (videos), and paradoxically, while he was able to source material that was new to him, the technology involved in obtaining videos through the Internet ultimately meant that he became frustrated and destroyed part of his collection.

In conclusion, while ES had always been a passionate collector of pornography, this became more extreme when he used the Internet, such that other interests, such as watching the television or reading, could not be met. This, in part, was because of the volume of pictures downloaded and the amount of time that by necessity had to go on sorting and cataloguing the images. Storage of material downloaded from the Internet was much easier, with none of the apparent risks involved in acquiring and storing hard-copy magazines. However, his cataloguing behaviour had an almost obsessive quality to it, and involved a seemingly endless number of subcategories. Again, this was possible in part because of the ease with which he could sort and index material on his computer.

ES illustrates most clearly the notion of process in collecting, and it is the development and features of this that characterise the collector in general. What ES also illustrates, however, is the significance of the Internet in enabling the process of collecting both to develop further and to exercise even greater control over his behaviour. Combined with the particular qualities of the material collected (in terms of fantasy and sexual potential), we see the emergence of a very powerful force.

Chapter 8

A model of problematic Internet use

Previous chapters in this book have explored the range of activities related to child pornography and the Internet. Although the issues raised are matters of considerable public concern, we have noted many times that there is little by way of consistent analysis in the area, and a marked absence of conceptual thinking from which more empirically based approaches to management of the problem can draw. As an attempt to address this gap, in the following we present a model of adult sexual interest in children and problematic Internet use. Such a model might serve several functions. It enables us to think of sexual offences against children that arise out of Internet use as being part of a complex array of behaviours, rather than any single activity. Such behaviours occur in relationship to each other, although, because of the process of offending, not all people who use the Internet will engage in offence-related behaviour to the same degree. For example, the person who downloads child pornography as part of an array of pornographies, but who does not communicate with others, trade or produce material, may be qualitatively different from the person who uses children within their social world to produce images to trade on the Internet. The latter has necessarily committed a contact offence against a child in the production of material, but has also had prior engagement with the Internet pornography world that necessitated the production of pictures. It is also evident that while there are people who have previously acknowledged a sexual interest in children, for whom the Internet becomes a medium for meeting their expressed preferences, there are equally those who seem to have had no prior knowledge that the images might be sexually arousing for them. In the latter case, we do not know whether such 'dormant' interests might ever have found expression without the Internet. This model also allows us to look at the cognitions or 'self-statements' that people generate in relation to their activities, that enable them to behave in ways that bring them into conflict with the law.

In developing the model, three issues seem important. The first is to note that adult sexual interest in children on the Internet embraces both illegal and legal activities. Collecting child pornography is illegal, but talking about fantasy or engaging in sexual role-plays while they may be inappropriate are not necessarily illegal. Sharing information about computer security is not illegal, but sharing information about access to children is illegal in many jurisdictions. Furthermore, as we have noted, not all pictures that are attractive to, and collected by adults with a sexual interest in children are necessarily illegal. Any model of behaviour in this area, therefore, must embrace not only clear offending behaviours, but also other related though not necessarily illegal activities. The second issue is to emphasise the notion of process as a key element in understanding the expression of the behaviour we are concerned with. As we have seen in earlier chapters, offending is a dynamic rather than static process, with individuals moving along a range of potential continua, related to satiation of sexual arousal, processes of engagement with both collecting and communities, and the exploration of different online personas. Previous history of contact offences, personal circumstances and opportunity are also critical elements.

The third issue is to note that the use of the Internet for sexual purposes extends beyond the relatively narrow confines of our concern with child pornography to embrace many other forms of sexual interest. What is referred to as 'cybersex' seems to be a major part of many people's experience of the Internet (Cooper *et al.* 2000a), and for some that experience may well have problematic qualities. In particular, a number of authors have made reference to its compulsive and addictive features (Cooper *et al.*, 2000b; Orzack and Ross 2000). The use of the Internet for sexual purposes, therefore, is not unique to the paedophile community, and the more general problematic qualities of cybersex may well find their parallels in paedophile behaviour and activity.

In the following we have adopted, as our starting-point for developing a conceptual model, a focus on research that emerges out of cognitive behaviour therapy, one therapeutic context to the management of offenders guilty of sexually related offences against children. This is an appropriate starting-point, because it is in the management of offenders that issues related to causative factors become most prominent. In addition, the model presented quite explicitly draws on the discussions in earlier chapters related to processes of collecting, notions of virtual communities, changing notions of identity and the sexual qualities of pictures. It seeks to pull together the various discussion threads from previous chapters into a conceptual framework, drawing on cognitive-behavioural approaches to the management of offenders.

A MODEL: CONCEPTUAL CONTEXT

The theoretical perspective that dominates both our understanding and treatment of adults who are sexually interested in children is a cognitive-behavioural one. In this context, as we discussed in Chapter 3, offender differences in empathy, social skills and cognitive processes have been a major focus for research and therapy (Geer *et al.* 2000). Distortions in the way offenders think are assumed to reflect attitudes and beliefs which are used to deny, minimise and rationalise behaviour, related to underlying belief systems or schema which play a role in precipitating and maintaining offending (Murphy 1990). While it is unclear whether such distortions are part of the aetiology of offending or are *post hoc* rationalisations, they are not only a focus of therapeutic intervention but have also been used to provide an index of risks of recidivism (Langevin 1991).

Authors such as Ward *et al.* (2000) suggest that the problem for the offender can be viewed as partially arising from deficits in one central mechanism: the ability to infer mental states. This has the result that the offender has difficulties in being aware of other people's beliefs, desires, perspectives or needs. Such an inability is clearly context-specific, however, as many people who have committed a contact offence are able to describe in detail how they targeted a child perceived to be vulnerable and how time was spent in 'grooming' the child to increase the opportunity of offending. Given this, it might be argued that the grooming process in particular shows a highly developed understanding of at least this aspect of the child's vulnerabilities and needs.

Cognitive Behavioural Therapy (CBT) approaches are largely based on such an understanding of offender behaviour and are guided by a relapse prevention framework. Marshall *et al.* (1998) asserted that the majority of programmes are predominantly derived from the same conceptualisation of treatment and are being increasingly applied to diverse populations, and they suggest that 'Care providers are trained in skills that are meant to equip offenders with the capacity to meet their needs in more appropriate ways, and clients are taught to apply these skills to avoid or abort an identified relapse process' (477). Typically CBT programmes include modules that focus on victim awareness/empathy, fantasy in offending, sexuality and relationships, and assertiveness and anger management (e.g. Eldridge and Wyre 1998).

In this book we have identified and discussed what in many ways is essentially a new category of sexual offender, whose offence relates to downloading, distributing and perhaps also producing pornographic pictures of children. In terms of offences related to downloading child pornography, such offenders may have no known contact with a victim, and may appear to be more similar in some ways to the voyeur (Quayle *et al.* 2000) than contact offenders. In earlier chapters we have discussed the limited research about such people and noted that we have little knowledge even as to whether they share the same characteristics and behaviours as contact offenders. However, given the wide use of the Internet, and the thousands of pornographic images of children available to those who wish to look (Taylor *et al.* 2001b), the use of the Internet by sexual offenders has remained largely unexplored. Even very recent reviews of those committing sexual offences against children (e.g. Geer *et al.*, 2000; Ward *et al.*, 2000 and Ivey and Simpson 1998) make no reference to the Internet and the possible relationship between offending and child pornography, or indeed pornography in general.

King (1999) has called for basic research about the Internet and human sexuality that might help practitioners. He has argued that it is not the simple availability of pornography online that has created this need, but the fact that people now have access to types of material that were previously available only at great expense and/or personal risk. This, added to the current anarchical nature of Internet communications, means the possibility of increasing social problems as people are faced with conflicts related to self-regulation of their behaviour. This broad issue clearly goes beyond sexuality and the Internet, and other authors have suggested that in extreme circumstances what we are seeing is a trend of people spending increasingly more time with technology than with other people (Kennedy-Souza 1998).

Despite the growth in numbers of Internet-related offenders within the judicial system, there has been little therapeutic research that has focused on either the assessment or treatment of people who download child pornography from the Internet, or who use the Internet in other ways to express sexual interest in children. Earlier research (Quayle and Taylor 2002b) has identified difficulties experienced by professionals who work in this area both in understanding the nature of the offence and accommodating this as part of existing sex offender programmes. Related to this, Marshall *et al.* (1998) asked us to consider in what ways we need to modify our programmes in order to educate ourselves to treat different types of sex offender effectively.

Within the last few years one way of conceptualising problematic Internet use has emerged in the concept of 'Internet Addiction' (Griffiths 1998). This is seen as a kind of technological addiction, falling within a subset of behavioural addictions, and involves excessive human–machine interaction, which can be either passive (such as television) or active (such as computer games). Such interaction is thought to 'usually contain inducing and reinforcing features which may contribute to the promotion of addictive tendencies' (Griffiths 2000: 171). Cooper *et al.* (2000a) have also focused on addictive and compulsive qualities related to Internet use, emphasising sexuality as the critical factor, rather than Internet processes *per se*. The label of addiction may be seen as problematic (Davis 1999), however, and diagnostic tools such as DSM-IV (APA 1994) use instead the term dependence, while others such as Cooper *et al.* (1999) talked of pathological use. However, with regard to people who download child pornography, none of these labels appears satisfactory, as they seem to both suggest a model of Internet use as an illness, and also relegate it to an extreme end of a continuum of behaviour. In contrast, in the context of the model proposed here, it would seem more helpful to think of the downloading of child pornography as 'problematic'.

Davis (2001) has presented a specific cognitive-behavioural model of Pathological Internet Use (PIU), which focused on associated maladaptive cognitions. The model he presented distinguished between specific PIU and generalised PIU. Specific PIU referred to a condition in which an individual pathologically used the Internet for a particular purpose, such as online sex or gambling, while generalised PIU referred to general 'time wasting' activities on the Internet, such as repeatedly checking e-mails and surfing through different web sites. Specific PIU usage was purposive and tended to be content-specific, and as such is particularly relevant to the problems associated with downloading child pornography. Generalised PIU in contrast related to multidimensional over-use, resulting in dysfunctional behaviours across a broad spectrum.

In identifying the aetiology of Pathological Internet Use, Davis suggested that it resulted from problematic cognitions that either intensified or maintained the maladaptive response. He presented a model, within a diathesis–stress framework, emphasising cognitions (or thoughts) as the main source of problem behaviour. According to such a framework, any abnormal behaviour is a result of a predisposed vulnerability (diathesis) and a life event (stress). Distal contributory causes identified in this model were the diathesis element in the diathesis–stress model, and were described by Davis as underlying psychopathology (such as depression, social anxiety and substance dependence); these were seen as a distal, necessary cause of Pathological Internet Use. The stressor was identified as the introduction of the Internet or some new technology related to the Internet. One example given in relation to this might be the first time an individual locates pornography on the Internet, or goes into a chat room. The event becomes a catalyst for the developmental process of PIU. Davis (2001) suggested that if the event is reinforcing, this increases the likelihood of the individual repeating the activity and becoming susceptible to forms of secondary reinforcement, such as the sound of the computer connecting with the Internet.

The central element to this model is the presence of 'maladaptive cognitions'. Such cognitions were seen to be 'proximal sufficient causes of PIU, in that they are sufficient to cause the set of symptoms associated with PIU' (191). Maladaptive cognitions were broken down into two main subtypes: thoughts either about the self or about the world. Davis gave very general examples of such cognitions, but it is not clear where these are drawn from. Davis (2001) gave an example of specific PIU as someone who compulsively and pathologically uses pornography, 'pornography is an immediate stimulus–response condition. Internet users are able to immediately locate pornography online, and get immediate reinforcement from it. This behavioural association becomes strong, and the need for more explicit materials becomes stronger. As a result, the individual demonstrates symptoms of specific PIU' (192). As the problem is content-specific, it is suggested that the problem might still have occurred even if the Internet had not been a factor.

In a similar vein, Putman and Maheu (2000) have suggested that people at risk of developing problems related to compulsive online sexual behaviour may be vulnerable owing to underlying depressive symptoms and difficulty coping with stress, where factors unique to the Internet result in their engaging in levels of sexual behaviour that interfere with everyday life. Once using the Internet, 'behavioral factors can combine with individual vulnerabilities to establish and maintain problematic online sexuality. Individual vulnerabilities such as anxiety, depression, stress, and interpersonal difficulties may increase a person's susceptibility to behavioural conditioning because the online sexual behaviour temporarily removes the dysphoric state' (93).

The work in this area is interesting, as it suggests some sort of dynamic interaction between the person and social context, rather than emphasising inherent and static qualities of the individual. There is still, however, lack of clarity in relation to both the diathesis and the stress elements of the model. Does the notion of pre-existing or underlying pathology refer to current mood state or some earlier experience? Are there 'critical periods' in terms of the development of such pathology? How do we make sense of pathological Internet use where such pathology cannot be identified? Equally, the notion of maladaptive cognitions is not straightforward. Are such cognitions in existence prior to engagement with new technologies, or do they arise out of it? Such issues are problematic in many such diathesis–stress accounts and are not unique to this model.

However, the emphasis on maladaptive cognitions in Davis's model gives a useful starting-point to develop thinking more generally about adult sexual interest in children and problematic Internet use. Of course, there is a sense in which it might be argued that in this case the presumed cognitions are highly adaptive, in that they enable the individual to gain access to, and use in some way, preferred material. Such cognitions are, however, problematic in the sense that they support behaviour that ultimately is exploitative of others who are more vulnerable. Figure 8.1 below presents a model of potential problematic Internet use, drawing on the broad notion of PIU described by Davis, but extends it to focus specifically on factors related to adult sexual interest in children and the Internet. The model relates concepts already emerging from the COPINE research programme, such as Setting Events, Process Factors and Cognitive and Social Factors discussed in Chapter 4, to both problematic cognitions and behaviours.

While the focus of the model is the person expressing a sexual interest in children, it also allows us to think about the many ways in which children are victimised by such engagement with the Internet. What is apparent from previous chapters is that there is not only one category of behaviour that relates to such sexual interest, but an array of behaviours, all of which potentially function in relation to each other. However, central to the sexual exploitation of children on the Internet, and central to the model proposed here, is the role of child pornography. As well as aiding our general understanding, in expressing relationships in this way, this model has the potential to be adapted to form the basis of a focused and specific treatment module to be used as part of a sex offender programme. It also aids the development of notions of dangerousness of offenders in the relationship between child pornography possession and the potential to engage in contact offences. This would also be in keeping with authors such as Gelder (1997) who have stressed the importance of a focused approach to psychopathology, particularly in relation to abnormalities of cognition.

A MODEL OF POTENTIAL PROBLEMATIC INTERNET USE

The schematic model presented in Figure 8.1 facilitates the examination of behaviours and cognitions related to problematic Internet use outside a pathological framework. In the model, such problematic cognitions are assumed to support problem behaviours such as accessing illegal material, sustain engagement with the Internet and may lead to the commission of further offences. These cognitive distortions are characteristic of a set of attitudes and values that support the legitimacy of sexual interest in relation to children, and in particular the use of the Internet as a means of meeting this. The characteristics of such cognitions (drawn from the discussion in Chapter 4) are that they:

1 justify the downloading of child pornography because they are only pictures and do not involve actual contact with a child;
2 normalise this behaviour because of the large number of people who are also engaged in the same online behaviour;
3 objectify the images through a process of collecting which distances the offender from the illegal content;
4 justify other forms of engagement with the images or, on occasions, real children through colluding in an online social network.

As in earlier chapters, the data on which this model is based derives from the research of the COPINE project. For the purpose of the discussion here, illustrative examples are drawn from interviews with twenty-three men, all of whom have been convicted of downloading child pornography as part of their offence behaviour. The methodology related to these interviews has been previously described in Chapter 4.

Setting events

In the model, the concept of distal and proximal setting events replaces 'contributory causes' used by Davis (2001). Given the discussion in previous chapters, this seems more properly to describe the array of factors that contribute to setting the scene for offending, and moves the discussion away from notions of pathology. It must also be emphasised that this is not an attempt to generate a static or essentialist framework, where, for example, sexual abuse is a necessary setting event for the subsequent development of problems. In attempting to make sense of our experiences we generate accounts for ourselves that we also use in a more public domain. In doing so, we select elements of our experiences, both past and present, that we feel have some salience or credibility. In part this is reflected in current social discourses, and it is perhaps inevitable that our current focus on child sexual abuse should find its place in offenders' accounts. This moves us away from notions of 'accuracy' or 'truthfulness' to examine how individuals construct their world. In talking about offences, this sample of offenders frequently, but not exclusively, gave examples of distal setting events which included early sexualised experience and poor adolescent or adult socialisation, while more proximal events were in relation to an existing sexual interest in children, the commission of a prior contact offence and dissatisfaction with a current persona. Offenders often used these setting events as an explanation of offending behaviour. Examples of distal cognitions related to earlier sexualised experiences included:

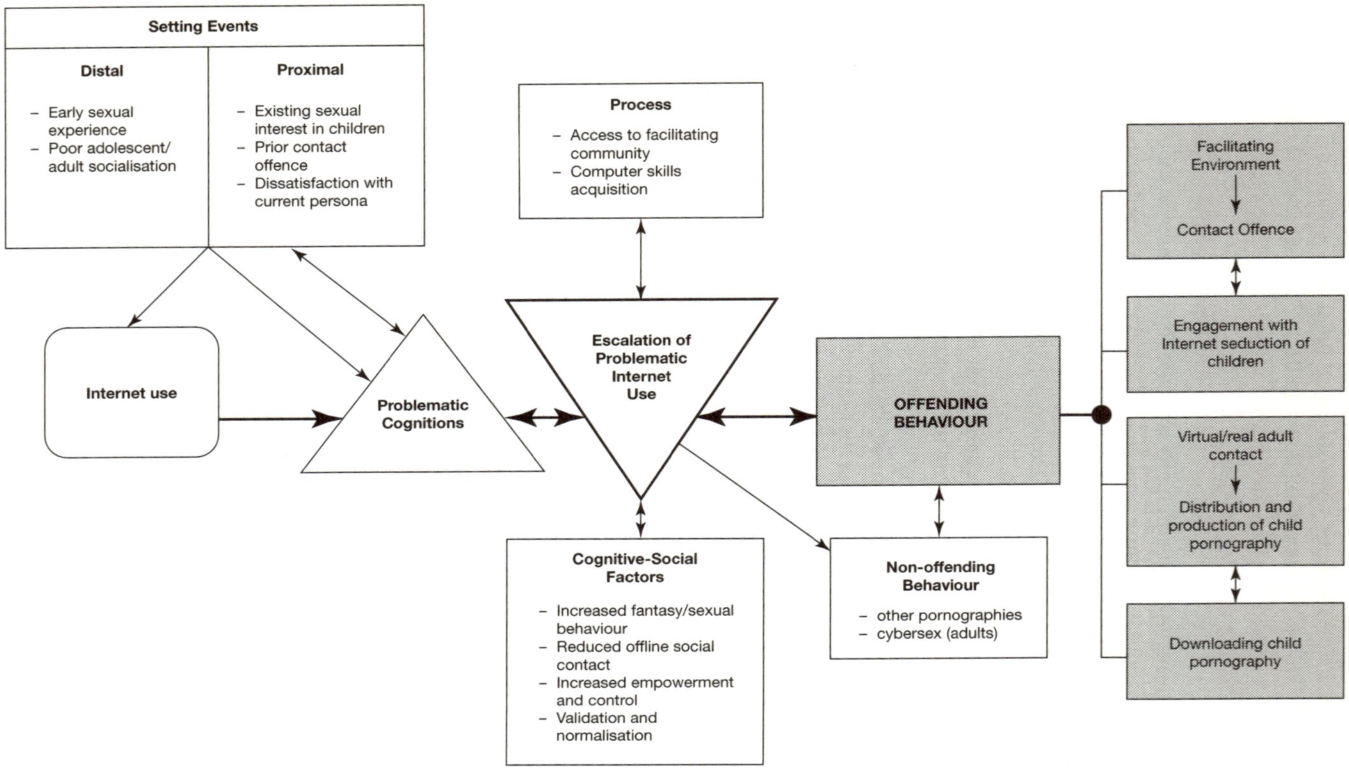

Figure 8.1 A model of potential problematic Internet use.

> John got down these magazines and we were all being very quiet and we were sitting on the floor and looking at them. It was basically pornography . . . they were pictures of Paul doing stuff . . . doing all sorts of things I mean. (EI: 55)

This quotation is from the account of EI's first introduction to sexual abuse as a child, which involved viewing pornographic photographs involving his friend (John). Cognitions like these appear to normalise the involvement with child pornography and act as a way of explaining, or justifying, continued adult interest in this area. Explanations of this kind are often juxtaposed with statements of how traumatic that personal abuse or exposure had been, which seems rather paradoxical, given that the same person may go on to talk about own adult sexual involvement with children as an expression of love. It leaves unanswered how apparently traumatic events might play a part in inflicting further such events on others, and inevitably raises questions about the relationship between fantasy and fact, or the interpretations based on accounts of this kind. Other examples of distal setting events made reference to long-lasting difficulties in relating to adults, with the Internet providing the means for sexual exploration or expression that involved no actual contact with people:

> I wouldn't talk to them . . . you know . . . unless they spoke to me I always acted nervous around them . . . and I think it was because of that . . . that it was more easier . . . it was easily accessible on the Internet . . . just to erm . . . just to look at the images there. (LD: 15)

The following quotations are illustrative of what might be seen as examples of more proximal setting events, either in terms of providing a way of effectively dealing with current dissatisfactions in the individual's life, or as a means of engaging in sexual interest in children without necessitating the abuse of a child within the offender's immediate social world:

> I think it mattered to the extent that it shut out the . . . part of my life that I was finding difficult to deal with . . . it was sort of my time, it was my space . . . I got to the stage where I started to feel . . . annoyed if I felt . . . other people were intruding on that. (MQ: 33)

> I told them that my whole philosophy was we're paedos . . . let's look at the pics . . . let's jerk off but let's not hurt any kids. (QH: 24)

ENGAGING WITH THE INTERNET AND THE BEGINNING OF PROBLEMATIC INTERNET USE

The setting events identified relate both to Internet use and the development of problematic cognitions. The decision to go online, on the basis of evidence from the COPINE interviews, may be a way of generating solutions to both distal and proximal setting events. The majority of respondents in the interview sample had taught themselves how to use the Internet, and gaining access to it brought opportunity to find pornography. While some respondents developed skills sufficient only to help them gain access to such material, most quickly acquired high levels of skill either through chatting to others, reading Internet magazines, or buying or downloading software packages. Long periods of time spent on the Internet provided opportunity for practice that was highly reinforcing. This can be conceptualised as part of the process of engagement, which was facilitated by cognitive and social factors. It is worth noting that there was often a rapid increase in feelings of power associated with being able to find material, bypass security measures and gain credibility with other Internet users. This is reflected in cognitions that indicate an emergent sense of power and control:

> But it was by going through and searching and . . . I suppose practice they say makes perfect . . . that I found these sites in Russia which had a whole sort of data base. (MQ: 17)

> yes a lovely little world that you'd get into . . . and you knew you could be in control of it. Nobody was going to stop me . . . seeing what I wanted to see. (DX: 60)

As respondents started to download, what emerged was the increasing normalisation of accessing and collecting pornographic material. Cognitions supporting this make reference to others engaged in similar behaviour:

> I was finding more explicit stuff on the computer and I was looking at the computer and thinking oh . . . they're doing it . . . it can't be that bad . . . it's there you know. (KQ: 7)

> there was the knowledge that at least a lot of the material was of interest not only to myself but to other people. (II: 9)

For all respondents there was a rapid increase in the amount of time spent online and a reduction in actual social behaviour. There was a sense of not wanting to or not needing to move away from the computer in order to be with people. This was seen particularly where participants moved from picture- to text-based material and where they sought out 'chat' with others through IRC. Cognitions reflect the difference between the social world offline and the more exciting online environment:

> you're not getting anywhere . . . it was like I was doing overtime I was doing stupid overtimes like double shifts sometimes you know I used to work . . . I think like when it became like me only social outlet. (TQ: 13)

> er it was a little . . . it was a fantasy world for me . . . and it was so different from the mundane existence I'd been leading. Here was something that was dangerous . . . it was exciting . . . it was new. (II: 15)

ESCALATION OF PROBLEMATIC INTERNET USE

Engagement with the Internet is a dynamic process, and in the case of offending activity, it seems to involve a process of escalation. Given this, it is important to note that presumably some individuals, having reached this point, reduce their level of engagement with the Internet, rather than increase it. Access to this information is difficult, for, of course, we only see in offender accounts the result of escalating involvement. Perhaps the issue here relates to the nature and personal significance of the setting events as factors sustaining involvement with the Internet. For those for whom escalation occurred, there were frequent references made to the addictive qualities of the Internet, as an explanation of continuing and escalating involvement with the child pornography world:

> it was a real sense of addiction. Every opportunity that I had to get online when my wife wasn't in I would do it. (II: 15)

> and the first thing I do like any drug addict looking for his next fix is I go on the Web for . . . paedophilia . . . especially pictures. (QH: 5)

> and I'd stopped for a while but it was like constantly in my head . . . I wanted to get back to it. (DX: 18)

These cognitions were used as a way of rationalising staying online and looking for child pornography, and engaging in other forms of sexualised activity. Downloading behaviour, therefore, was often seen as a form of illness over which the respondent has little or no control. However, one relevant difference to note in relation to the Internet is that there are few external controls, by way of people or situations, which are going to influence this behaviour. Once online, downloading pornography is not censured but is reinforced by the community engaged in similar behaviour. To challenge that community by expressing doubts about what one is doing is to run the risk of censure or even of losing the social contact with others.

OFFENDING BEHAVIOUR

As a result of these processes, the model proposes a number of behavioural outcomes, some of which are clearly forms of illegal behaviour (termed offending behaviour) and others drawing on the same roots that are not illegal (referred to below as non-offending behaviour). The model proposes four forms of offending behaviour: downloading; trading; seduction; and contact offences. All revolve around engagement with the Internet and the possession of child pornography.

Downloading

Given such circumstances, spending time online was associated with an increase in the number of images downloaded and a corresponding expansion and/or focus in collecting. Collecting behaviour taking this form generated cognitions that appeared to distance the respondent from the content of the collection and objectified the children within such images:

> Well I had a good collection. I had a strong collection actually 'cause er . . . there were very few duplicate pictures in it . . . See most people when they'd organize their collection there'd be a lot of duplicate pictures and it was all of this disheveled mess . . . my organizational skills were er quite excellent. (QH: 17)

> well in the pictures folder there'd probably be a folder called er panties and there'd be like front and behind. (OC: 60)

In many cases, preference was shown for some pornographic images over others. In the main this involved downloading large numbers of images and then sorting and cataloguing new images, identifying as part of this those pictures that were attractive. Some respondents looked for images to complete a series, and kept the series name; others liked to complete a series but changed the name to suit either the child or a particular fantasy:

> I began to collect certain series . . . of pictures erm one at a time . . . erm. You know you'd get a particular series that you'd particularly like. (OK: 22)

The fact that sexual activity involved masturbation to images as opposed to real children was used as a justification of this behaviour:

> it was purely a visual image to allow me to achieve an erection so I could go into the bathroom and masturbate. (KQ: 22)

> it wasn't a person at all it was . . . it was just a flat image . . . it was a nothing. (OC: 54)

Sometimes the images had a specific sexual focus: for example, one respondent liked to look at circumcised penises and would collect, but not exclusively, pictures that related to this. Another liked pictures of 'Aryan' boys, whereas one respondent indicated a preference for 'action shots' that depicted actual penetration. For all respondents, however, collecting was driven by a search for new material, sometimes to complete a series and at other times with reference to a particular sexual fantasy. This meant that 'old pictures' once catalogued might seldom be looked at again. Newness was also referred to as part of a socialisation process – it legitimised exchange, whereas old material did not:

> I would tend to look at what . . . what had recently been posted so it wasn't about tracking through to find specifics but a half dozen or so or a dozen or so and new this week. (JK: 27)

> it kind of legitimised my . . . sort of personality on the Net . . . in that I can show you I liked this . . . you can talk to me because I can show you I like this material. (II: 16)

Collecting pictures from the Internet led to an increase in both fantasy and sexual activity. Many of the participants had had a very low level of sexual engagement with others (even where there was a sexual partner) and solitary sexual activity increased, for some dramatically, while downloading and sorting material (both pictures and text):

> I would say after probably two or three hours I would say . . . about two or three hours and then I would masturbate. If I hadn't found anything particular that I liked on the Internet I could always go back to me disks and feed off them. (DX: 9)

Cognitions that supported such sexual activity made reference to the fact that it was only fantasy, or made comparisons with adult heterosexual relationships:

> and as long as you keep your sense . . . that it's fantasy . . . then it's OK. (MQ: 19)

> But the big thing I kept saying and I believed it . . . with every inch of my body . . . was that this was OK because I'm not touching . . . I'm not touching anybody . . . it's better for me to sit here fantasising and looking at pictures . . . and I'm not I'm not doing anything else. (OK: 68)

Being able to access images at will for the purposes of masturbation was also accompanied by feelings of control, often absent in real-life relationships. This notion of control was also evidenced in some of the preferred fantasy material about 'teaching' children about love and sex:

> and then I started to . . . wonder if he's old enough to clim(ax). I mean this is the thought that came into it with the pictures . . . I meant to tell you that as well . . . you know about making their first time really good. (OK: 58)

Downloading pictures was not necessarily the end point in this form of offending behaviour. Closely related was an involvement in collecting text material, which may substitute for pictures as a stimulus for sexual arousal.

Trading child pornography and the importance of virtual/real adult contact

Not all collectors of child pornography moved from collecting to contact or communication with others (either adults or children). Some people seemed to prefer to engage only with the Internet as an individual, taking pictures or text from others but in the absence of any social exchange. But for all respondents who sought to communicate with others, the relationships formed assumed importance and were selective, and access to both material and relationships were often through a carefully policed private channel. Several respondents contacted people they had met through the Internet and arranged physically to meet them. These contacts often had a mundane quality about them, including telephone calls, sending flowers and cards. For all respondents who made contact with others, the 'reality' of the relationship was important in legitimising and normalising their interests:

> my rule was that they had to be decent . . . stable, not police officers and have some pictures. They didn't have to have a huge collection . . . if they had stuff I didn't have great . . . if they didn't I wasn't going to lose any sleep over it. (QH: 21)

For those respondents who engaged in any social interaction with the Internet through IRC (Internet Relay Chat) or other forms of person-to-person contact, the process of sustaining that engagement required the participant to have credibility. Such credibility often related to qualities of pornographic picture collections, which served to illustrate the centrality of child pornography to the broader issue of adult sexual interest in children and the Internet. Credibility and status could be achieved through the size of the collection of photographs or through the exchange or trade of new or 'rare' material such as pictures or text. The latter would consist of fantasy stories, or talk of previous 'contact activities'. Again, cognitions that supported such behaviour tended to emphasise the feeling of importance gained from owning and distributing such images, while at the same time equating the pictures with more socially desirable commodities, such as works of art:

> Well like I said I was very good at finding people to trade with. I was a good negotiator so to speak and I would tend to find pictures . . . I managed to find the whole series from somebody and I let the channel operators know

> . . . and they were deeply grateful. It's kind of like an art collector who finds a lost Picasso. (QH: 13)

It appeared that there had to be 'input' of some sort both to engage in such relationships and to sustain them (in a similar way to real-life relationships). This might be achieved by keeping a file of 'vital statistics' in relation to nicknames, so that when a nickname came up they could immediately respond with personal material that helped build the relationship. The adoption of nicknames was also a way of reinforcing fantasies about the self, and, of course, drew on notions of identity and manipulation of self-representation. For example, one respondent took on the name Harry Mudd as being a fictional character that he saw as being similar to the real him – the mischievous rogue – but a part of his persona that he could never express. Another used Mutznutz as a cartoon dog character – friendly and boisterous – and would follow this through by signing on and off IRC with a woof.

For those respondents who traded, or distributed, images, the notion of images as currency appeared to be important. They are currency in terms of trading for new material but they are also currency in maintaining existing online relationships and giving credibility. An important aspect of this is the notion of a community of collectors serving to normalise the process of collecting but also legitimising the downloading and saving of images that in other contexts may have been aversive to the respondent:

> some of them I kept with the idea well these again don't appeal to me but I might be able to use these some time in the future perhaps for swapping with somebody else . . . something perhaps more that I do like or whatever. (OK: 40)

Engagement with Internet seduction of children

Within the sample of respondents available to the COPINE Project, one person used both a child and an adult persona to effect contact with other children through the Internet. This was accomplished through chat rooms. As noted in Chapter 5, assuming a child's persona (sustained over a number of months) allowed this respondent easily to win the trust of others he supposed to be children and to engage in cybersex with them. These necessarily had to be geographically distant relationships, as revealing himself physically would have destroyed the persona he had created for himself. The creation and maintenance of this persona lasted for over twelve months and in itself is evidence of a distorted cognitive style that was at odds with his offline world. Chatting to others as if he was a child allowed this respondent to justify his behaviour, as then the activity was taking place between children rather than between an adult and a child.

However, self-representing as an adult male allowed him to chat to under-age males, to engage in sexual activity with them both online and via the telephone, and to arrange physical meetings with them. Justification of such behaviour was largely achieved through talking to other adults online, and feeling that here in this community were the only people who would understand.

Public concern about Internet seduction of children is very high, but it is difficult to gain any true sense of the nature and scale of the problem. For it to occur, it requires a degree of engagement by both parties, in a sense making real the fantasy of the compliant and sexualised child. Presumably the frequent accounts of Law Enforcement 'sting' operations in this area, when adults engage with what they think is a child who later turns out to be a police officer, draws on this 'shared' fantasy. Unquestionably there really are children on the Internet who do in fact fulfil these fantasy requirements, but it may be that 'sting' operations are as much an indicator of the prevalence of that fantasy, rather than a reflection of risk as such.

Commission of a contact offence

For some respondents, the commission of a contact offence was presented as an extension of online behaviour, where the fantasy engaged with online was acted out in real life. A critical limiting factor is, of course, opportunity to access a child in circumstances where a contact offence could occur. The cognitions that supported contact offences made reference to the pictures reflecting others having engaged in similar behaviour, along with passive acceptance by the child:

> I was finding more and more explicit stuff on the computer and I was looking at the computer and thinking oh . . . they're doing it . . . it can't be that bad . . . it's there you know . . . I'm not doing any harm and she doesn't seem to mind . . . and it just gradually built up over a period of time. (KQ: 7)

> 'cause by the time I had those images yes so I'd look at those erm . . . and all I wanted to do was abuse her really . . . make sure she was asleep in bed, stalk on the stairs and keep watching . . . to make sure she was asleep and then I abused. (DX: 24)

Contact offences may be limited to sexual assaults, but may also include the production of pornographic material. In some cases self-statements that supported such production lean heavily on the legitimacy of the behaviour because it was a copy of what had been seen online:

> when I made this video tape I was copying these er movie clips . . . that I'd downloaded er . . . I wanted to be . . . doing what they were doing. (KQ: 32)

Such justifications share many of the same qualities as those that accompany downloading, raising important issues about the relationship between downloading and contact offences. In terms of risk assessment, this is a very important issue.

In other cases, contact offences were related to the need to sustain and increase credibility amongst others, as a means of gaining further desired pornographic material. The following is an account from an offender (ET) of how he became involved in the production of pornographic videos of his young daughter both to meet demands from people he encountered online and to gain access to material that he wanted:

> Well, that came about where . . . I was in the chat room and obviously chatting to a lot of people who were trading images.
>
> It was like . . . people send lists of material that they had. They might have 10,000 and videos and that . . . and they were reluctant to give me access to any of that material unless I could come up with some new material
>
> I was sort of left out of this arena that was going on, this trading of new pictures.
>
> My motivation then was to come up with some pictures that I could trade for . . . for these images.
>
> It was then that I thought about steps of involving my daughter . . . in in creating video to actually trade to get the material that I wanted.
>
> When I actually started offending it was . . . my aims were to produce a video without necessarily abusing my daughter . . . that's how I think I began justifying it to myself.
>
> I think the first instance was when I'd got back into the chatrooms and . . . I was sort of talking about I may be able to provide something and in return . . . and I'm sort of asking what would I get in return if I did sort of thing . . . and they came up with like longer snippets of videos that were available that they were prepared to trade with me if I did. And that was like what really made up my mind to carry out the acts themselves.

Central to this account is how the offender 'talked himself' into sexual contact with his child that he then photographed and distributed. Having arrived at that point, he justifies his behaviour as not really being abusive, in part because he involved her in the production of the material. What this also emphasised is the importance of newness as being a factor in the production of material and its currency for trading images.

NON-OFFENDING BEHAVIOUR

The model presented here reflects the fact that not all people who engage in problematic Internet use either go on to commit an offence through downloading child pornography or attempting to seduce children through the Internet. Within our sample of respondents (all of whom had been convicted), there was also evidence of a movement between pornographies and of using the Internet to further adult sexual relationships. This is often expressed in terms of boredom or satiation, so that cognitions that support accessing new material are in relation to increasing the levels of sexual stimulation. Indeed, in time this might lead to a movement away from collecting and even viewing child pornography:

> I was actually getting quite bored as it were . . . erm . . . with the sort of child pornography . . . I was becoming sort of much more obsessed with bondage . . . and sort of torture . . . imagery. So . . . I'd kind of exhausted . . . the potential that it had for sexual arousal. (II: 20)

For some respondents, non-offending behaviour took the form of collecting erotica, rather than material that would meet the legal definition for child pornography (Taylor *et al.*, 2001). This material appeared to function in the same way as child pornography (as a sexual stimulus, as a collectible item, as a means of exchange and so on), but could be justified because it did not constitute pornography, and was often described as 'artistic'. The fact that such material was relatively easy to obtain and was sometimes in the public domain was used to legitimise the behaviour, even when the person acknowledged that it functioned in exactly the same way as material that was frankly pornographic.

A further parallel feature of Internet behaviour for many people involved in adult sexual interest in children is a preoccupation with issues related to security. Whilst gaining information on how best to protect a computer, or how to hide material, does not constitute an offence in itself, it is clearly associated with offending behaviour and the desire to avoid detection. Thus, engagement through the Internet with other people with a sexual interest in children does not necessarily focus only on pictures, or seductive relationships or fantasy. Bulletin Boards and newsgroups, for example, frequently contain material relevant to the security concerns of their readers.

PROCESSES

Previous literature, in the context of people with a sexual interest in children, has focused on a cognitive behavioural model both to help us understand the nature of the problem and to provide a framework for therapeutic intervention. While such research is not without its critics (e.g. Geer *et al.*, 2000), it still informs the majority of treatment approaches for offenders, yet so far it fails to accommodate behaviour that relates to the new technologies. Recent research that has examined the role of cognitions in Pathological Internet Use (e.g. Davis 2001), suggested that cognitive distortions and reinforcement facilitate symptoms and behaviours associated with spending too much time online. The model that has been developed in this chapter draws attention to a process model of problematic Internet use that is mediated by distorted cognitions. This model allows us to examine the various stages that offenders move through in engaging with the Internet, and the cognitions that support and sustain engagement. While it is not supposed that this represents the totality of problematic cognitions related to such offending, it is suggested that this provides a useful conceptual framework that may inform therapeutic assessment and intervention.

Such a conceptual framework is desirable in the context of our understanding of offenders and the management of their offences, because it suggests that offenders move through stages of involvement with the Internet that are largely maintained by problematic cognitions about the self and the material being viewed. Such cognitions may facilitate an increase in the level of problematic behaviour (for example, moving from downloading child pornography to the commission of a contact offence) or may allow for the move to other sexually exciting, but legal, behaviour.

Within this model, it is clear that cognitions change when the offender moves from a relatively isolated position as 'downloader' to be involved in a larger social network that has many of the characteristics of a 'community' (Linehan *et al.*, 2002). Within the more benign context of education, it has been argued that the Internet provides the opportunity for the development of a 'community of learners' (Ingram *et al.* 2000). The model proposed here addresses this in its account of two crimes that relate to community: the production and trade of child pornography, and engagement with Internet seduction of children. Communities facilitate such behaviour through coaching users in the skills needed to engage with the Internet and avoid detection. They also allow offenders to justify their behaviour, and the absence of an offline audience means that such distorted cognitions go unchallenged. It is also important to note that for most, if not all, downloaders of child pornography, increased Internet activity results in, or is a function of, decreased social engagement with the 'real' world. This is very similar to the findings of Kraut *et al.* (1998) who suggested that greater use of the Internet was associated with declines in participants' communication with family members and larger social circle, as well as increases in depression and loneliness. In the work reported here, the amount of time spent on the Internet precluded many social relationships and limited any 'reality checks' on the appropriateness of downloading child pornography.

It is apparent from this model not only that for some individuals the Internet presents an opportunity to access material that may be problematic from a judicial perspective, but that the nature of the Internet itself may be problematic for the user (Davis 2001; Morahan-Martin and Schumacher 2000). Granic and Lamey (2000) suggested that the Internet has provided people with experiences that have led to a reinterpretation of society, relationships and the self. This is very relevant for people with a sexual interest in children. Through the Internet we see a potential change in the offenders' beliefs, values and cognitive styles, as they act and interact outside the confines of a conventional hierarchy. It is possible that such experiences may empower sex offenders, who have otherwise felt marginalised within a conventional society.

King (1999) discussed the problems that some people clearly have in abstaining from problematic Internet content. The respondents in the work reported here rationalised this by talking about their addiction to the Internet in general and child pornography in particular. It may be that this is a peculiarity of this sample, in that the police had apprehended all respondents and their downloading activities had been taken out of their control. Whether more of this sample would have gone on to commit contact offences remains unknown.

Clearly the anarchic nature of the Internet (King 1999) means that it will continue to effect social, cultural and psychological changes. However, the model proposed here is a first step to increasing understanding of the role that the Internet may play in offending behaviour and, in particular, offences related to the abuse of children.

Chapter 9

Issues for concern and conclusions

In this book, we have tried to develop a broad and comprehensive view of child pornography, in terms of the features, qualities and processes that might be involved in its collection, distribution and production. In this final chapter, we will attempt to pull together some of the major issues that emerge from the book, and in doing so try to extend the debate towards conceptual and policy gaps and practice as we see them.

By way of review and conclusion, perhaps the single issue most clearly to emerge is the fact that child pornography can have a variety of functions for individuals who collect, produce and distribute it. However we define child pornography, its role for those involved with it can be quite complex. Whilst sexual fantasy may in one sense lie at its heart, there are also ways in which the pictures are a commodity which those concerned with them use in different ways, and which can meet a number of different needs for those individuals. Furthermore, it seems that these functions for the individual can change over time, and that whilst we might identify a range of processes in which child pornography plays a part, not all individuals are involved with these processes in the same way, and similarly the functions of child pornography for any given individual may change over time.

A further principal issue addressed by this book relates to the specific role of the Internet in the production, distribution and collection of child pornography, as well as the broader associated issue of the role of the Internet in the sexual exploitation of children through child pornography. Two problems can be identified in drawing conclusions with respect to this issue. The first is our general lack of knowledge about the role of child pornography in the sexual exploitation of children *per se*; the second relates to a historical comparative perspective and concerns the extent and nature of child pornography before the Internet. To properly understand the current situation, we need to better define its context, but we are ill-prepared to do this. Is the extent and nature of child pornography growing because of the Internet, or are we simply more aware of something that has always been there, but hidden? With respect to new pictures, when they emerge are we seeing something that would have happened anyway, but in the absence of the Internet did not have an accessible forum through which to emerge, or are we seeing a genuine growth of something that was not happening before? The Internet certainly makes child pornography more accessible, and ease of access presumably means that psychological barriers such as inhibitions or fear of exposure are less effective in limiting access. Should we perhaps look on this in market terms, where increased demand caused by the relative ease of access on the Internet results in an increased supply? In absolute terms it is difficult to make accurate judgements about issues related to growth in quantity, but what is clear is that we are now much more aware than we were that it is a problem, and furthermore a problem in which the Internet plays a significant role.

However, even given these gaps in our knowledge, there are some things we can say with reasonable certainty. It does seem that there are different kinds of involvement with child pornography as we noted above, which may in part be a reflection of both Internet processes, and the ready availability of child pornography on the Internet, creating a new situation when compared to pre-Internet days. The Internet as a network is bounded by specific communication protocols which focus and shape what is possible, but which may also increase the likelihood of particular types of behaviour. The isolated quality of engagement with the Internet, the assumed anonymity, and the possibilities for changing self-representation are all factors that might lead some people to become increasingly involved with deviant activities such as child pornography. However, this applies not only to involvement with child pornography, of course, but to many other areas as well.

COMPLEXITY OF DEFINING AND UNDERSTANDING CHILD PORNOGRAPHY

In Chapter 2, we discussed at some length what we mean by child pornography. Two broad contrasting perspectives were identified: definitions related to legal specification, and definitions related to more psychological qualities of what people with a sexual interest in children themselves regard as sexually attractive. In a way, this is a false dichotomy, because these different approaches to definition address different issues; in any event, at the extreme end of pictures portraying explicit sexual behaviour, both views converge. It only becomes potentially more problematic, however, when less extreme pictures are considered. But, by making this distinction, we did not mean to argue for a substitution of one definition for the other. Legal definitions are necessarily precise and have to be grounded in some objective criteria. The alternative, more psychological approach supplements the legal definition, because it helps us to place the rather arbitrary qualities any legal approach will have in practice into some kind of context.

The core quality of any psychological approach to child pornography based on preferences of adults with a sexual interest in children will necessarily relate to fantasy. But whilst fantasy is clearly an element in the distorted cognitions that we have suggested underpin engagement with child pornography, the management of fantasy *per se* is something that the law is ill-equipped to address, and indeed many would feel should not attempt to address. Many people have many kinds of fantasies; provided such fantasies remain private, and provided they are not expressed in some form of behaviour that impinges on others, the law can have no effective role. Indeed, unless such fantasies are expressed in some way, how can anyone know they are there? Drawing attention to the psychological qualities of child pornography aids our understanding of the nature of the problem, but does not necessarily solve the difficult issues related to resolving what constitutes child pornography. Psychological approaches might help the law to be better refined, or may play a part in placing into context collecting behaviours, for example, that may be indicative of a sexual interest in children. It is not, however, a competing kind of definition.

Whilst the central and core quality of child pornography is its capacity to generate and sustain sexual fantasy, child pornographic pictures can also be seen to be important as objects for collecting, and as a focus for social interaction. In Chapter 7 we reviewed the sense in which qualities relating to collecting *per se*, rather than sexual fantasy, may be factors in determining some aspects of collecting behaviour. In this respect, notions of completeness along some attribute or dimension seem to be important. In Chapter 6 we also reviewed the sense in which child pornography can be the 'vehicle' around which social interaction between people can grow. Such social interaction has an important role in normalising adult sexual interest in children. It also facilitates the provision of information related both to the availability of photographs and to issues of security in both maintaining collections and accessing the Internet. For some people, social activities also include the opportunity to engage in fantasy role-play, and sometimes, real role-play leading to meetings, centred on sexual encounters with children. Given this, therefore, our understanding of child pornography needs to be broadened beyond a narrow concern with pictures, to embrace a much more comprehensive agenda related to sexual abuse of children. Sexual fantasy may lie at the core of child pornography, but other issues are also significant.

The central quality of pictures that are attractive to adults with a sexual interest in children, therefore, is that they enable the generation and sustenance of sexual fantasy about children. This is expressed primarily in terms of solitary sexual activity such as masturbation, but may, as we have noted, include other more social activities. However, the pictures that are used as a vehicle for sexual fantasy and behaviour are not confined to those we refer to, within a legal framework, as child pornography. Child pornography in most jurisdictions refers to pictures that meet some legal criteria. For example, it may be that to be defined as pornography, such pictures have to portray children in sexual acts, or have to meet some benchmark with regard to what is considered obscene. Such criteria vary both between countries and even within countries, such that what may be considered pornographic in one state of the United States, for example, may not be considered pornographic within another. Child pornographic pictures at their worst are pictures of sexual assault in progress, and in this sense, therefore, are at the extreme end (in terms of sexual victimisation) of a continuum of pictures that adults with a sexual interest in children fantasise over. Fantasy, however, is both an ephemeral and fickle thing. What constitutes a sexually arousing fantasy can change over time, as a result of continued exposure (perhaps related to a form of habituation), changing circumstance (availability of pictures) and learning experiences.

According to offenders, and also through inspection of the child pornographic pictures available on the Internet, core fantasy qualities that seem to be important in child pornography often emphasise notions of innocence, conventional prettiness, wholesomeness and, paradoxically, knowing compliance: on the whole, contradictory elements. Depiction of explicit sexual behaviour is not always, and appears not necessarily to be, a central quality of attractiveness, although nakedness, and/or sexually provocative position do seem to be. White, blonde boys and girls aged between 9 and 12 seem to be the preferred ethnic background and age for the community that collects child pornography from the Internet (probably a reflection of the primarily Western white community that uses the Internet).

Given that child pornography is, at its core, about sexual fantasy, and recognising that the law has a limited role to play in the regulation of fantasy when that fantasy does not include third parties, why then is viewing child pornography so problematic? In Chapter 2 we outlined some of the reasons why this should be the case, and it is worth restating them here.

Perhaps the primary reason is that the production of child pornography requires a child to be sexually abused in some sense. The process of production requires the photographer to create a situation where a child is either physically abused, or posed in sexualised ways, and as such it is a product of an illegal and inappropriate act. The production of child pornography is not an act of fantasy – it is an abusive act. The viewer, even though distant from both the child and the producer, is in a sense aiding and abetting that process, by providing a market for the supplier of the material and similarly for making evident (through Internet activity, private contact or through payment for commercial material) a demand.

A further reason why viewing child pornography is problematic is that a photographic record in whatever media preserves the pictures of that abuse. At worst, therefore, it is a permanent record of crime, and serves to perpetuate the images and memory of that abuse for as long as it exists. Distributing and viewing child pornography, therefore, ensures the continued and even increased availability of the record of the abuse. As we have noted, the implications of this for the family of the child and the child itself may be very severe and traumatic. It also represents a violation of the child and his or her family's privacy, and generally a visible demonstration of abuse of position or relationship. This becomes of greater significance in the context of the Internet. Once a photograph is digitised and distributed on the Internet, it can be perfectly reproduced or modified endlessly by anyone in possession of it. In the case of a normal photograph, destruction of the negative severely limits the likelihood of that photograph being reproduced; in the case of Internet images, the only way to control reproduction of a photograph is to destroy all copies – an impossible task once a picture has been posted to an Internet source.

A more complex argument relates to the effects on cognitive functioning of exposure to child pornography. By generating such inappropriate sexual fantasy in an individual, we must be concerned about the risk of fantasy becoming reality; we must be concerned that by watching a sexual assault, the viewer is encouraged subsequently to commit such an assault. Intellectually this may seem a reasonable fear, although empirically the evidence, such as there is, is difficult to interpret. In the context of adult rape, it appears that the use of pornography by offenders may be evidence of an engagement in a deviant array of sexual behaviours, rather than, as we noted in Chapter 4, a cause of offending. On the other hand, some research has suggested that child molesters were more likely to use such pornographic pictures prior to and during the commission of an offence. Given the importance of this issue and in the absence of definitive knowledge, for practical purposes prudence suggests we must err on the side of caution and assume the balance lies in terms of the dangers of fantasy becoming reality. There is a much clearer identifiable risk that lies (albeit for a small number of people) in pornographic material becoming the model that encourages and generates viewers to take photographs themselves – in other words, for some people it provides the stimulus (when other circumstances allow) to cross the boundary from viewing to abusing. It is not clear whether child pornography *per se* creates that stimulus, whether the social context in which child pornography is traded (especially on the Internet) is the critical factor, or whether it facilitates and gives expression to an intention already formed. However, that there is a relationship of some kind for some individuals is quite clear, and we must take the potential danger of this seriously. It is, however, important to maintain a sense of proportion, and risk factors here, of course, also relate to the access an individual has to children, and the context and circumstances of that access.

We also know that child pornography for some individuals can be used as a learning instrument in the 'grooming' process, whereby a child is de-sensitised to sexual demands and encouraged to normalise inappropriate activities. Finally, in a more general sense, we can reasonably assert that a consequence of viewing sexual pictures of children is that it may sexualise other aspects of childhood and family life. In contemporary Western society there is a broad, if confused, consensus that childhood and family life should not be encroached on in this way.

The reasons why possession of child pornography should be criminalised, therefore, seem clear enough, and its links with sexual abuse need to be clearly stressed and understood. However, it is important also to stress that not all those who have an interest in child pornography are necessarily actual or even potential child molesters in reality rather than fantasy. For some people, a sense of progression seems to be evident, where child pornography represents a step on the way to sexual assaults on children. But, as can be seen in the model of offending presented in Chapter 8, others may stay at one phase, or shift to other elements without necessarily going through all other phases. Some offenders clearly progress from a history of contact offences, discover child pornography, collect and eventually produce their own material for trading on the Internet. Others seem to engage in solitary collecting through non-interactive protocols (such as newsgroups), and, as far as can be judged, never engage in contact offences. For yet other people, the social context to collecting seems to become of greater importance than the material itself; and perhaps for others sexual fantasy associated with a strong attraction to risk taking is important. Adler (2001) emphasises the potential significance of risk taking from an unusual legal perspective, and extends the argument to suggest that there will always be people within our society who are attracted to what is socially constructed as taboo. A further group seems to pass through child pornography as part of a progression through a range of pornographies; perhaps these people can be characterised as seeking sexual stimulation through novel or extreme materials.

What we can say is that the dynamic processes associated with child pornography are at the moment complex and obscure, and it seems likely that not all individuals who collect child pornography do so for the same reasons, or indeed necessarily have the same degree of sexual interest in children. The significance of the factors influencing this may also change over time. In terms of making judgements about the extent to which people in possession of child pornography represent a serious threat to children, there is a need for more research to better identify the issues involved. However, whatever we might say of individual risk, it also needs to be stressed that engagement with the processes we have identified is a serious threat to children, and involvement with these processes represents endorsement and facilitation of them. On conviction, possession of child pornography should therefore attract heavy sentences regardless of the extent of risk for an individual of contact offence. In our view, the issue revolves around the identification and management of risk, and subsequent provision of treatment, rather than sentencing practices *per se*.

Contact offences

How then do we make sense of child pornography in relation to contact offences? The original evidence cited in this book largely comes from interviews with offenders and the people who work with them. Many of these offenders appear to have no history of contact offences, and the offence for which they were convicted generally involved downloading and possession of child pornography. Few of these offenders admitted to intentions to commit contact offences, and most spoke about the barriers they felt that hindered the actual real-life expression of their sexual fantasy. Some even denied sexual arousal by the photographs they were found in possession of. On the basis of this evidence, and on the basis of the limited literature in this area, there are grounds for supposing that there is a group of offenders who focus not on actual sexual assaults on children, but on fantasy contact with children – fantasy driven by child pornography. This fantasy world gains support from its social context, and from the ready availability of child pornography in which the Internet plays a crucial role. There are even some limited grounds for suggesting that, in some cases, access to child pornography may protect against actual sexual assault, by offering the adult with a sexual interest in children the opportunity to express sexual activity with a surrogate child (a photograph) rather than a real child.

However, making inferences in this area is difficult. Most of the published literature, and the evidence cited from the COPINE interviews used in this book, involves convicted offenders. As a general rule, convicted offenders are unlikely to admit to offences they have not been convicted of (although that in fact has happened), and inevitably, because of hindsight and the fact of being either in prison, or under probation supervision, and perhaps exposed to therapy, there is a very human tendency for individuals to put the best light on their actions. Perhaps more importantly, however, all were stopped in their actual or potential offending behaviour by being arrested. Would the offenders whose voices you have heard in this book have committed a contact offence if they had not been apprehended? There is, of course, no answer to this. We do know, however, that the numbers of new pictures that emerge are very, very much less than the number of people who collect pictures. Similarly, we also know that producers of child pornography appear to be relatively rare (at least in terms of those photographs that are publicly distributed and identified). What we do not know, however (and what inevitably complicates the analysis), is the extent to which taking photographs is a factor in sexual assaults against children (involving photographs that are never distributed or disclosed to third parties). Anecdotal reports would suggest that many offenders take pictures of their victims to keep as trophies or reminders of what the child looked like at their preferred age. Such photographs may be shared with others, and may appear in the collections of child pornography we see, but many are more likely to be kept as personal memorabilia.

We need to maintain a sense of proportion in making judgements related to predicting the extent to which an individual possessing child pornography might engage in contact offences. Quite clearly, producers of child pornography are involved in sexual assaults against children. Where opportunity allows, some collectors of child pornography may become involved in assaults (which may or may not involve photographs) through exposure to child pornography, and some people may become involved in other forms of assault or potentially assaultive behaviour through activities such as seeking to meet children through chat rooms. There is also the possibility of individuals 'commissioning' the production of photographs or engaging in the direction of sexual assaults through video-conferencing. The evidence, such as it is, suggests that all of these groups are in a minority when compared to the very large numbers of people who in some way or another access child pornography on the Internet.

One way of representing the structure of offending suggested in this book can be seen in Figure 9.1 which illustrates the relationship between the three different kinds of involvement with child pornography we have identified.

The figure shows how producers of child pornography trade pictures with other producers, and with others who collect pictures (collectors), and others who might both collect and trade pictures with others (distributors). It illustrates that not all producers necessarily trade pictures, that not all collectors and distributors necessarily have contact with producers (although some may), and that the numbers involved in the differing activities are in all probability very different. Consistent

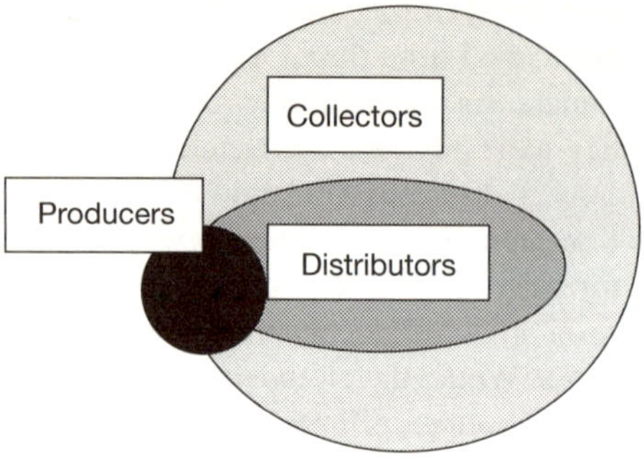

Figure 9.1 The relationship between the three different kinds of involvement with child pornography.

with the notion of process introduced in this book, individuals may move between different roles, depending on circumstances.

Once a picture moves out of the hands of the producer, its distribution is effectively out of control. We know that pictures can rapidly pass from person to person through the different Internet protocols, and indeed there is evidence that some individuals specialise in (and gain status by) providing the channel whereby privately produced pictures are given wider distribution through reposting material. What this means is that any particular photograph may have passed through many hands before it eventually emerges in some public forum, such as the newsgroups. It therefore follows that the individual in possession of a photograph cannot be assumed to have anything other than a tenuous link with the original producer. If there are clear linkages, these can only be identified from the context to the individual's collection.

One of the major challenges in this area is the development of assessment tools that will enable effective discrimination between those involved in child pornography who represent little threat and those who represent a real threat of committing a contact offence, either in terms of producing child pornography, or in another form of assaultive behaviour. In terms of Figure 9.1, we need to discriminate between the sense of risk associated with the relative position of an individual in the offending process, and also (but probably of different character) the degree of risk of an individual moving towards more extreme involvement with child pornography.

If the above is correct, and there is indeed a high proportion of individuals who only collect child pornography, what this also suggests is that whilst the numbers involved are unknown, sexual interest in children is much more widespread than we might imagine. In the present climate, few people would openly acknowledge this, but, in a sense, the numbers engaged in behaviours associated with accessing child pornography on the Internet gives us an indication of the extent of such interest.

Some practitioners find conclusions of this kind difficult to accept. Sometimes this may be because they have a vested interest in maintaining a particular personal position. But a more coherent objection relates to a fear that by introducing questions about the relationship between involvement with child pornography and contact offences, we are in effect suggesting two categories of offender, and furthermore, in a sense, saying that one is of lesser significance than the other. This is certainly not the position put forward in this book. As noted above, we would strongly argue that possession of child pornography *per se* should be subject to severe legal sanctions, and, regardless of its relationship to offending, this can be argued simply on the grounds that production of child pornography depends upon an audience for the sexual abuse of children. But we would also argue that one consequence of an undiscriminating view of the role of child pornography might be a failure to develop the most effective strategies for dealing with the behaviour of offenders. This would also be the case with attempts more generally to control the problem, particularly in the context of the Internet. This issue is developed in greater detail below.

The Internet

What does the Internet bring to this? We have identified in the preceding chapters a range of issues that seem to be particularly relevant as far as the Internet is concerned. One major issue is that the Internet has enabled child pornography to be more widely distributed than ever before, and associated with this increased distribution has been unrivalled ease of access with limited risk of exposure or detection. Thus, until the advent of the Internet, access to child pornography was relatively difficult and required a deliberate effort on the part of the collector to acquire it and to safeguard himself in the process. Also the media used in pre-Internet times was relatively bulky – hard-copy magazines, photographic prints, cine file and videos being the most common.

These two simple issues have important consequences. First, Internet-based collections of child pornography are no longer bulky. Digitised images do not make the same storage demands that hard-copy images do, a fact of considerable importance in terms of hiding material, and general personal and collection security. This also means that collections can become large, because storage is in the main no longer a significant limiting factor. Second, ease of access means that large collections can be relatively easily acquired and developed, which is obviously associated with ease of storage of digitised images. Perhaps of greater significance, however, is that ease of access and low risk of detection also means that individuals who might not have engaged with child pornography because of the risk, or because of lack of opportunity, can now do so. It also means that people who in other circumstances would never experience child pornography may well do so with relative ease, either through expression of a latent sexual interest in children, or as a result of adventitious access.

These factors are of considerable significance in explaining why the Internet has become such an important forum for child pornography. But there are other issues as well that can be identified as being both of significance and specific to the Internet. As we have noted, child pornography on the Internet has important functions other than simply sexual arousal. It is at the centre of the sexual exploitation of children on the Internet, and it facilitates a number of important social processes. Perhaps the greatest source of concern is that the social engagement on the Internet around and with child pornography both de-sensitises and normalises adult sexual interest in children. What might have been a personal fantasy becomes less fantastic and more real through social engagement around these issues. Furthermore, objectification of children becomes more possible, when sexualised pictures of children become objects to trade or collect.

Internet processes also enable and drive the production of new material. The sheer volume of material available means that in the main, specific and perhaps obscure fantasies can be met. But continued exposure associated with ease of availability also, in a sense, reduces 'the value' of pictures to individuals. Newness therefore becomes an attribute of continued sexual interest and arousal. The Internet also seems to serve for some people as a stepping-stone to other forms of abuse. Normalisation processes, which allow of open discussion of kinds and methods of sexual exploitation of children, for example, presumably contribute to this.

Conceptual issues

From our discussion to date, we can draw together a number of issues that merit further attention. The first relates to the paucity of knowledge on the changing interplay between adult sexuality, the Internet, adult sexual interest in children and child pornography. Research in this area has been very limited, with little by way of systematic investment in understanding the processes that may be involved. This is very troubling, given that the issue of child pornography has attracted major political interest, and that as a consequence prison sentences resulting from prosecutions for possession of child pornography are generally very severe. There has been a rapid growth in law in this area, associated with a number of important policy developments. The issue of child pornography has become one of the major driving forces for the development of law enforcement co-operation, and press interest assures high exposure to any arrest or new development. But, as we have noted above, there are many issues that remain obscure and poorly understood. It is difficult to imagine any other substantive policy area where significant resources are committed with so little understanding of the underlying processes. (See Adler 2001 for a discussion of these issues from a legal perspective.) Some of these issues have already been discussed above, but include:

- our concept of the sex offender;
- the role and significance of child pornographies in the context of other pornographies on the Internet;
- the paucity of research on pornography and the Internet, especially as related to both the offender and the victim;

- paucity of knowledge on links between child pornography and contact offences;
- lack of understanding of the effect on future offending of exposing young people to child pornography, either adventitiously or purposively.

Where does this leave us?

We can identify a range of issues that seem relevant to dealing with the problems presented by child pornography and the Internet. The first relates to controlling the problem, through regulating the Internet and the broader issue of censorship, and the role of Internet Service Providers (ISPs).

REGULATING THE INTERNET AND CENSORSHIP

The inescapable conclusion of much of the above discussion is for the development of some form of regulatory framework for the Internet. Individuals collect and produce child pornography, but the Internet itself seems to have a critical role. It is often said that the Internet was designed to make it effectively uncontrollable. Certainly, its international character means that no single national jurisdiction can exercise control over it or unilaterally limit any particular aspect of it. Similarly, the structure of the various communication protocols means that their operation is largely automatic and resistant to unilateral modification. However, perhaps the greatest problem exaggerating lack of control relates to the volume of users. Many millions of people each day access the Internet in some way, and the technical and physical resources required to track each access on any scale would be enormous. But it is important to note that with respect to an individual's activities, tracking and monitoring is not necessarily technically difficult, although it may be costly.

Other aspects of the Internet that are often thought to be necessary qualities of unregulation may be much less significant. In particular, the anonymity, which the Internet is thought to provide, can be much less in practice than in theory. Sophisticated users can certainly hide themselves through a variety of connections, and there are commercial services that offer anonymous access. But in all cases, point-to-point communication protocols require Internet addresses to send information to, and these addresses are necessarily accessible given adequate tracking resources. The use of nicknames, etc. in IRC may give the appearance of anonymity, but any person logged into a network can be identified through their unique Internet address. The issue of anonymity, of such importance in discussion related to the distribution of child pornography, is primarily, therefore, an issue only because we allow it to be, by allowing access to anonymiser services, by allowing anonymous postings to newsgroups, and by not monitoring and recording information at critical points of access. That to do so would require investment of additional resources is beside the point.

Clearly the issue of regulating the Internet gives rise to many concerns. The distinctive and valuable culture that has grown around the Internet is important, and should be preserved; e-commerce is potentially an important source of wealth creation, and powerful pressures will be deployed against anything that might limit the capacity of business to generate wealth from the Internet. However, choices have to be made that might involve setting the limitation of some freedoms against the capacity to generate and sustain sexual abuse of children. Arguments around the issue of censorship are politically and morally complex, and, of course, extend beyond issues related to child pornography and child protection. Ironically, one of the strongest arguments against censorship relates to an emphasis on the dignity of the individual and the choices an individual might make, and against anything that interferes with self-development and self-fulfilment. Notions of freedom of expression are clearly related to this, especially in the context of government regulation of means of expression. But is it really censorship to strive to abolish something that is a source of abuse and a reduction in dignity? Freedom of expression rests upon notions of the common good, and on a framework where rights are matched by duties. The liberty and sense of empowerment that the Internet has offered marginalised groups has to be set within a framework where the exercise of that liberty does not victimise other marginalised and powerless groups. The law is probably an ineffective way of achieving this balance, but in the absence of other avenues, it may be the only option available.

The role of ISPs

The agencies that can effect change outside legal proscription and law enforcement are the Internet Service Providers (ISPs). They alone control access to the Internet for most consumers, and represent the medium through which access to Internet networks is possible. There is strong pressure towards the development of self-regulation within the Internet industry, but the regulatory pressure often seems to be tempered by commercial considerations. Unilateral limitations implemented by one service provider in some circumstances may be seen as placing that organisation at a commercial disadvantage in comparison to others who have not imposed such limitations. For example, where one service provider limits access to newsgroups known to carry child pornography and others don't, presumably adults with a sexual interest in children will tend to subscribe to those ISPs that do carry unrestricted and uncensored access to newsgroups. This, of course, may represent lost revenue to the first ISP. Most ISPs would no doubt publicly reject that this is a factor in the decisions they make about access to newsgroups, but the existence of companies providing 'uncensored' access to newsgroups suggests that there is at least a commercially viable market related to this.

One difficulty is that individual ISPs, or even national groupings, cannot 'control' access to the Internet, because the determined subscriber can always seek access through a third-party service, located elsewhere. However, what is disappointing is that, even at national levels, there seems to be little co-operation or co-ordination between ISPs to formulate coherent collective strategies to limit access to child pornography. As a first step to reducing the amount of child pornography available on the Internet, this must have a high priority. It is difficult, for example, to see why newsgroups which are known to carry child pornography are allowed to survive, let alone made available to ISP subscribers.

Yet what is needed if self-regulation is to be meaningful is a coherent *international* structure to be created that would begin to address these problems on a global scale. Improved co-operation between ISPs and law enforcement agencies, as reflected in the aspirations of the Cybercrime Convention, does not substitute for a proactive approach to self-regulation, deploying the technical capacities of the ISPs to limit and control access to child pornography. The aspiration here should not be to eliminate child pornography from the Internet, which is probably an unachievable aim. More realistically, we should seek to eliminate easy points of access (such as newsgroups) and exercise more control and monitoring over point-to-point communication and web site hosting. In a similar vein, ISPs should not seek moral authority by distorting claims that they are in some sense guardians of privacy on the Internet. Freedom as an abstract moral concept sits very uneasily in organisations created for commercial gain, and ISPs have no role in the defence of presumed freedoms in the absence of a clear sense of rights and obligations. If international regulation became a reality, however, identifying 'rogue' ISPs would then be an important step in focusing attention for governments and other institutions to develop strategies to limit or control access to such companies; an achievable aim. It is disappointing to note that the United Nations in general, and UNICEF in particular, have taken so little action in this area (Taylor 2001).

There is a broader challenge to the ISP industry in this, however. Conceding the legitimacy of control over child pornography will no doubt be seen as the thin end of a wedge of greater public attention to the problem of pornography in general on the Internet. Lane (2000) has drawn our attention to the scale of pornography on the Internet, and the very considerable amounts of money made from it. This money is made at an individual and social cost, however. Cooper *et al.* (2000a) reported one of the few quantitative examinations of patterns of problematic and compulsive use of the Internet for sexual purposes, based on a survey of 9,265 adults. They suggest that 17 per cent of their sample fell within the problematic range for sexual compulsivity in terms of the characteristics and usage patterns of Internet users, and they further suggest that this group seems to spend between 35 and 45 hours per week online. Some 8 per cent of this group (and around 7 per cent of the sample as a whole) reported pursuing sexual material solely from work. This study was not at all about child pornography, but, given the discussion in earlier chapters in this book about processes of offending, it would be naïve to not assume some links between broader sexual activity related to pornography on the Internet and developing interests in child pornography. Clearly this is a contentious issue, and the evidence is far from clear. But it does give rise to a number of questions that might be put to ISPs about their role in the distribution of pornography in general, about web site hosting practices, and more generally on their social responsibility in this area.

Effective investigative strategies

At the moment, the principal lead in the control of child pornography on the Internet is taken by law enforcement agencies. Networks of hotlines, which act as points of referral for members of the public to report inappropriate or illegal material, complement the efforts of law enforcement agencies as sources of information and investigative skills. Other agencies, whilst expressing concern, seem to have limited roles in actually addressing the problems. The European Union, through its STOP and Daphne programmes, has been particularly active in funding innovative initiatives for both law enforcement agencies and non-government agencies to develop research or practice-based initiatives.

By its very nature, law enforcement agencies tend to address individuals or groups of offenders, rather than processes or victims. Efforts by law enforcement agencies to apprehend offenders tend to attract enormous publicity, but headlines emphasising the scale of collections, or the conspiratorial nature of the networks often seem designed to generate political consequences and perhaps allay public fears, rather than control of the problem. Despite very high expectations (and very considerable resource commitment) associated with high-profile cases such as Operation Cathedral, the actual effect on the amount of child pornography available, or the degree and extent of distribution and collection, is minimal. Even more important, however, operations designed to disrupt networks involved in the exchange of photographs give a false sense of achievement related to the apprehension of producers of child pornography. Very few children who appear in child pornographic photographs and videos are ever identified, and the discussions in earlier chapters of this book related to the multiple functions of child pornography might give some indications as to why efforts to disrupt trading networks are unlikely to have high success rates in relation to the identification of child victims.

Recognition that there are a variety of kinds of involvement with child pornography has obvious implications in terms of the development of policing strategies in this area. At the moment, because an unfocused and undifferentiated view is taken of offenders as noted above, it is unlikely that appropriate victim-focused interventions can develop. This is not to say, of course, that in disrupting networks, some producers will not be identified – the new material that is of so much importance in sustaining collecting is, of course, fed into private networks and broader distribution from somewhere, and the points of entry of material into networks is obviously of significance. But given the sheer scale of trading of child pornography on the Internet, disruption of individual networks is unlikely to have any significant impact.

More importantly, however, a lack of targeted intervention means that resources justified as preventing the abuse of children are, in fact, directed at individuals involved in the collection of child pornography, which, as argued here, may constitute a potentially different group. A focus on evidential issues related to specific children particularly at risk who are known about from pictures, or picture series, for example, tends not to be the driving force behind investigations. A symptom of this is the way in which, when reporting operations, an emphasis is placed on the number of child pornography pictures recovered, as if this in some sense represented a measure of risk, or a reduction in the vulnerability of children. The reality is that large collections are more a reflection of an individual's ability to use the Internet, and perhaps a measure of an individual's engagement with other collectors in collecting networks. Disruption of networks, however, does have attractions in terms of police deployment, in that such investigations offer attractive targets for learning about high tech crime in general, and readily fit into policy initiatives that look for quick results that lend themselves to, at times, spurious quantification.

The discussion in this book suggests that disruption of the social context that allows the transition from solitary collecting of child pornography to engagement with some form of community is a critical point in the development of adult sexual interest in children and the Internet. To the extent that disruption of the distribution processes of child pornography achieves this, it is clearly a worthwhile activity. However, if more general disruption of distribution processes is the principal objective, law enforcement intervention is unlikely to provide the most cost-effective approach. Given that trading on the Internet in child pornography requires access to an Internet Service Provider, it is likely to be much more cost-effective to place the burden of control on the Internet Service Providers who provide the Internet access, whose technology enables trading to take place, and whose proprietary and generic network protocols are used to exchange photographs and video clips.

The emergence of a regulatory framework, perhaps akin to those used in Health and Safety Regulations, would place the burden of control on those who have immediate control over the environment (the ISPs). This then leaves law enforcement (or regulatory agencies) the task of ensuring and enforcing compliance with regulations. This would seem a much more satisfactory arrangement, and more likely to effect rapid and permanent change.

A much more effective and strategic use of focused police resources would be to target specific pictures with a view to the identification of the children involved. This would imply a shift of attention away from offenders to victims, something that police services in general are not particularly effective at. Pictures can provide considerable evidence about such issues as location, and there have been a number of notable cases where children have been identified from evidence contained in, or related to, pornographic images. This is much less high-profile work than breaking up networks of traders, and does not yield immediate results that can be publicly characterised as 'fighting child pornography' or 'waging war on pornographers'. It also probably does not fit readily with the popular contemporary imagery of policing, emphasising glamour, action and drama. In most cases, this is primarily a sordid domestic world, one where private betrayal, bribery and inducements and hidden secrets characterise what happens. But the identification of the children involved seems a much more important primary activity for law enforcement agencies than disrupting trading networks. It is also much more difficult, much more resource-intensive, and much more challenging.

A substantive criticism of the criminal justice system's response to child pornography is that it has over-focused on offender issues, at the expense of victim issues. At its worst, the child victim becomes an object around which adults (offenders, police and social services) devote resources to sustain their own construction of events, and their own vested interests, rather than those of the child. We need to engage in a major reappraisal of activity in this area.

The identification of victims of child pornography itself presents considerable difficulties, however. One central operational factor for the police is the identification of new pictures from old. New pictures are examples of a crime currently in progress, a child at risk of current sexual abuse. But obviously to make this judgement it is necessary to be able to recognise new pictures from old. There are examples where police resources have been committed to investigations of pictures 30 or 40 years old, on the assumption that they were current cases. This is a complex area, and requires special knowledge to engage in investigations which not all police forces or even specialist paedophile units have. Recent investments in databases of child pornography photographs, although presented as aids to the identification of victims, will contribute little if anything to this issue. Face or background recognition software, for example, amounts to little more than expensive and complex indexing techniques, and seems to be premised on the assumption that child pornography production is a complex conspiracy that can involve multiple children in multiple locations. The regrettable reality is, however, that people who have legitimate access to a child produce most child pornography in domestic settings. Complex conspiracies may occur, and certainly should be investigated, but not at the expense of the probable greater incidence of domestic production of child pornography.

Investigating the identity of children involved in child pornography can give rise in some circumstances to significant moral dilemmas. It may seem reasonable to launch investigations into cases where there is evidence of a recent sexual assault; this can be justified as preventive action against a serious crime against a child, who by definition cannot give consent to what may be happening, and is presumably at risk. Mobilising significant resources in these circumstances is appropriate, and investigations may even need to be supplemented by other strategies, such as the release of information to the media to aid identification of locations or individuals. Clearly decisions related to this must be made carefully, with a balance struck between the risks associated with publicity and the danger a child may be subjected to through continued exposure to sexual assaults.

It is less easy to justify commitment of resources to seek to identify children who are now adults who were involved in older pictures. There are two reasons for this: unless detection is very straightforward, the deployment of the specialist resources necessary should presumably focus on ongoing abuse, rather than past abuse, because this is where need is greatest. However, another and more important issue relates to the effects of identification of a child on that individual as an adult, and their family. Victims' rights to retain control over their own experiences are important here. When an individual seeks help, by disclosing events in the past, then it is reasonable to follow through on such disclosure. But it cannot be right to force disclosure on to someone who has come to terms with his or her own past, and who fears the loss of control over that experience which will inevitably come about in a police investigation. This is a very complex issue, where policy guidelines are poorly thought through and expressed. It is not an easy issue, but one that has direct practical relevance for both the psychological health of victims and police policy. Relentless pursuit of the offender is not always an appropriate policy for the adult victim.

An area of sexual abuse of children on the Internet that attracts considerable attention is the use of chat rooms to seduce children into actual meetings. Child pornography may play a role in this, but the concern here relates to the potential for actual assault, rather than fantasy. However, given the role of fantasy in sexual activity on the Internet, particularly in chat rooms, concern must be expressed about the extent to which the entrapment activities that are used by law enforcement agencies in these circumstances are actually encouraging the behaviour they seek to control. As we have noted in earlier chapters, there is a complex relationship between fantasy and reality on the Internet. The processes involved in establishing a successful entrapment scenario may well blur the boundaries, resulting in a false sense of the scale of the problem.

Perhaps a critical distinction to make when considering investigative policy related to the production of child pornography relates to organised profit making, perhaps by organised criminal groups, or associated with domestic production. A central and primary task of any offender-focused law enforcement activity in this area must be to remove the capacity to make profits from the production and distribution of child pornography. Networks of distribution of child pornography that we are aware of at the moment (such as the wØnderland conspiracy, for example) were not involved in making profit either from distribution, or from the production and trading of new material. However, there is evidence of individual producers seeking to make financial gain from their own domestic production of child pornography.

One of the most alarming new developments in this area, however, is the growth in what appears to be organised criminal involvement. Commercial web sites selling child pornography videos exist, many of which appear to have their origins in Eastern Europe. Not all these web sites sell material portraying explicit sexual activity, and not all owners of such sites are responsible for producing the material which they sell access to. But, quite clearly, there is a market for this material and unscrupulous individuals and organisations are moving into it. The potential for links with child trafficking and child prostitution are obvious further areas for concern. Dealing with this requires a major investment of law enforcement resources, at an international level, and must be regarded as a high priority. Given that the children that seem to be involved in this material appear to come from economically disadvantaged regions, a focus on the identification of children in those locations must also be of the highest priority. Unfortunately, international investments of this kind in law enforcement activity are complex, and we lack the structures for effective implementation. However, we should not be distracted from these objectives by easy options focusing on disruption of trading networks in countries with more effective law enforcement systems; these limitations should not be allowed to hinder policy development.

In exploring what intervention strategies should seek to achieve, perhaps one gap in policy thinking in this area is a failure to learn from what we already know about crime and criminal behaviour. The model presented in Chapter 8 focuses on the behaviour of offending, and as such, can be readily absorbed within criminological frameworks such as the Rational Choice Perspective (Cornish and Clarke 1986; Clarke and Felson 1993). This approach to crime analysis, amongst other things, focuses attention on points for intervention to control the expression of criminal behaviour. Within the context of concern to us, the model presented in Chapter 8 suggests that intervention to address escalating Internet use, targeted at those individuals at risk and associated with the emergence of problematic cognitions, may have utility. Two issues follow from this:

1 those individuals may not of course be aware of the extent of their problematic behaviour, and therefore may need assistance in recognising both its emergence and the consequence of increasing involvement (perhaps in terms of heightened risk of commission of contact offences);
2 it is likely that the expression of such behaviour already involves engagement with illegal images.

This seems to argue for the development of strategies to limit access to child pornography on the Internet (as argued above) associated with appropriate self-help provision to enable potential offenders to escape from and control the process of escalating involvement. The natural and appropriate medium for this is, of course, the Internet.

THE MANAGEMENT OF PRODUCTS AND PROBLEMS

The products and problems associated with child pornography fall into two broad classes: those associated with perpetrators, and those associated with victims.

Perpetrator issues

The current debate about the management of offenders guilty of sexual offences against children seems to have a one-dimensional quality to it. There seems to be a sense of impotence associated with the child sex offender, such that there is little confidence in any of the efforts made to reduce future likelihood of offending. Highly politicised trials, associated with a focus in the media on extreme and tragic cases, has created a climate where the offender is demonised and where the only solution to 'protecting' children is permanently to incarcerate the offender. Undoubtedly, there are some offenders who, no matter what, will remain a threat to children; there are some offenders who seem to structure their lives around molesting children, and who are unlikely ever to be able to control their offending. As with other forms of offending, therefore, there are groups of incorrigible offenders who seem to represent an enduring threat. But are all offenders involved with child pornography the same? Do they all necessarily represent the same degree of threat, or even a threat at all, in terms of contact offences? We have discussed this earlier in this chapter and in previous chapters of this book, and the conclusions seem to be that there may be evidence to support a more differentiated view of offending related to child pornography. However, what we really need is much more research to explore this issue. Political or moral posturing is not a substitute for balanced assessment in this area, as in others.

Current sex offender treatment programmes appear to make no assumptions about kinds of offender, which may be problematic when applied to Internet-related offences. Whether or not possession of child pornography is necessarily a precursor to a contact offence, an increasing number of people are coming into the criminal justice system guilty of possession of child pornography involving the Internet with no apparent history of contact offences. Is it prudent, let alone effective, to mix such people in therapeutic programmes with acknowledged contact offenders? Anecdotally, we know that possession offenders gain knowledge of grooming practices through exposure to contact offenders. We also have anecdotal information that contact offenders learn about the Internet and child pornography through exposure to child pornography offenders.

If intervention programmes are intended to address the problems offenders present with, then there is a *prima facie* case to be made for a more differentiated approach to therapeutic intervention programmes. At present, sentencing and therapy often reflect a standpoint that seeks to deny offender access to the Internet. However, what we may be conveying to the offender is that they cannot learn to control or limit their behaviour, but rather have to avoid or abstain from Internet use. The viability of this position, given the dramatic increase in both the availability and use of the Internet in everyday life, is questionable. Associated with this is a need for more effective and specific assessment of individuals. If we see offending behaviour in terms of a process, rather than a set of attributes, such assessments need to be ideographic; they need to focus on the individual, their context, and the processes related to his or her offending. An emphasis on functional analysis of offending behaviour would also seem to be appropriate.

At present, police resources are deployed to apprehend those involved in accessing, distributing and producing child pornography. The forensic analysis of computer hard drives, CD-ROMs and disks is largely focused on detecting sufficient material that might secure a conviction. This largely reflects the illegal nature of the photographs or video clips themselves, and may be substantiated by quantification of the types of image and the overall number collected. However, while such an approach is successful in that it facilitates a conviction, it does little to further our understanding of the offender or the process of offending. Such forensic analysis rarely takes into account the ways in which an individual's collection was structured and organised, or the relationships between aspects of the collection. Indeed, there is a possibility that the evidence is largely destroyed by the renaming of series of pictures or fracturing of files. Highly structured collections may, for example, be indicative of an individual who not only collects pictures but who trades them. The collection in itself may yield information about a network of which the offender is a part. This information is not simply academic. It may provide vital information that informs the assessment of risk, and which would also enable therapeutic intervention.

Sentencing practices are necessarily bound up with issues related to offender-intervention issues. There is unquestionably strong current public demand for high sentences for offences related to sexual exploitation of children. However, it is important that a sense of proportionality is maintained, both between these offences and other serious offences, and between different kinds of sexual offence against children. A particular problem relates to the objectives of sentencing in this area. Punishment, protection of the public, effective control and therapeutic intervention are obvious factors that relate to sentencing, but in this context the balance between these factors often seems confused. Aside from issues about absolute length of sentence, and consistency of sentencing practices between judges, a particular issue relates to the role of the Sex Offenders Register, which needs to be more fully explored.

At the moment, in the public eye (if not the authority's), entry on to the Register is seen as an element in the punishment process as much as a means of effecting control over an offender once released into the community. If this is what it is meant to be, and entry on to the register is, in some sense, a substitute for prison, then procedures and resources need to be put in place to ensure offender compliance. If entry on to the register is related to control, and perhaps therapeutic assistance, however, then again appropriate but different resources need to be put in place. In the absence of a clear investment, it is unlikely that the Register will achieve anything in terms of control over further offending.

Victim issues

Earlier in this chapter, we discussed some of the victim-related issues in our discussion of law enforcement practice. The identification of victims is difficult, and it is much easier for the police to focus on offenders, both in terms of opportunities for detection and in terms of the publicity derived from successful operations. Yet surely any concern with child pornography must focus on protection of the child victims. Victim issues need to be at the very top of the agenda in both investigations and social welfare or probation interventions.

However, there is no point in developing strategies for the identification of victims, if the necessary support structures are not available, or sufficiently developed. Necessarily, a focus on victims will involve close inter-agency liaison, which can be both personally and professionally challenging. This can be illustrated in a simple way. In the main, children involved in the production of child pornography are identified through investigation, rather than disclosure. In addition, victims of child pornography, as with victims of other kinds of sexual abuse, often are reluctant to disclose what has happened to them. Pornographic pictures are, of course, clear evidence of some elements of the abuse, but the children involved may often only disclose to the police what they feel the police already know. This can result in the difficult situation that the offender may effectively be the principal source of information about the extent and nature of victimisation of the child; the offender in effect can control what is known about the abuse. In terms of assessment of the child's needs, therefore, there needs to be close communication between the police officers investigating the offence and the social welfare or therapeutic teams dealing with the child. This implies a much greater degree of commonality of approach and a sharing of information than is currently the case.

Earlier we made a distinction between new and old photographs, in terms of structuring policing priorities. This distinction is critical if a focus on the control of current abuse is to be maintained. Child pornography gives a view into the hidden world of child sexual exploitation, and, consistent with what we know about that world, it is primarily domestic in character, with perpetrators having legitimate access to the child. High-profile examples of sex rings involving the multiple stranger abuse of children should not distract attention from the 'mundane' but more extensive domestic abuse which constitutes the core of new child pornography as it appears on the Internet. This is not to underestimate the consequences of abuse in the past involving the production of child pornography for the individual concerned, nor is it to say that there are different categories of victim, some more deserving of attention than others. But the realities of old pictures (which as we noted may have been produced 20 or 30 years ago) are that they involve people who are now adults and who, for good or ill, have accommodated to the world they find themselves in. Further education about the effects of child pornography, and the development of facilities to support adults who disclose past abuse would perhaps change this analysis. But above all the needs of the individual involved must always remain paramount, and social welfare or law enforcement agencies should have as their primary objective the empowerment of victims, however administratively or politically inconvenient that might be.

We have very little knowledge of the long-term consequences for victims of involvement in child pornography. The knowledge for the victim that a highly sexualised picture may continue to circulate long after that child has grown up and matured must be a source of concern, in terms of the psychological well-being of the victim. But because both the Internet and its role in the distribution of child pornography are relatively new, we have not yet seen much evidence on which to base strategic interventions. Fears of identification and the intrusion of traumatic memories are obvious sources for concern.

Does the Internet add a distinctive element to the trauma of sexual exploitation? For the moment we cannot answer that question with any authority, but anecdotal accounts suggest that we should take the risk of this seriously. This, of course, adds even greater weight to the need to prioritise the identification of victims in law enforcement initiatives in this area, as well as to emphasise the need for greater efforts to diminish access and availability through effective ISP actions.

SOCIAL CONTEXT

Castells (1998) in his brief discussion of child pornography, in the context of the broader issue of social effects of the new technologies, makes the following point: 'It is easier to blame the messenger than to question the sources of the message; that is, to ask why our informational society engages in this activity on such a large scale' (156). He identifies the following as factors that contribute to the development of child pornography: globalisation of markets; anonymity; and the search for further sexual excitement in a society of normalised sexuality fuelling the demand for new emotions, associated with poverty, and the crisis of the family identified as significant supply side factors. His chilling conclusion is that 'the network society devours itself, as it consumes/destroys enough of its own children to lose the sense of continuity of life across generations, so denying the future of humans as a humane species' (157).

The extent and nature of child pornography certainly seems to question whether we have indeed created a humane society. Perhaps the answers to why this has occurred lie at one level in terms of the emergence and/or more public expression of aspects of human sexuality. Or, perhaps, more accurately, we should refer to the recognition of aspects of sexuality that have until now been either ignored or repressed. Child sexual abuse is not something new, nor is child pornography. The Internet has certainly made child pornography more available, and through some of the distinctive processes of the Internet has probably enhanced the sexual exploitation of children. The lesson to emerge from our review of the nature and qualities of child pornography is that in terms of those who collect child pornography, there are no particular attributes or qualities that we can identify; offenders are in the main depressingly ordinary individuals.

But offending takes place within a social context. Castells above has identified one aspect of that context, as it might relate to the emergence of the new technologies. But an equally significant element of that context is the sexualisation of childhood that we have seen over recent years. Kincaid (1998) has drawn our attention to the paradoxical qualities of this; we seek to protect children from sexual exploitation in ways that we have never done before, often drawing on notions of romantic innocence to justify this. Yet, through advertising and through the emergence of youth culture, we encourage younger and younger children to wear make up, and to wear what in adults would be seen as sexualised clothing. Designers 'dress little girls as adults, undress teens (Brooke Shield's "There's nothing between me and my jeans") and disguise adult women as little girls' (Kincaid 1998: 104).

Our understanding of child pornography needs to be grounded in this broader social context. Our preoccupation with child pornography, both in terms of the activities of collectors and in terms of the almost excessive media preoccupation with reports of child abuse related to child pornography, draws on this social context. In demonising the child sex offender through failing to make distinctions between kinds of offender, and the over-concern with elements of the process of controlling the distribution of child pornography at the expense of more cost-effective strategies, we reveal a confused and at times contradictory approach to the problem. The production and distribution of child pornography is a major social problem: it is a major child protection issue; it is undoubtedly a factor that contributes to the sexual exploitation of children; and its management does require it being placed high on the list of social priority areas. But in order effectively to control the problem, we need to move away from strategies grounded in assumptions to more empirically based approaches.

We also need to invest in education. Professionals involved in managing child sexual abuse (including the judiciary) need to be made aware of the role that the Internet might play; parents need to be educated in enabling safe Internet access; policy makers need to be educated in the broader context of child pornography in order that informed initiatives can be developed; politicians need to be educated in the causes and consequences of this aspect of the new technologies. Reducing the availability of child pornography on the Internet will not eliminate this problem, but a more informed society might begin the process of dealing with child pornography in a effective and rational way, and in so doing produce a safer environment for our children to grow and develop in.

References

Abel, G. G., Becker, J. V. and Cunningham-Rathner, J. (1984) 'Complications, consent and cognitions in sex between children and adults', *International Journal of Law and Psychiatry*, 7, 89–103.

Abel, G. G., Gore, D. K., Holland, C. L., Camp, N., Becker, J. V. and Cunningham-Rathner, J. (1989) 'The measurement of cognitive distortions of child molesters', *Annals of Sex Research*, 2, 135–53.

Abel, G., Lawry, S., Karlstrom, E., Osborn, C. and Gillespie, C. (1994) 'Screening tests for pedophilia', *Criminal Justice and Behavior*, 21(1), 115–31.

Abel, G. G., Jordan, A., Hand, C. G., Holland, L. A. and Phipps, A. (2001) 'Classification models of child molesters utilizing the Abel Assessment for sexual interest', *Child Abuse and Neglect: The International Journal*, 25, 703–18.

Adler, A. (2001) 'The perverse law of child pornography', *Columbia Law Review*, 101(March), 209–73.

Akdeniz, Y. (1997) 'Governance of pornography and child pornography on the global internet: a multi-layered approach', in L. Edwards and C. Waelde (eds), *Law and the Internet: Regulating Cyberspace*, Oxford: Hart Publishing.

Allen, C. M. (1991) *Women and Men who Sexually Abuse Children: A Comparative Analysis*, Orwell, VT: Safer Society Press.

APA (1994) *Diagnostic and Statistical Manual of Mental Disorders* (4th edn), Washington, DC: American Psychiatric Association.

Araji, S. K. (1997) *Sexually Aggressive Children: Coming to Understand Them*, Thousand Oaks, CA: Sage Publications.

Aylwin, A. S., Clelland, S. R., Kirkby, L., Reddon, J. R., Studer, L. H. and Johnston, J. (2000) 'Sexual offense severity and victim gender preference: a comparison of adolescent and adult sex offenders', *International Journal of Law and Psychiatry*, 23(2), 113–24.

Ba, S. (2001) 'Establishing online trust through a community responsibility system', *Decision Support Systems*, 31, 323–36.

Back, S. and Lips, H. (1998) 'Child sexual abuse: victim age, victim gender and observer gender as factors contributing to attributions of responsibility', *Child Abuse and Neglect: The International Journal*, 22(12), 1239–52.

Bandura, A. (1977) *Social Learning Theory*, Englewood Cliffs, NJ: Prentice-Hall.

Barlow, D. H., Abel, G. G., Blanchard, E. B., Bristow, A. R. and Young, L. D. (1977) 'An heterosocial skills behavior checklist for males', *Behaviour Therapy*, 8, 229–39.

Barron, M. and Kimmel, M. (2000) 'Sexual violence in three pornographic media: toward a sociological explanation', *The Journal of Sex Research*, 37(2), 161–8.

Bechar-Israeli, H. (1995) 'From <Bonehead> to <cLoNehEAd>: nicknames, play, and identity on Internet Relay Chat', *Play and Performance in Computer-Mediated Communication*, 1(2); available at http://www.ascusc.org/jcmc/vol1/issue2/bechar.html.

Belk, R. W. (1995a) 'Collecting as luxury consumption: effects on individuals and households', *Journal of Economic Psychology*, 16, 477–90.

Belk, R. W. (1995b) *Collecting in a Consumer Society*, London: Routledge.

Belk, R. W. and Wallendorf, M. (1997) 'Of Mice and Men: gender identity and collecting', in K. Ames and K. Martinez (eds), *The Material Culture of Gender; the Gender of Material Culture*, Ann Arbor, MI: University of Michigan Press, pp. 1–22.

Blumenthal, S., Gudjonsson, G. and Burns, J. (1999) 'Cognitive distortions and blame attribution in sex offenders against adults and children', *Child Abuse and Neglect: The International Journal*, 23(2), 129–43.

Bogaert, A. F. (2001) 'Handedness, criminality, and sexual offending', *Neuropsychologia*, 39(5), 465–9.

Boshier, R. (1990) 'Social-psychological factors in electronic networking', *International Journal of Lifelong Education*, 9(1), 49–64.

Boyd, N., Hagan, M. and Cho, M. (2000) 'Characteristics of adolescent sex offenders: a review of the research', *Aggression and Violent Behaviour*, 5(2), 137–46.

Boyle, K. (2000) 'The pornography debates: beyond cause and effect', *Women's Studies International Forum*, 23(2), 187–95.

Briere, J. and Runtz, M. (1990) 'Differential adult symptomatology associated with three types of child abuse histories', *Child Abuse and Neglect: The International Journal*, 14, 357–64.

Bromberg, H. (1996) 'Are MUDs communities? Identity, belonging and consciousness in virtual worlds', in R. Shields (ed), *Cultures of the Internet: Virtual Spaces, Real Histories, Living Bodies*, London: Sage, pp. 143–52.

Bumby, K. M. (1996) 'Assessing the cognitive distortions of child molesters and rapists: development and validation of the MOLEST and RAPE scales', *Sexual Abuse*, 8, 37–54.

Burgess, A. W. and Hartman, C. (1987) 'Child abuse aspects of child pornography', *Psychiatric Annals*, 248–53.

Carter, D., Prentky, R., Knight, R., Vanderveer, P. and Boucher, R. (1987) 'Use of pornography in criminal and developmental histories of sexual offenders', *Journal of Interpersonal Violence*, 2(2), 196–211.

Castells, M. (1998) *The Information Age: Economy, Society and Culture*, vol. 3: *End of Millennium*, Oxford: Blackwell Publishers Ltd.

Chandler, D. (1997) 'Writing oneself into cyberspace'. Retrieved, from the World Wide Web: www.aber.ac.uk/media/Documents/short/homepgid.html

Chou, C. and Hsiao, M. C. (2000) 'Internet addiction, usage, gratification, and pleasure experience: the Taiwan college students' case', *Computers and Education*, 35, 65–80.

Clarke, R.V. and Felson, M. (eds) (1993) *Routine Activity and Rational Choice*, New Brunswick, NJ: Transaction Publishers.

Collings, S. J. (1995) 'The long-term effects of contact and noncontact forms of child sexual abuse in a sample of university men', *Child Abuse and Neglect: The International Journal*, 19, 1–6.

Condron, M. K. and Nutter, D. E. (1988) 'A preliminary examination of the pornography experience of sex offenders, paraphiliacs, sexual dysfunction patients, and controls based on Meese Commission recommendations', *Journal of Sex and Marital Therapy*, 14, 285–98.

Cooper, A., Swaminath, S., Baxter, D. and Poulin, C. (1990) 'A female sex offender with multiple paraphilias: a psychologic, physiologic (laboratory sexual arousal) and endocrine case study', *Canadian Journal of Psychiatry*, 35, 334–7.

Cooper, A. and Sportolari, L. (1997) 'Romance in cyberspace: understanding online attraction', *Journal of Sex Education and Therapy*, 22(1), 7–14.

Cooper, A., Scherer, C. R., Boies, S. C. and Gordon, B. L. (1999) 'Sexuality on the Internet: from sexual exploration to pathological expression', *Professional Psychology: Research and Practice*, 30(2), 154–64.

Cooper, A., Delmonico, D. L. and Burg, R. (2000a) 'Cybersex. Users, abusers, and compulsives: new findings and implications: a special issue of the journal *Sexual Addiction and Compulsivity*', in A. Cooper (ed), *Cybersex: The Dark Side of the Force*, Philadelphia: Brunner-Routledge, pp. 5–29.

Cooper, A., McLaughlin, I. P. and Campbell, K. M. (2000b) 'Sexuality in cyberspace: update for the 21st century', *CyberPsychology & Behavior*, 3(4), 521–36.

Cornish, D. B. and Clarke, R. V. (eds) (1986) *The Reasoning Criminal: Rational Choice Perspectives on Offending*, New York: Springer-Verlag.

Cornwell, B. and Lundgren, D. C. (2001) 'Love on the Internet: involvement and misrepresentation in romantic relationships in cyberspace vs. realspace', *Computers in Human Behavior*, 17, 197–211.

Cowburn, M. and Pringle, K. (2000) 'The effects of pornography on men', *The Journal of Sexual Aggression*, 6, 52–66.

Curtis, P. (1997) 'MUDding: social phenomena in text-based virtual realities', in S. Kiesler (ed), *Culture of the Internet*, Mahwah, NJ: Lawrence Erlbaum Associates.

Danet, B. (1998) 'Text as mask: gender, play and performance on the internet', in S. G. Jones (ed), *Cyber-society 2.0: Revisiting Computer-Mediated Community*, Thousand Oaks, CA.: Sage, pp. 129–58.

Davis, G. E. and Lietenberg, H. (1987) 'Adolescent sex offenders', *Psychological Bulletin*, 10(3), 417–27.

Davis, M. H. (1983) 'Measuring individual differences in empathy: evidence for a multidimensional approach', *Journal of Personality and Social Psychology*, 44, 113–26.

Davis, R. A. (1999) 'Internet addiction: is it real?', *Catalyst*. Retrieved, from the World Wide Web: http://www.victoriapoint.com/Addiction%20or%20net.htm

Davis, R. A. (2001) 'A cognitive-behavioural model of pathological Internet use', *Computers in Human Behavior*, 17, 187–95.

DeYoung, M. (1989) 'The world according to NAMBLA: accounting for deviance', *Journal of Sociology and Social Deviance*, 16, 111–26.

Dhawan, S. and Marshall, W. L. (1996) 'Sexual abuse histories of sex offenders', *Sexual Abusing: A Journal of Treatment and Research*, 8(1), 7–17.

Donath, J. S. (2000) 'Identity and deception in the virtual community', in M. A. Smith and P. Kollock (eds), *Communities in Cyberspace*, London: Routledge.

Döring, N. A. (2000) 'Feminist views of cybersex: victimization, liberation and empowerment', *CyberPsychology & Behavior*, 3(5), 863–84.

Durkin, K. (1997) 'Misuse of the Internet by paedophiles: implications for law enforcement and probation practice', *Federal Probation*, 61(2), 14–18.

Durkin, K. F. and Bryant, C. D. (1995) 'Log on to sex: some notes on the carnal computer and erotic cyberspace as an emerging research frontier', *Deviant Behavior: An Interdisciplinary Journal*, 16, 179–2000.

Durkin, K. and Bryant, C. (1999) 'Propagandizing pederasty: a thematic analysis of the online exculpatory accounts of unrepentant paedophiles', *Deviant Behavior: An Interdisciplinary Journal*, 20, 103–27.

Edwards, S. (1994) 'Pretty babies: art, erotica or kiddie porn?', *History of Photography*, 18(1), 34–6.

Edwards, S. S. M. (2000) 'The failure of British obscenity law in the regulation of pornography', *The Journal of Sexual Aggression*, 6(1/2), 111–27.

Eldridge, H. and Wyre, R. (1998) 'The Lucy Faithful Foundation residential programme for sexual offenders', in W. L. Marshall, Y. M. Fernandez, S. M. Hudson and T. Ward (eds), *Sourcebook of Treatment Programmes for Sexual Offenders*, New York: Plenum.

Elliott, M. (1994) 'What survivors tell us – an overview', in M. Elliott (ed), *Female Sexual Abuse of Children*, New York: Guilford, pp. 5–13.

Evans, R. D. (2001) 'Examining the informal sanctioning of deviance in a chat room culture', *Deviant Behavior: An Interdisciplinary Journal*, 22, 192–210.

Falk, J. (1998) 'The meaning of the web', *Information Society*, 14, 285–94.

Faller, K. C. (1995) 'A clinical sample of women who have sexually abused children', *Journal of Child Sexual Abuse*, 4, 13–30.

Fernback, J. (1999) 'The individual within the collective: virtual ideology and the realization of collective principles', in S. S. Jones (ed), *Virtual Culture: Identity and Communication in Cybersociety*, Thousand Oaks, CA.: Sage Publications Inc.

Finkelhor, D. (ed.) (1984) *Child Sexual Abuse: New Theory and Research*, New York: Free Press.

Finkelhor, D. (1994) 'The international epidemiology of child abuse', *Child Abuse and Neglect: The International Journal*, 18, 409–17.

Finkelhor, D. and Russell, D. (1984) 'Women and perpetrators: review of the evidence', in D. Finkelhor (ed), *Child Sexual Abuse: New Theory and Research*, New York: Free Press, pp. 171–87.

Finkelhor, D. and Araji, S. (1986) 'Explanations of pedophilia: a four factor model', *Journal of Sex Research*, 22, 145–61.

Finkelhor, D., Hotaling, G., Lewis, I. A. and Smith, C. (1990) 'Sexual abuse in a national survey of adult men and women: prevalence, characteristics and risk factors', *Child Abuse and Neglect: The International Journal*, 14, 19–28.

Fisher, D. and Howells, K. (1993) 'Social relationships in sexual offenders', *Sexual and Marital Therapy*, 8, 123–36.

Fisher, D. and Thornton, D. (1993) 'Assessing risk of reoffending in sexual offenders', *Journal of Mental Health*, 2, 105–17.

Fraser, M. (1976) *The Death of Narcissus*, London: Secker and Warburg.

Freeman, K. and Morris, T. (2001) 'Investigative interviewing with children: evaluation of the effectiveness of a training programme for child protective service workers', *Child Abuse and Neglect: The International Journal*, 23(7), 701–13.

Freud, S. (1975) *Three Essays on the Theory of Sexuality*, New York: Basic Books.

Geer, J., Estupinan, L. and Manguno-Mire, J. (2000) 'Empathy, social skills and other relevant cognitive processes in rapists and child molesters', *Aggression and Violent Behavior*, 5, 99–126.

Gelder, M. (1997) 'The scientific foundations of cognitive-behaviour therapy', in D. M.

Clark and C. G. Fairburn (eds), *Science and Practice of Cognitive Behaviour Therapy*, Oxford: Oxford University Press, pp. 27–46.

Giese, A. A., Thomas, M. R., Dubovsky, S. L. and Hilty, S. (1998) 'The impact of a history of childhood abuse on hospital outcome of affective episodes', *Psychiatric Services*, 49(1), 77–81.

Gill, G. (1996) 'Discourse analysis: practical implementation', in J. T. E. Richardson (ed), *Handbook of Qualitative Research Methods*, Leicester: BPS Books.

Goldstein, S. L. (1999) *The Sexual Exploitation of Children: A Practical Guide to Assessment, Investigation, and Intervention*, Boca Raton, FA: CRC Press.

Granic, I. and Lamey, A. V. (2000) 'The self-organization of the Internet and changing modes of thought', *New Ideas in Psychology*, 18, 93–107.

Grasz, L. S. and Pfaltzgraf, P. J. (1998) 'Child pornography and child nudity: why and how states may constitutionally regulate the production, possession and distribution of nude visual depictions of children', *Temple Law Review*, 71, 609–35.

Grayston, A., D. and De Luca, R. V. (1999) 'Female perpetrators of child sexual abuse: a review of the clinical and empirical literature', *Aggression and Violent Behavior*, 4(1), 93–106.

Green, A. H. and Kaplan, M. S. (1994) 'Psychiatric impairment and childhood victimization experiences in female child molesters', *Journal of the American Academy of Child and Adolescent Psychiatry*, 33, 954–61.

Greenberg, D., Bradford, J., Firestone, P. and Curry, S. (2000) 'Recidivism of child molesters: a study of victim relationship with the perpetrator', *Child Abuse and Neglect: The International Journal*, 24(11), 1485–94.

Griffiths, M. (1998) 'Internet addiction: does it really exist?' in J. Gackenbach (ed), *Psychology and the Internet: Intrapersonal, Interpersonal and Transpersonal Implications*, San Diego: Academic Press.

Griffiths, M. (2000) 'Sex on the Internet', in C. Von Feilitzen and U. Carlsson (eds), *Issues, Concerns and Implications: Children in the New Media Landscape*, Goteborg: UNESCO.

Groth, A. N., Hobson, W. F. and Gary, T. S. (1982) 'The child molester: clinical observations', in J. Conte and D. A. Shore (eds), *Social Work and Child Sexual Abuse*, New York: Howarth.

Grubin, D. and Wingate, S. (1996) 'Sexual offence recidivism: prediction versus understanding', *Criminal Behaviour and Mental Health*, 6, 349–59.

Hagel, J. and Armstrong, A. G. (1997) *Net Gain: Expanding Markets Through Virtual Communities*, Boston MA: Harvard Business School Press.

Hamman, R. (1996) 'Cybersex amongst multiple-selves and Cyborgs in the narrow-bandwidth space of America Online chat rooms', unpublished MA thesis, Essex.

Hamman, R. B. (1998) 'Debunking some myths about AOL users and the affects of their being online upon offline friendships and offline community', unpublished M. Phil. thesis, Liverpool.

Hanson, R. (1998) 'What do we know about Sex Offender Risk Assessment?', *Psychology, Public Policy and Law*, 4(1/2), 50–72.

Hanson, R. K. and Bussiere, M. T. (1996) *Predictors of Sexual Offender Recidivism: A Meta-analysis* (User Report: Catalogue No. JS4-/1996-4E), Ottawa: Solicitor-General, Canada.

Hanson, R. K. and Harris, A. J. R. (2000) *The Sex Offender Need Assessment Rating (SONAR): A Method for Measuring Change in Risk Levels*, Ottawa: Department of the Solicitor-General, Canada.

Hartman, C. R., Burgess, A. W. and Lanning, K. V. (1984) 'Typology of collections', in A. W. Burgess (ed), *Child Pornography and Sex Rings*, Lexington, MA: D.C. Health.

Hauben, M. F. (1997) 'The netizens and community networks', *CMC Magazine*, Retrieved, from the World Wide Web: http://www.december.com/cmc/mag/1997/feb/hauben.html

Healy, M. (1997) 'Child pornography: an international perspective', prepared as a working document for the World Congress Against Commercial Sexual Exploitation of Children. Retrieved, from the World Wide Web: http://www.usis.usemb.se/children/csec/215e.htm

Hogan, R. (1969) 'Development of an empathy scale', *Journal of Consulting and Clinical Psychology*, 33(3), 307–16.

Hollway, W. and Jefferson, T. (2000) *Doing Qualitative Research Differently*, London: Sage.

Holmes, R., Tewksbury, R. and Holmes, S. (1998) 'Hidden JPGs: a functional alternative to voyeurism', *Journal of Popular Culture*, 17–29.

Horley, J. (2000) 'Cognitions supportive of child molestation', *Aggression and Violent Behaviour*, 5(6), 551–64.

Horn, S. (1998) *Cybersville: Clicks, Culture and the Creation of an Online Town*, New York: Warner Books.

Howitt, D. (1995) 'Pornography and the paedophile: is it criminogenic?', *British Journal of Medical Psychiatry*, 68, 15–25.

Hsu, L. K. G. and Starzynski, J. (1990) 'Adolescent rapists and adolescent child sexual assaulters', *International Journal of Offender Therapy and Comparative Criminology*, 34(1), 23–30.

Hudson, S. M. and Ward, T. (1997) 'Intimacy, loneliness and attachment style in sex offenders', *Journal of Interpersonal Violence*, 12, 323–39.

Hunter, J. A. and Becker, J. V. (1999) 'Motivators of adolescent sex offenders and treatment perspectives', in J. A. Shaw (ed), *Sexual Aggression*, Washington DC: American Psychiatric Press, pp. 211–34.

Hunter, J. A., Lexier, L. J., Goodwin, D. W. and Browne, P. A. (1993) 'Psychosexual, attitudinal and developmental characteristics of juvenile female perpetrators in a residential treatment setting', *Journal of Child and Family Studies*, 2(4), 317–26.

Ingram, A. L., Hathorn, L. G. and Evans, A. (2000) 'Beyond chat on the Internet', *Computers and Education*, 35, 21–35.

Itzin, C. (1997) 'Pornography and the organization of intrafamilial and extrafamilial child sexual abuse: developing a conceptual model', *Child Abuse Review*, 6, 94–106.

Ivey, G. and Simpson, P. (1998) 'The psychological life of paedophiles: a phenomenological study', *South African Journal of Psychology*, 28, 15–20.

Jenkins, P. (2001) *Beyond Tolerance: Child Pornography on the Internet*, New York and London: New York University Press.

Johnson, T. C. (1989) 'Female child perpetrators: children who molest other children', *Child Abuse and Neglect: The International Journal*, 13(4), 571–85.

Johnson, T. (1996) 'The assessment aned treatment of sexually molestive children', Paper presented at the Doctors for Sexual Abuse Care seminar, Auckland, New Zealand (cited in Lightfoot and Evans, 2000).

Jones, S. (1997) *Virtual Culture: Identity and Communication in Cybersociety*, London: Sage.

Jones, S. (1999) *Doing Internet Research: Critical Issues and Methods for Examining the Net*, Thousand Oaks, CA: Sage.

Kalichman, S. (1991) 'Psychopathology and personality characteristics of criminal sexual offenders as a function of victim age', *Archives of Sexual Behaviour*, 20(2), 187–97.

Kaufman, K. L., Wallace, A. M., Johnson, C. F. and Reeder, M. L. (1995) 'Comparing female and male perpetrators' modus operandi', *Journal of Interpersonal Violence*, 10(3), 322–33.

Kendall, L. (1999) 'Recontextualizing "Cyberspace": methodological considerations for on-line research', in S. G. Jones (ed), *Doing Internet Research: Critical Issues and Methods for Examining the Net*, Thousand Oaks, CA: Sage, pp. 57–74.

Kennedy-Souza, B. L. (1998) 'Internet addiction disorder', *Interpersonal Computing and Technology*, 6, 1–2.

Kincaid, J. R. (1998) *Erotic Innocence: The Culture of Child Molesting*, Durham, NC, and London: Duke University Press.

King, S. (1999) 'Internet gambling and pornography: illustrative examples of the psychological consequences of communication anarchy', *CyberPsychology & Behavior*, 2, 175–93.

Knight, R., Carter, D. and Prentky, R. (1989) 'A system for the classification of child molesters', *Journal of Interpersonal Violence*, 4(1), 3–23.

Kollock, P. and Smith, M. A. (1999) 'Communities in Cyberspace', in M. A. Smith and P. Kollock (eds), *Communities in Cyberspace*, London: Routledge, pp. 3–28.

Krauss, D. A., Sales, B. D., Becker, J. V. and Figueredo, A. J. (2000) 'Beyond prediction to explanation in risk assessment research', *International Journal of Law and Psychiatry*, 23(2), 91–112.

Kraut, R., Patterson, M., Lundmark, V., Kiesler, S., Mukophadhyay, T. and Scherlis, W. (1998) 'Internet paradox: a social technology that reduces social involvement and psychological well-being?', *American Psychologist*, 53, 1017–31.

Kron, J. (1983) *Home Psych: The Psychology of Home and Decoration*, New York: Clarkson N. Potter.

Lamb, M. (1998) 'Cybersex: research notes on the characteristics of the visitors to online chat rooms', *Deviant Behaviour: An Interdisciplinary Journal*, 19, 121–35.

Lane III, F. S. (2000) *Obscene Profits: The Entrepreneurs of Pornography in the Cyber Age*, New York and London: Routledge.

Langevin, R. (1983) *Sexual Strands*, Hillsdale, NJ: Erlbaum.

Langevin, R. (1991) 'A note on the problem of response set in measuring cognitive distortions', *Annals of Sex Research*, 4, 287–92.

Lanning, K. (1992) *Child Molesters: A Behavioral Analysis*, Washington, DC: National Center for Missing and Exploited Children.

Lanning, K. (1995) 'Child molestation: law enforcement typology', in R. R. Hazelwood and A. W. Burgess (eds), *Practical Aspects of Rape Investigation*, 2nd edn, Boca Raton, FA: CRC Press.

Lanning, K. and Burgess, A. W. (1989) 'Child pornography and sex rings', in D. Zillman and J. Bryant (eds), *Pornography: Research Advances and Policy Considerations*, Hillside, NJ: Lawrence Erlbaum.

Lanyon, R. L. (1991) 'Theories of sex offending', in C. R. Hollin and K. Howells (eds), *Clinical Approaches to Sex Offenders and their Victims*, Chichester: John Wiley and Sons.

Laws, D. R. and Marshall, W. L. (1990) 'A conditioning theory of the etiology and maintenance of deviant sexual preference and behavior', in W. L. Marshall, D. R. Laws and H. E. Barbaree (eds), *Handbook of Sexual Assault: Issues, Theories and Treatment of the Offender*, New York: Plenum, pp. 209–29.

Lewis, D. O., Shankock, S. S. and Pincas, J. H. (1981) 'Juvenile male sexual asaulters: psychiatric, neurological, psychoeducational and abuse factors', in D. O. Lewis (ed), *Vulnerabilities to Delinquency*, Jamaica, NY: Spectrum Publications, pp. 29–105.

Lévy, P. (1998) *Becoming Virtual: Reality in the Digital Age*, trans. R. Bononno, New York: Plenum Press.

Lightfoot, S. and Evans, I. M. (2000) 'Risk factors for a New Zealand sample of sexually abusive children and adolescents', *Child Abuse and Neglect: The International Journal*, 24, 1185–98.

Lindsay, W. R., Law, J., Quinn, K., Smart, N. and Smith, A. H. W. (2001) 'A comparison of physical and sexual abuse: histories of sexual and non-sexual offenders with intellectual disability', *Child Abuse and Neglect: The International Journal*, 25, 989–95.

Linehan, C., Quayle, E., Holland, G. and Taylor, M. (2002) 'Virtual paedophile communities', *Journal of Sexual Aggression*, in press.

Longo, R. E. and Groth, A. N. (1983) 'Juvenile sexual offenses in the histories of adult rapists and child molesters', *International Journal of Offender Therapy and Comparative Criminology*, 27, 150–5.

McCabe, K. A. (2000) 'Child pornography on the Internet', *Social Science Computer Review*, 18(1), 73–6.

McCabe, K. A. and Gregory, S. S. (1998) 'Recognizing the illegal activities of computer users', *Social Science Computer Review*, 16(4), 419–22.

McConaghy, N. (1998) 'Paedophilia: a review of the evidence', *Australian and New Zealand Journal of Psychiatry*, 32, 252–65.

McFall, R. M. (1982) 'A review and reformulation of the concept of social skills', *Behavioral Assessment*, 4, 1–33.

McLaughlin, M., Osborne, K. and Smith, R. (1995) 'Standard of conduct on Usenet', in S. G. Jones (ed), *Cybersociety: Computer-Mediated Communication and Community*, Thousand Oaks, CA: Sage, pp. 90–111.

McLaughlin, M. L., Osborne, K. K. and Ellison, N. B. (1998) 'Virtual community in a telepresence environment', in S. G. Jones (ed), *Virtual Culture: Identity and Communication in Cybersociety*, London: Sage.

Mahoney, D. and Faulkner, N. (1997) 'Brief overview of pedophiles on the Web', submitted by request to the Internet online summit, Focus on Children, Washington DC. Retrieved, from the World Wide Web: http://www.healthyplace.com/communities/abuse/socum/articles/pedophiles.htm

Malamuth, N. M. and Check, J. V. P. (1985) 'The effects of aggressive pornography on beliefs in rape myths: individual differences', *Journal of Research in Personality*, 19, 299–320.

Maltz, T. (1996) 'Customary law and power in Internet communities', *Journal of Computer-Mediated Communication*, 2(1).

Mantovani, F. (2001) 'Networked seduction: a test-bed for the study of strategic communication on the Internet', *CyberPsychology & Behavior*, 4(1), 147–54.

Margison, F. R. (1997) 'Abnormalities of sexual function and interest: origins and interventions', *Current Opinion in Psychiatry*, 10(2), 127–31.

Marshall, W. L. (1988) 'The use of sexually explicit stimuli by rapists, child molesters and nonoffenders', *Journal of Sex Research*, 25(2), 267–88.

Marshall, W. L. (1989) 'Pornography and sex offenders', in D. Zillman and J. Bryant (eds), *Pornography: Research Advances and Policy Considerations*, Hillsdale, NJ: Lawrence Erlbaum Associates, pp. 185–214.

Marshall, W. L. (2000) 'Revisiting the use of pornography by sexual offenders: implications for theory and practice', *The Journal of Sexual Aggression*, 6(1/2), 67–77.

Marshall, W. L. and Barrett, S. (1990) *Criminal Neglect: Why Sex Offenders Go Free*, Toronto: Doubleday.

Marshall, W. L., Jones, R. L., Hudson, S. M. and McDonald, E. (1993) 'Generalized empathy in child molesters', *Journal of Child Sexual Abuse*, 2, 61–8.

Marshall, W. L., Hudson, S. M., Jones, R. and Fernandez, Y. M. (1995) 'Empathy in sex offenders', *Clinical Psychology Review*, 15(2), 99–113.

Marshall, W. L., Fernandez, Y. M., Hudson, S.M. and Ward, T. (1998) *Sourcebook of Treatment Programs for Sexual Offenders*, New York and London: Plenum Press.

Marshall, W. L. and Fernandez, Y. M. (2000) 'Phallometric testing with sexual offenders: limits to its value', *Clinical Psychology Review*, 20(7), 807–22.

Marx, B., Miranda, R. and Meyerson, L. (1999) 'Cognitive-behavioural treatment for rapists: can we do better?', *Clinical Psychology Review*, 19(7), 875–94.

Matthews, J. K., Mathews, R. and Speltz, K. (1991) 'Female sexual offenders: a typology', in M. Q. Patton (ed), *Family Sexual Abuse: Frontline Research and Evaluation*, Newbury Park, CA: Sage Publications, pp. 199–219.

Mehrabian, A. and Epstein, N. (1972) 'A measure of emotional empathy', *Journal of Personality*, 40, 525–43.

Morahan-Martin, J. and Schumacher, P. (2000) 'Incidence and correlates of pathological Internet use among college students', *Computers in Human Behaviour*, 16, 13–29.

Mosher, D. L. (1988) 'Pornography defined: sexual involvement theory, narrative context, and goodness-of-fit', *Journal of Psychology and Human Sexuality*, 1, 67–85.

Muensterberger, W. (1994) *Collecting: An Unruly Passion*, Princeton, NJ: Princeton University Press.

Murphy, W. D. (1990) 'Assessment and modification of cognitive distortions in sex offenders', in W. L. Marshall, D.R. Laws and H. E. Barbaree (eds), *Handbook of Sexual Assault: Issues, Theories, and Treatment of the Offender*, New York: Plenum, pp. 331–42.

Nelson, C., Miner, M., Marques, J., Russell, K. and Achterkirchen, J. (1988) 'Relapse prevention: a cognitive-behavioral model for treatment of the rapist and child molester', *Journal of Social Work and Human Sexuality*, 7, 125–43.

Newson, J. and Newson, E. (1968) *Four-year-old in an Urban Community*, Chicago, IL: Aldine.

National Task Force on Juvenile Sex Offending (1993) 'National Adolescent Perpetrator Network revised report', *Juvenile and Family Court Journal*, 44(4), 1–120.

Orzack, M. H. and Ross, C. J. (2000) 'Should virtual sex be treated like other addictions?', *Sexual Addiction and Compulsivity*, 7, 113–25.

Ostrom, E. (1990) *Governing the Commons: The Evolution of Institutions for Collective Action*, New York: Cambridge University Press.

Overholser, J. C. and Beck, S. (1986) 'Multimethod assessment of rapists, child molesters, and three control groups on behavioral and psychological measures', *Journal of Consulting and Clinical Psychology*, 54, 682–7.

Palandri, M. and Green, L. (2000) 'Image management in a bondage, discipline, sadomasochist subculture: a cyber-ethnographic study', *CyberPsychology & Behavior*, 3(4), 631–41.

Phelen, P. (1995) 'Incest and its meaning: the perspectives of fathers and daughters', *Child Abuse and Neglect: The International Journal*, 19, 7–24.

Pierce, R. (1984) 'Child pornography: a hidden dimension of child abuse', *Child Abuse and Neglect*, 8, 483–93.

Postman, N. (1993) *Technology: The Surrender of Culture to Technology*, New York: Vintage Books.

Prentky, R., Knight, R. and Lee, A. (1997) *Child Sexual Molestation: Research Issues*, Washington: US Department of Justice.

Proulx, J., Perreult, C. and Ouimet, M. (1999) 'Pathways in the offending process of extrafamilial sexual child molesters', *Journal of Research and Treatment*, 11(2), 117–29.

Putman, D. E. and Maheu, M. M. (2000) 'Online sexual addiction and compulsivity: integrating web resources and behavioural telehealth in treatment', *Sexual Addiction and Compulsivity*, 7, 91–112.

Quayle, E., Holland, G., Linehan, C. and Taylor, M. (2000) 'The Internet and offending behaviour: a case study', *Journal of Sexual Aggression*, 6(1/2), 78–96.

Quayle, E. and Taylor, M. (2001) 'Child seduction and self-representation on the Internet: a case study', *CyberPsychology & Behavior*, 4(5), 597–608.

Quayle, E. and Taylor, M. (2002a) 'Child pornography and the Internet: perpetuating a cycle of abuse', *Deviant Behaviour*, 23, 365–95.

Quayle, E. and Taylor, M. (2002b) 'Paedophiles, pornography and the Internet: assessment issues', *British Journal of Social Work*, 32, 863–75.

Quinsey, V., Rice, M. and Harris, G. (1995) 'Actuarial prediction of sexual recidivism', *Journal of Interpersonal Violence*, 10(1), 85–105.

Reid, E. (1998) 'The self and the Internet: variations on the illusion of one self', in J. Gackenbach (ed), *Psychology and the Internet: Intrapersonal, Interpersonal and Transpersonal Implications*, San Diego: Academic Press.

Rheingold, H. (1993) *The Virtual Community: Homesteading on the Electronic Frontier*, Reading, MA: Addison-Wesley.

Riva, G. and Galimberti, C. (1998) 'Interbrain frame: interaction and cognition in computer-mediated communication', *CyberPsychology and Behavior*, 1, 295–309.

Rosenberg, R. and Knight, R. (1988) 'Determining male sexual offender subtypes using cluster analysis', *Journal of Quantitative Research*, 4(4), 383–411.

Rothaermel, F. T. and Sugiyama, S. (2001) 'Virtual Internet communities and commercial success: individual and community-level theory grounded in the atypical case of TimeZone.com', *Journal of Management*, 27, 297–312.

Scott, M. B. and Lyman, S. (1968) 'Accounts', *American Sociological Review*, 31, 46.

Segal, Z. V. and Marshall, W. L. (1985) 'Heterosexual social skills in a population of rapists and child molesters', *Journal of Consulting and Clinical Psychology*, 53, 55–63.

Segal, Z. V. and Stermac, L. E. (1990) 'The role of cognitions in sexual assault', in W. L. Marshall, D. R. Laws and H. E. Barbaree (eds), *Handbook of Sexual Assault: Issues, Theories and Treatment of the Offender*, New York: Plenum, pp. 161–74.

Sentencing Advisory Panel (2002) Sentencing Advisory Panel's Advice to the Court of Appeal on Sentences Involving Child Pornography. Retrieved from World Wide Web: http://www.sentencing-advisory-panel.gov.uk/c_and_a/advice/child_offences/advice_child_porn.pdf

Seto, M. C., Maric, A. and Barbaree, H. E. (2001) 'The role of pornography in the etiology of sexual aggression', *Aggression and Violent Behavior*, 6, 35–53.

Shaw, D. F. (1997) 'Gay men and computer communication: a discourse of sex and identity in cyberspace', in S. G. Jones (ed), *Virtual Culture: Identity and Communication in Cybersociety*, London: Sage.

Shaw, J. A. (1999) 'Sexually aggressive behaviour', in J. A. Shaw (ed), *Sexual Aggression*, Washington, DC: American Psychiatric Press, pp. 3–40.

Shaw, J. A., Lewis, J. E., Loeb, A., Rosado, J. and Rodriguez, R. A. (2000) 'Child on child sexual abuse: psychological perspectives', *Child Abuse and Neglect: The International Journal*, 24(12), 1591–600.

Shirky, C. (1995) *Voices from the Net*, Emeryville, CA: Ziff-Davis Press.

Silbert, M. H. (1989) 'The effects on juveniles of being used for pornography and prostitution', in D. Zillman and C. Bryant (eds), *Pornography: Research Advances and Policy Considerations*, Hillside, NJ: Lawrence Erlbaum.

Smith, A. D. (2000) 'Problems of conflict management in virtual communities', in M. A. Smith and P. Kollock (eds), *Communities in Cyberspace*, London: Routledge, pp. 134–66.

Smith, J. A. (1995) 'Semi-structured interviewing and qualitative analysis', in J. A. Smith, R. Harre and L. Van Langenhove (eds), *Rethinking Methods in Psychology*, London: Sage, pp. 9–26.

Stahl, S. S. and Sacco, U. P. (1995) 'Heterosocial perception in child molesters and rapists', *Cognitive Therapy and Research*, 19(6), 695–706.

Stermac, L. and Segal, Z. (1989) 'Adult sexual contact with children: an examination of cognitive factors', *Behaviour Therapy*, 20, 573–84.

Studer, L. H., Clelland, S. R., Aylwin, A. S., Reddon, J. R. and Monro, A. (2000) 'Rethinking risk assessment for incest offenders', *International Journal of Law and Psychiatry*, 23(1), 15–22.

Svedin, C. G. and Back, K. (1996) *Children Who Don't Speak Out*, Stockholm, Sweden: Swedish Save the Children.

Talamo, A. and Ligorio, B. (2001) 'Strategic identities in cyberspace', *CyberPsychology & Behavior*, 4(1), 109–20.

Tate, T. (1990) *Child Pornography*, St. Ives: Methuen.

Taylor, M. (1999) *The Nature and Dimensions of Child Pornography on the Internet, 1999*. Retrieved, from the World Wide Web: http://www.asem.org/Documents/aaconfvienna/pa_taylor.html

Taylor, M. (2001) 'Challenges and gaps', paper presented to the Second World Congress Against Commercial Sexual Exploitation of Children, Yokohama.

Taylor, M., Holland, G. and Quayle, E. (2001a) 'Typology of paedophile picture collections', *The Police Journal*, 74(2), 97–107.

Taylor, M., Quayle, E. and Holland, G. (2001b) 'Child pornography, the Internet and offending', *ISUMA, The Canadian Journal of Policy Research*, 2(Summer), 94–100.

Tikkanen, R. and Ross, M. W. (2000) 'Looking for sexual compatibility; experiences among Swedish men in visiting Internet gay chat rooms', *CyberPsychology & Behavior*, 3(4), 605–16.

Tönnies, F. (1967) 'Gemeinschaft and Gesellschaft', in C. Bell and H. Newby (eds), *The Sociology of Community*, London: Frank Cass and Co. Ltd.

Travin, S., Cullen, K. and Protter, B. (1990) 'Female sex offenders: severe victims and victimizers', *Journal of Forensic Sciences*, 35, 140–50.

Turkle, S. (1995) *Life on the Screen: Identity in the Age of the Internet*, New York: Simon and Schuster.

Tyler, R. P. and Stone, L. E. (1985) 'Child pornography: perpetuating the sexual victimization of children', *Child Abuse and Neglect: The International Journal*, 9, 313–18.

Wakefield, H. and Underwager, R. C. (1991) 'Female child sexual abusers: a critical review of the literature', paper presented at the Seventh Annual Symposium in Forensic Psychology, Tyler, TX.

Wallace, P. (2001) *The Psychology of the Internet*, New York: Cambridge University Press.

Ward, T. (2000) 'Sexual offenders' cognitive distortions as implicit theories', *Aggression and Violent Behavior*, 5(5), 491–507.

Ward, T., Hudson, S. M. and Johnston, L. (1997) 'Cognitive distortions in sex offenders: an integrative review', *Clinical Psychology Review*, 17(5), 479–507.

Ward, T., Fon, C., Hudson, S. M. and McCormack, J. (1998) 'Classification of cognition in sex offenders: a descriptive model', *Journal of Interpersonal Violence*, 13, 129–55.

Ward, T., Keenan, T. and Hudson, S. M. (2000) 'Understanding cognitive, affective, and intimacy deficits in sexual offenders: a developmental perspective', *Aggression and Violent Behavior*, 5(1), 41–62.

Wasserman, H. J. (1998) 'Note Virtual.Child.Porn.Com: Defending the constitutionality of the criminalisation of computer-generated child pornography by the Child Pornography Prevention Act of 1996 – a reply to Professor Burke and other critics', *Harvard Journal on Legislation*, 35, 245–83.

Watson, N. (1998) 'Why should we argue about virtual community? A case study of the Phish.net Fan Community', in S. G. Jones (ed), *Virtual Culture: Identity and Communication in Cybersociety*, London: Sage.

Webley, P. and Lea, S. E. G. (1993) 'Towards a more realistic psychology of economic socialization', *Journal of Economic Psychology*, 14, 461–72.

Wellman, B., Carrington, P. and Hall, A. (1988) 'Networks as personal communities', in B. Wellman and S. D. Berkowitz (eds), *Social Structures: A Network Approach*, Cambridge: Cambridge University Press.

Wellman, B. and Gulia, M. (2000) 'Net surfers don't ride alone: virtual community as community', in P. Kollock and M. Smith (eds), *Communities in Cyberspace*, London: Routledge.

Wetherell, M. (1998) 'Positioning and interpretative repertoires: conversation analysis and post-structuralism in dialogue', *Discourse and Society*, 9(3), 387–412.

Widdicome, S. (1998) 'Identity as an analyst's and a participant's resource', in C. Antaki and S. Widdicombe (eds), *Identities in Talk*, London: Sage.

Wood, A. F. and Smith, M. J. (2001) *Online Communication: Linking Technology, Identity and Culture*, Mahwah, NJ: Lawrence Erlbaum Associates Inc.

Wynn, E. and Katz, J. E. (1997) 'Hyperbole over cyberspace: self-presentation and social boundaries in Internet Home Pages and discourse', *Information Society*, 13(4), 297–328.

Index